COMPLETE CONDITIONING FOR HOCKEY

Ryan van Asten, CSCS

Director of Sports Performance

Calgary Flames

HUMAN KINETICS

Library of Congress Cataloging-in-Publication Data

Names: Asten, Ryan van, 1980- author.
Title: Complete conditioning for hockey / Ryan van Asten.
Description: Champaign, IL : Human Kinetics, [2023] | Includes
  bibliographical references.
Identifiers: LCCN 2021054980 (print) | LCCN 2021054981 (ebook) | ISBN
  9781718208872 (paperback) | ISBN 9781718208889 (epub) | ISBN
  9781718208896 (pdf)
Subjects: LCSH: Hockey--Training. | BISAC: SPORTS & RECREATION / Winter
  Sports / Hockey | SPORTS & RECREATION / Bodybuilding & Weight Training
Classification: LCC GV848.3 .A88 2023 (print) | LCC GV848.3 (ebook) | DDC
  796.356--dc23
LC record available at https://lccn.loc.gov/2021054980
LC ebook record available at https://lccn.loc.gov/2021054981

ISBN: 978-1-7182-0887-2 (print)

Acquisitions Editors: Michael Mejia, Diana Vincer; **Senior Developmental Editor:** Cynthia McEntire; **Managing Editor:** Shawn Donnelly; **Copyeditor:** Marissa Wold Uhrina; **Proofreader:** Rodelinde Albrecht; **Permissions Manager:** Martha Gullo; **Graphic Designer:** Denise Lowry; **Cover Designer:** Keri Evans; **Cover Design Specialist:** Susan Rothermel Allen; **Photograph (cover):** Tom Pennington / Getty Images; **Photographs (interior):** Candice Ward; **Photo Production Specialist:** Amy M. Rose; **Photo Production Manager:** Jason Allen; **Senior Art Manager:** Kelly Hendren; **Illustrations:** © Human Kinetics; **Printer:** Versa Press

Human Kinetics
1607 N. Market Street
Champaign, IL 61820
USA

United States and International
Website: **US.HumanKinetics.com**
Email: info@hkusa.com
Phone: 1-800-747-4457

Canada
Website: **Canada.HumanKinetics.com**
Email: info@hkcanada.com

E8425

Tell us what you think!
Human Kinetics would love to hear what we can do to improve the customer experience. Use this QR code to take our brief survey.

COMPLETE CONDITIONING FOR HOCKEY

Contents

Foreword

As an undrafted player in the NHL, I realized early on that I would have to outwork and outperform my peers if I was going to turn the passion I have for the game of hockey into a career. As essentially a walk-on, it was clear that I would not get the opportunities handed to me that are generally reserved for high draft picks. I very quickly realized I would have to develop a strategy that would catch me up and give me an edge long-term. Ryan van Asten would end up being a big part of my progress.

Demanding work would have to be the cornerstone of what I needed to do. I learned that if I were to excel at the game, outworking the competition alone would only take me so far. To prepare for the game's unique challenges, I had to focus my efforts on meeting the unique physical demands the game requires of us all. To have speed, power, strength, and endurance, in addition to the skill I had, was more important than the skill itself. Many great young players possessed unparalleled skill and were drafted ahead of players like me and never played a single NHL game. They learned far too late what hockey at the NHL level required of them.

Ryan helped me understand that the game's rigors required that I strike a more effective balance in my training, and to not focus as much on the heavy lifting I did when I was younger as most players do. (This is a product of coaches harping on us to get stronger when we first reach the pros.)

As you will learn in the pages that follow, Ryan taught me and will teach you that strength alone is not enough. Getting stronger in certain positions that are beneficial to a stronger skating stride, for example, is essential. Little nuances like this made a significant difference in my game. I soon found I could perform better and execute more effectively from various positions on the ice.

His in-season workout plan is dramatically different than that of any other trainer I have had. It has helped me to recover effectively and maintain my strength throughout an 82-game schedule when the loss of muscle mass tends to occur. It is almost impossible to be in the gym consistently during the season without wearing down. Ryan's focus on an effective balance here is critical.

Ryan's effectiveness extends to helping to learn to move effectively and efficiently in ways that optimize performance and reduce the risk of injury. The latter is critical if you want to have a long professional career and stay off the injured reserve list. Many believe movement efficiency is only important as an athlete gets older, but it is essential for all age groups, and it must be developed from an early age. Combining all of these factors has been a crucial contributor to my longevity.

I have worked with Ryan van Asten for eight years. His level of care, attention to detail, and ability to convey complex ideas in simple terms so athletes can comprehend them are significant assets in his ability to get the most out of his players. He has been in the trenches of professional hockey for over a decade, and this hands-on experience has shaped his coaching philosophy and style. He is innovative and continuously pushes the limits of performance through different exercise techniques, program design, and technology implementation.

The athletic demands of hockey are constantly evolving, particularly in the speed and skill possessed by the younger generations of players entering the NHL. To stay relevant, players must take pride in their off-ice training. This book is an excellent resource to build the foundation for these athletic demands for players of all levels. I wish I had it in my arsenal at a younger age. As athletes, we must continually strive to improve, and I believe this book will help all hockey players take steps in the right direction on the road to optimizing their performance on the ice.

Ryan has been a great partner of mine and has been a vital part of my success. He is approachable, and he cares. I believe any young man or woman looking to reach their potential would be wise to consider the wisdom Ryan shares in *Complete Conditioning for Hockey*.

Mark Giordano, Three-time NHL All-Star

Preface

Complete Conditioning for Hockey is the culmination of many years of hands-on training experience at both the elite and youth levels of hockey. This breadth of experience, along with my academic training, has molded my training philosophy, which I am delighted to share with you in this book. My philosophy, however, continues to evolve and adapt in parallel with my experiences and available scientific evidence. As all good strength and conditioning practitioners know, there are many ways to attain the desired results. Therefore, I am offering my unique perspective on high-performance training to optimize and support your athletes' ability to perform on-demand when it matters the most.

Chapter 1 focuses on the physical demands of hockey, outlining the movement capacity, energy systems, strength, power, acceleration, speed, and agility characteristics needed to excel in the sport. However, to build an individualized training plan, these characteristics must be assessed. Therefore, chapter 2 outlines assessments and tests that can be utilized to map out a complete picture of the individual athlete. From the data obtained through these assessments, the coach and athlete can determine the best course of action for the tailor-made training plan. The foundation of the training plan is movement optimization. Hockey players must have adequate joint range of motion, mobility, flexibility, and stability to attain specific biomechanical positions on the ice while skating and performing movements at high velocities. The concepts of movement optimization are outlined in chapter 3.

A hockey player, just like a race car, must have a high-powered engine to perform at the highest levels. Not only do they have to possess high amounts of power output (horsepower), but they also require large energy reserves (fuel tank) and the ability to replenish the energy (fuel) that has been expended. The game of hockey is multi-dimensional and requires a well-rounded approach to conditioning. Chapter 4, energy systems development, focuses on developing these characteristics to optimize on-ice performance and the ability to maintain this performance throughout a game and a long season. Chapters 5 through 8 outline the theory and exercise selection for developing systemic strength, functional power, acceleration, speed, and agility. These chapters are presented in a specific sequence as each topic or concept builds from the previous one.

Hockey players must train with purpose and intent. Still, they must also recover with a purpose to realize the full benefits of the long and grueling hours spent developing the performance characteristics outlined in this book. Chapter 9 takes a deep dive into monitoring fatigue and the many recovery modalities, both passive and active, that can be used to mitigate this fatigue. Recovery modalities discussed include sleep, nutrition and hydration, active recovery, bodywork, hydrotherapy, compression, breathing, and mindfulness. Chapter 10 outlines several technological advancements that help to monitor how athletes respond to training and recovery modalities and innovative ways to accumulate load during strength and power training.

A goal without a plan is just a wish. Therefore, chapter 11 provides the blueprint for developing a yearly training plan by dissecting the calendar year into smaller, digestible segments. This concept is known as periodization, and within this framework, the acute training variables are also discussed. Chapters 12 through 15 combine all the concepts outlined in the book by presenting sample programs for postseason, off-season, preseason, and in-season training.

This book aims to provide an adaptable training framework that is grounded in science and experience for coaches and hockey players. I intend to offer a unique perspective on training, and I am optimistic that this text will advance and push the boundaries of physical preparation for hockey.

Enjoy the book!

Acknowledgments

The opportunity to thank the many people and organizations that have supported and helped me on my career journey is something I cherish deeply. I am fortunate to have accumulated many unique experiences in sport science and strength and conditioning and have been influenced by many people along the way. It's impossible to thank everyone who has impacted my career, but I will attempt to thank as many of them as possible.

The first person I want to thank is my wife, Jackie. Without your unwavering love and support, my career goals and aspirations may never have come to fruition. Your support allowed me to pursue every opportunity that presented itself, and you have been by my side every step of the way, without hesitation. You are my rock and continue to make me a better person by setting the bar for determination and work ethic.

I also thank my parents, John and Carol van Asten. To my dad, thank you for showing me the value of hard work and pushing me to be my best. To my mom, thank you for believing in me even when I didn't believe in myself and for teaching me how to write, one of the most underrated skills for any profession. To my brother, Brandon van Asten, thank you for the mentorship. I've looked up to you my whole life, and we have learned many valuable lessons together along the way.

I would like to thank all my mentors, specifically Dr. David Smith and Dr. Stephen Norris, for teaching me the value of critical thinking and attention to detail. To Anthony Slater and Matt Jordan, thank you for sparking my interest in strength and conditioning. Without you, I may never have known about this career path.

To Alan Selby, Chris O'Neil, and Ricky Davis, thank you for allowing me to bounce ideas off you during the writing process, as well as providing multiple sets of critical eyes on the material.

Thank you to the folks at the Canadian Sport Institute—Calgary, specifically Jason Poole, for taking a chance on me and giving me my first job in high-performance sport. Thank you to Hockey Canada for allowing me to be a part of something special in Vancouver 2010. To the Los Angeles Kings, thank you for allowing me to realize my boyhood dream of working in the NHL. Thank you to the Calgary Flames for giving me the opportunity to come home and continue to do what I love most.

To Human Kinetics, thank you for asking me to do something I may never have had the courage to do otherwise. I am grateful for the help and expertise you have provided along the way.

Lastly, I want to thank all the athletes I have had the pleasure of working with throughout my career. You have shaped who I am today as a coach, and you are the reason I love every moment of what I do.

Chapter 1

Physical Demands of Ice Hockey

The date was June 13, 2014, and the Los Angeles Kings and New York Rangers were in double overtime in game 5 of the Stanley Cup Finals. With 5:17 remaining in the second overtime period, Alec Martinez of the Kings scored off a rebound to capture their second Stanley Cup in three seasons. The players poured onto the ice in celebration of winning arguably the toughest trophy to capture in sports. As the Kings' strength and conditioning coach, I witnessed this moment as the culmination of 7 preseason, 82 regular season, and 26 playoff games, for a total of 115 games played that season. This was an extraordinary number of games to be played. When combined with one of the league's most grueling travel schedules, the players' physical resiliency was tested to their fullest. Starting with the 2011-2012 season, the Kings had played 291 games leading to that championship moment, which solidified the team's legacy as one of the most dominant National Hockey League (NHL) teams of the era. The players' ability to endure such physical demands resulted from years of planned on- and off-ice training and an immeasurable amount of unstructured play and practice, particularly in their early development stages.

Physical development for ice hockey is continuously evolving. This evolution is a direct result of many factors including changes to the style of play due to rule modifications at the NHL level and an influx of international players who sometimes play a more skill- and speed-based game. Scientific advances in game analysis, motion analysis, and identification of physical qualities have also contributed to the evolution of elite hockey performance. For example, the average player on the Calgary Flames' 1989 Stanley Cup championship team had a body weight of 192.0 pounds (87.1 kg), was 72.4 inches (183.8 cm) tall, had a body fat percentage of 9.3 percent, and had an anaerobic peak power of 28.0 watts per pound (12.7 W/kg). Fast forward 15 years, and the average player on the Calgary Flames' 2004 Western Conference championship team had a body weight of 205.0 pounds (93.0 kg), was 73.5 inches (186.8 cm) tall, had a body fat percentage of 8.8 percent, and had an anaerobic peak power of 32.2 watts per pound (14.6 W/kg). In contrast, the average player on the Calgary Flames in 2019 had a body weight of 198.4 pounds (90.0 kg), was 73.1 inches (185.7 cm) tall, had 9.0 percent body fat, and had an anaerobic peak power of 35.9 watts per pound (16.3 W/kg) (figure 1.1). These data demonstrate that even though the players' average size and body composition have not changed significantly over the decades, their anaerobic peak power continues to increase. That being said, every team, position, and individual athlete has a different style of play and set of physicals demands. The physical preparation must match these requirements to be successful. Therefore, a one-size-fits-all approach to training hockey players does not exist. For example, a small skilled forward such as Johnny Gaudreau or Patrick Kane might be significantly different than a big stay-at-home defender such as Matt Greene, reinforcing the need for individualization.

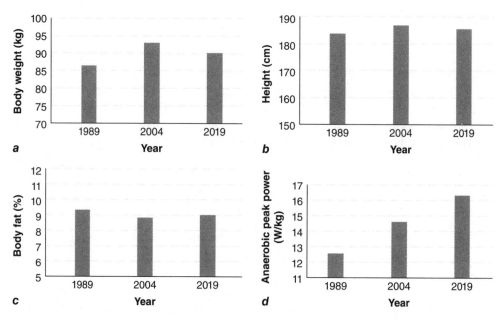

Figure 1.1 Comparison of physical characteristics of Calgary Flames players between 1989 and 2019: *(a)* body weight, *(b)* height, *(c)* body fat, and *(d)* anaerobic peak power.

The game of hockey is a multiple-sprint sport with repeating bouts of high-intensity, sprint, and low-intensity skating (Lignell et al. 2018). Lignell et al. (2018) showed that players performed 390 ± 26 feet per minute (119 ± 8 and 31 ± 3 m/min) of high-intensity and sprint skating, respectively, during a 60-minute game. The total distance covered was 15,111 ± 719 feet (4,606 ± 219 m), of which high-intensity distance was 6,699 ± 318 feet (2042 ± 97 m) (table 1.1).

If skating were the only metric that required attention, our job as coaches would be relatively straightforward. At most levels, ice hockey is a full-contact

Table 1.1   Skating Distances Traveled Based on Velocity During an NHL Hockey Game

	Total distance	Fast skating (17.0-20.9 km/hr)	Very fast skating (21.0-24.0 km/hr)	Sprint skating (>24.0 km/hr)
Distance (m)	4606 ± 219	1011 ± 53	547 ± 32	484 ± 34

Data from E. Lignell, D. Fransson, P. Krustrup, and M. Mohr, "Analysis of High-Intensity Skating in Top-Class Ice Hockey Match-Play in Relation to Training Status and Muscle Damage," *Journal of Strength and Conditioning Research* 32, no. 5: 1303-1310.

sport in which battles with opposing players and high-velocity collisions occur almost every shift. Combine those with high-intensity rotational movements and numerous changes of direction and accelerations under the external load of equipment, and the picture becomes more complex. These additional requirements are almost always multiplanar and are often difficult to quantify but must be accounted for when developing training plans for hockey athletes. The purpose of this chapter is to discuss these physical qualities and demands concerning position, style of play, gender, and athlete age as well as to provide a general understanding for the context of designing solid training plans for hockey teams and individual athletes.

POSITION-SPECIFIC PHYSICAL DEMANDS

The three position categories within the sport of ice hockey are forward, defense, and goaltending. The forward position can be subdivided further into the center and wing (figure 1.2).

In general, each position has its own set of individual physical demands. On average, the center position will cover more ice surface relative to the wingers. The center also is responsible for taking most of the game's faceoffs. According to Lignell et al. (2018), defense covered 29 percent more skating

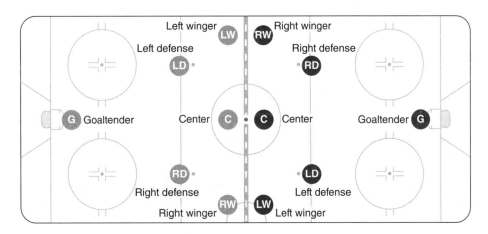

Figure 1.2   Ice hockey positions.

distance than forwards and were on the ice 47 percent longer. In contrast, forwards performed 54 percent more high-intensity skating per minute than defense (table 1.2). Lignell et al. (2018) also noted no significant difference in peak or mean sprint speeds between forwards and defense.

Table 1.2 Differences in Skating Metrics Between Forwards and Defense During an NHL Hockey Game

	Total skating (m)	High-intensity skating (m)	High-intensity skating per unit of time (m/min)
Defense	5445 ± 337	1938 ± 114	90 ± 6
Forwards	4237 ± 248	2087 ± 131	139 ± 4

Data from E. Lignell, D. Fransson, P. Krustrup, and M. Mohr, "Analysis of High-Intensity Skating in Top-Class Ice Hockey Match-Play in Relation to Training Status and Muscle Damage," *Journal of Strength and Conditioning Research* 32, no. 5: 1303-1310.

These data suggest that relative energy demands for skating vary significantly between forwards and defense, with forwards potentially requiring a greater contribution from anaerobic energy sources than defense positions do throughout a game. These facts are supported by the NHL combine's cumulative data that show forwards had higher relative peak anaerobic power than the defense and goalie positions (Burr et al. 2008). Lignell et al. (2018) also highlighted that the average sprint skating speed decreased significantly in the third and overtime periods. The ability to sustain such skating speeds is paramount to outperforming an opponent as the game progresses and should be a significant focus of any team's or player's training plan. Many variables such as movement capacity, energy systems, muscular strength qualities, and power production qualities contribute to the sustainability of high-intensity and sprint skating performance. If any of these variables is not optimized, athletes will not reach their full potential either acutely or from a performance sustainability standpoint.

MOVEMENT CAPACITY

The capacity to move effectively and efficiently is a critical quality for on-ice performance in hockey. The addition of fitness to dysfunctional movement will limit the global ability of the individual to perform optimally. Many high performers often lack specific movement qualities and capacity. Still, they should be considered outliers that might never reach their full movement potential and therefore their full athletic potential as hockey players.

The skating positions (forward and defense) differ from the goalie position regarding movement capacity demands and requirements. Because the butterfly goaltending style is more prevalent, nearly the default style of play, the hip range of motion required of and movement demands experienced by goalies significantly differ from those demanded of the skating positions.

Movement capacity is the foundation on which the bricks of all performance characteristics and qualities will be laid. As Cook (2003) described, this foundation is composed of both hardware and software components.

Hardware components include the following:

- Skeletal structure
- Joint range of motion
- Aspects of fascial and muscle tissue quality and length (structural)

Software components include the following:

- Aspects of fascial and muscle tissue quality and length (neurological)
- Functional stability and motor or neurological control
- Mechanics of movement

Compromised movement might be a result of hardware or software malfunctioning or a combination of both. These areas must be considered when analyzing an individual's global movement capacity.

ENERGY SYSTEMS

The energy system demands on ice hockey athletes might be the broadest in all of sports. The energy systems provide the fuel to support elite performance both on and off the ice. Energy demands differ depending on several factors, including the position of play, style of play, opponent's style of play, special teams play, and stage of a game. For example, a defender who is killing a penalty in overtime might have significantly different demands on their energy systems than a forward on the power play in the first period.

The two energy systems are the aerobic energy system (oxidative) and the anaerobic energy system. The anaerobic energy system is further broken down into the glycolytic (lactic acid) and alactic (phosphagen, ATP-PCr) systems.

To best capture how these energy systems fuel human movement, think of an automobile. The ATP-PCr system determines the amount of horsepower an individual has. The lactic acid system is the size of the gas tank available to support the horsepower, and the aerobic energy system is the ability to replenish or refill the gas tank. Each of these systems alone is not enough for optimal performance. For example, horsepower might be very high, but it will not matter after a short time with a small gas tank since very little fuel will remain to keep the engine going. Conversely, if an athlete's ability to refill the gas tank is high but their horsepower is low, they will lose most races to loose pucks or lack breakaway speed to separate themselves from an opponent. These systems are interconnected. They drive each other downstream; therefore, any break or weak link in the chain might be limiting from an energy standpoint. These global systems are subdivided into multiple levels, discussed in chapter 4, and can be manipulated for specific positions and levels of play.

SYSTEMIC STRENGTH

Strength is one of the most critical performance characteristics because it forms the basis of support for many of the performance characteristics to follow. Strength is the ability to generate force. Often when we think of strength, we think of compound lifting patterns (e.g., squat, deadlift, bench press, chin-up) and neglect to consider using an inside-out or proximal to distal approach to strengthening. A common analogy is that if you fire a cannon from a canoe, the cannonball will not travel very far and the canoe will tip backward, even though the cannon can produce a significant amount of force. This analogy also applies to human athletic performance. Individuals who do not have the appropriate proximal (core) strength to support their application of force distally (extremities) will have compromised performance due to the presence of energy leaks within the system. Think of a puck battle in the corner. Player A might have the strength to bench press more weight than player B but lacks the core stability, strength, and control to support this application of force in a real game situation. As a result, player A might lose the battle to player B, who has less isolated upper-body strength but has more stability and control from their base of support in standing position.

In addition to proximal to distal strengthening, adequate core strength allows for sufficient distal mobility in the joints of the extremities (Kibler, Press, and Sciascia 2006). Moreside and McGill (2012) add to this philosophy by demonstrating that when rotation exercises are performed by an athlete who has higher core stability and stiffness, the axis of rotation is directed more at the hip joints, resulting in a greater range of motion. Strength and stability in certain areas allow for appropriate mobility and range of motion in others. Elite performers are typically masters of compensation. They innately find any way to perform at the highest level, usually through the path of least resistance. This type of movement philosophy gets the job done until it does not. If the preferred path is a compromised movement pattern, overuse injuries are usually inevitable and often irreversible, which may affect performance as the athlete ages.

FUNCTIONAL POWER

Power is defined as the velocity at which force is applied. Regardless of position, the athletes who generate the most power on average skate and move the fastest. Backed by more than 10 years of data at the NHL level, this fact cannot be understated. In hockey, that application of power is rarely linear. Power generation is multiplanar and often from compromised body positions. Although many traditional testing protocols measure linear power capabilities, for power generation to be functional in hockey, it must be dynamic and optimized in the three planes of movement: sagittal, frontal, and transverse. How many times have you seen some of the top players in the NHL score a goal while a defender is checking them and knocking them off balance? Or a goalie makes a miraculous cross-crease save when they should have been out of the play? The best hockey players can produce high power levels in different forms and planes from often significantly compromised positions.

Historically, defense and forwards typically outperform goalies in linear power development (e.g., vertical jump) (Burr et al. 2008). This might result from the specific movements required from the different positions. Goalies must generate power over very short distances in slightly different planes than the skating positions. That said, some of the most powerful goalies have experienced tremendous success at the highest levels. Jonathan Quick is arguably one of the most dynamic and athletic goalies in the NHL, and he guided his team to two Stanley Cups. He was also awarded the Conn Smythe Trophy as the playoff most valuable player in 2012. Goaltenders must strive to buck this historical trend of being the least fit or powerful athlete on the team. Goaltenders have their own unique set of demands, with starting goalies playing in upwards of 80 percent of the team's games. They must have adequate power and power endurance that can be sustained for 60 or more minutes of game time and most of the team's games throughout the season.

ACCELERATION AND SPEED

In the sport of hockey, top-end speed or maximum velocity is rarely realized. When coaches and managers refer to speed, they typically are referring to the athlete's ability to accelerate, with the majority of these accelerations being 16 feet (5 m) or less in distance. One major misconception prevalent in hockey circles is that foot speed is the name of the game when it comes to acceleration. However, to the contrary, ground contact times during skating are relatively long compared to sprint running; therefore, force production for a given mass is arguably the most critical factor when it comes to acceleration. Mechanics and the rate at which force is produced are also crucial variables to optimizing acceleration, but absolute strength is the starting point for many athletes, particularly younger athletes.

CHANGE OF DIRECTION AND REACTIVITY

Agility encompasses an athlete's ability to be reactive and quickly change the course of their motion. Agility builds on the concept of acceleration with two additional components: it is the ability to react to a stimulus resulting in quick deceleration, followed by altering or changing direction and accelerating once again. During a hockey game, this might occur over very short distances. The athlete might have to perform this task several times within a short period while trying to evade, track down, or cover an opposing player. Of note, hockey equipment can weigh up to 20 pounds (9 kg) depending on sweat absorption; therefore, all agility actions are under external load. If strength levels are not adequate to withstand such high deceleration loads, athletes might be compromised in performance and potentially expose themselves to a higher risk of injury.

GENDER DIFFERENCES AND CONSIDERATIONS

Ice hockey has grown considerably over the decades to become more gender inclusive with the development of programs for females alongside their male counterparts. The women's game has grown substantially since the first International Ice Hockey Federation (IIHF) Women's World Championship in 1990. As the head strength and conditioning coach for Hockey Canada's women's national teams between 2008 and 2011, I had the opportunity to work with and learn from some of the best women's hockey players and coaches in the world at various levels of development (i.e., U18, U22, and National Level). My time spent with Canada's Women's National Program peaked with the gold medal game at the 2010 Olympic Winter Games in Vancouver, Canada. One of the most common questions concerning gender differences is how differently males and females should train. Evidence-based practitioners need to look at the science to guide their training philosophies.

Two questions need to be asked:

1. Do female hockey players differ in the specific performance areas outlined earlier in the chapter?

2. How do these differences, if any, affect particular training requirements to optimize on-ice performance?

Regarding energy systems, the current body of literature suggests some differences exist between males and females at the game's elite levels. For example, Durocher et al. (2008) demonstrated that male hockey players had significantly higher aerobic capacity values at the college level than their female counterparts. In contrast, the female players had a higher ventilatory threshold as a percentage of their maximum heart rate. However, their lactate thresholds were not different as a percentage of maximum heart rate or maximum aerobic capacity. Maud and Shultz (1986) showed differences in anaerobic power and capacity between males and females but highlighted that these differences were significantly reduced when adjusted for lean body mass.

Analysis of the forward skating start demonstrated that males reached higher skating speeds than their female counterparts within a 49-foot (15 m) distance (Shell et al. 2017). The authors also found skating technique differences between males and females concerning hip and knee kinematics and stride width even though the females had a similar hip range of motion. Shell et al. (2017) speculated that this might result from a learned protective mechanism to avoid high valgus forces and strain to the knee's medial structures in female hockey players. The literature has not always corroborated these findings. Abbott (2014) suggested that forward skating mechanics are the same for male and female hockey players.

With the similarities and differences, the primary consideration needs to be the individual athlete. Gilenstam, Thorsen, and Henriksson-Larsén (2011) noted significant differences between male and female hockey players in various off- and on-ice performance tests. However, they showed that these gender differences were eliminated when the athlete's lean body mass was taken into consideration. When performance outcomes are measured relative to lean body mass, gender differences are significantly diminished and often do not exist. This fact has been corroborated repeatedly in the scientific literature. These data suggest that training programs must be tailored to the individual's specific needs regardless of gender. Proper testing and ongoing monitoring must be done to account for the particular training needs to optimize performance.

THE CASE FOR AN INDIVIDUALIZED APPROACH

Position and gender influence many variables when designing and implementing hockey players' training programs. However, these demographics should serve only as a starting point in program design. Since hockey players of the same age, gender, and caliber tend to be reasonably homogenous groups many program components will be applied across the board. But all athletes will present with their own set of specific requirements to achieve their best physical performances. Therefore, further fine-tuning of the training plan is required to individualize the program to the athlete.

YOUTH DIFFERENCES AND CONSIDERATIONS

Promotion of youth programs often involves slogans such as "Train Like the Pros," "Sport Specific," or "Hockey-Specific Training." Coaches and parents want the best for their children to help them succeed. Therefore, we often impose adult values and attributes onto children because that is what we know. The type of training that adult professional hockey players do is likely not appropriate in many youth development stages. With guidance from Sport Canada's long-term athlete development (LTAD) resource paper, Hockey Canada has devised a long-term player development (LTPD) model. Hockey Canada's LTPD is an eight-stage model based on a multifactorial approach to developing youth players. Factors such as physical, mental, emotional, and cognitive development are represented in the model. Stages one through three place an emphasis on physical literacy through a broad range of activities, whereas stages four through eight focus on development, competitive excellence, and being active for life.

Sport specialization is a hotly debated topic in hockey circles. Generally, there are two camps: early specialization and early diversification. Wall and Côté (2007) studied the various characteristics that influence whether athletes drop out or invest in organized hockey. This research concluded that early diversification does not hinder hockey-specific development, and it is likely preferable to early specialization. One of the significant findings of this work is that the athletes who did drop out of the sport began focused off-ice training at a younger age and participated in more off-ice training at ages 12 and 13 than those who remained active in hockey. The data presented in this study are corroborated by most of the scientific literature regarding team sports. For example, Black et al. (2019) demonstrated that the mean age of sport specialization for a sample of professional hockey players was 14.1 years. This age coincides with the Train to Train phase of the LTPD. The statistics are clear: less than 1 percent of players to ever play the game will play a full career in the NHL. Of course, hockey participation might be an avenue to other endeavors, even long playing careers in other professional leagues. Still, the goal from the onset is lifelong physical activity and participation in sport.

CHRONOLOGICAL, PHYSIOLOGICAL, AND TRAINING AGE

In youth hockey, athletes are typically grouped based on their chronological age (i.e., how old they are in years) without consideration of their physiological (physical maturity) or training age (how long they have been training or how much experience they have with a given task). Therefore, athletes might be grouped with others of the same chronological age but significantly different physiological and training ages. This is a dilemma that most youth coaches experience daily. In this scenario, the coach should have a specific plan for what needs to be accomplished within the training session. The athletes will then be divided into groups based on their physiological and training ages with specific regressions or progressions for a given task. For example, suppose the session's primary goal is lower-body strength development using the squat pattern. In that case, one group might simply execute the squat pattern with no external load, another group might perform a goblet squat, and the most advanced group performs a front squat (see chapter 5 for exercises). In all three cases, the athletes will improve their lower-body strength in that specific pattern with various degrees of technical and external loading demands.

SUMMARY

When designing hockey training plans, many variables need to be considered due to the game's multifactorial nature. Movement capacity, energy systems, strength, functional power, acceleration, and change of direction are all critical variables that must be addressed. Additionally, the position, gender, and age of the athlete require considerable attention. When combining these factors, it is easy to get overwhelmed, knowing that there might not be a one-size-fits-all approach. Therefore, strength and conditioning practitioners must identify the specific qualities that allow for optimal performance and then assess each of these areas individually. These assessments can take the form of preseason evaluations as well as ongoing monitoring throughout the season. The assessments' results can then be used to tailor individualized training programs regardless of the athlete's demographic. Chapter 2 will discuss the various protocols used to evaluate the physical characteristics and concurrent development of a hockey player.

Chapter 2

Assessing and Monitoring Hockey Fitness and Movement

Every team or organization has a different philosophy of what qualities an individual player must possess to succeed on the ice. As a result, there is no right or wrong testing battery as long as what is measured aligns with the governing philosophy of the organization and helps form a well-rounded hockey player. Chapter 1 outlined the physical demands of ice hockey and explained that testing protocols should strive to measure each of these demands. It is imperative to know what matters and to measure what matters in order to change what matters.

The physiological data is crucial, but the way it is collected is arguably the most critical variable. Testing modalities must have a high degree of reliability and validity. Reliability refers to the consistency of a measurement, where consistency is present over time (test-retest reliability), across items (internal consistency), and across different testers (interrater reliability) (Price, Jhangiani, and Chiang 2019). Validity is the extent to which the test measures what it intends to measure. If the way you collect data is not reliable and valid, your data is not meaningful and cannot assess the athlete's true capabilities.

This chapter will outline the appropriate physical assessments and the testing schedule throughout the phases of a season and off-season. Typically, physical assessments are completed at the beginning of the preseason and postseason. Still, to account for changes throughout the season, ongoing monitoring of specific qualities and characteristics must accompany and complement these traditional fitness assessments. With the development of particular technologies, monitoring capabilities have improved throughout the years. However, these specific technologies are not always necessary to better understand players on a daily or weekly basis. Preseason and postseason testing typically occur over one or two days and are a snapshot of one point in time. This snapshot might not tell the whole story. For example, if an athlete is ill or not feeling well on the testing day, their results might not accurately depict their physiological capabilities. In that case, ongoing monitoring becomes even more critical.

MODALITY OF ASSESSMENT

Regardless of the task at hand, whether in testing or training, the risks must be weighed against the rewards. Inherent risks must be outlined, evaluated, and minimized to reduce the chances of any unintentional injury to the athletes. Often, athletes are away for the entire off-season, and at many levels, communication with these athletes might be limited or even prohibited. Therefore, some athletes might have higher chances of injury in specific tests due to the nature of their off-season training. For example, if an athlete's energy systems training throughout the off-season was strictly performed on a stationary bike, running tests to assess these energy systems might pose a higher risk of injury. One main factor coaches need to consider is that physical assessments should test physiology only, not whether the athlete will be a good player on the ice. Does the athlete's current physiological state support the game's demands, and what qualities, if improved, will aid the athlete in becoming more effective on the ice? These are the questions such tests attempt to answer.

TESTING SCHEDULE

At all levels, time is a valuable commodity. Head coaches typically want to maximize practice time early in the preseason to work on the technical and tactical aspects of the game. Therefore, physical assessments usually occur on the first day of training camp in the preseason. Currently, at the NHL level, the collective bargaining agreement states that the player's testing window cannot exceed three hours in duration and prohibits on-ice testing on this first day. Therefore, all physical assessments must be completed within that time frame, which poses many challenges to sport scientists and strength and conditioning coaches who must obtain a physiological picture of the athlete safely, efficiently, and effectively. On the other hand, most other levels are not governed by these same constraints, and fitness testing can be performed over a more extended period if needed.

Although testing on the first day of training camp runs some inherent risks, it is essential to obtain the athlete's best physiological picture. If testing is completed later within training camp to allow the athlete to acclimatize, factors such as fatigue or injury might negatively influence the data. Additionally, testing athletes later in training camp might not be possible at many levels if preseason and exhibition competition begins within a week of the start of training camp.

Postseason assessments should be guided by several factors and might differ from year to year. For example, the postseason protocols for a team that does not make the playoffs will vary significantly from the protocols of the team that wins the championship. Typically, postseason testing is less invasive and physically demanding than preseason testing. Postseason testing is often deemed nonessential if the organization performs adequate ongoing monitoring throughout the season, both on and off the ice.

Ultimately, all assessments should be carefully planned and fully justified by the sport science and strength and conditioning team. It is also the athlete's responsibility to be physically prepared for all physical assessments that an organization has planned. The rest of the chapter breaks down the various physical assessments concerning the physical demands outlined in chapter 1.

MOVEMENT CAPACITY ASSESSMENTS

When physical capabilities are considered, the movement capacity assessments are typically the last qualities that are thought of, if at all. Actually, movement capacity assessments are some of the most essential assessments in our toolbox. Movement capacity is the athlete's foundation on which all physiological variables are built. Assessing movement capacity makes apparent any problem areas that might need to be resolved before or in conjunction with other training forms.

As outlined in chapter 1, movement capacity is divided into hardware and software categories. The following tests pertain to the significant areas of concern typically present with many hockey players.

Hardware Assessments

Hardware assessments focus mainly on slower-changing qualities within the human systems. These factors include bone structure, muscle systems, and fascial systems.

Modified Thomas Test

Equipment

Examination table

Purpose

The modified Thomas test's primary purpose is to examine hip extensibility and range of motion in the sagittal plane.

Setup

The athlete lies on their back on an examination table with the lower fold of the gluteal muscles at the table's edge.

Procedure

While the athlete is on their back, they pull one knee toward the chest, placing the hip into flexion. The other leg remains in the extended position, and a neutral pelvis position is maintained throughout the test

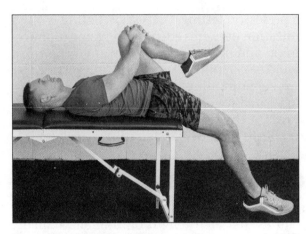

Figure 2.1   Modified Thomas test.

(figure 2.1). This position is held until the examiner has made the appropriate assessments. Once one side is completed, switch legs.

Assessment

The modified Thomas test is generally a pass-fail test. A positive or failed test is when there is noticeable hip flexion in the contralateral leg, known as a hip extension deficit, which usually indicates a tight iliopsoas (Vigotsky et al. 2016). However, one can gain three other vital pieces of information from performing the modified Thomas test. First, knee extension in the contralateral leg might indicate a tight rectus femoris muscle. Second, hip abduction in the contralateral leg might mean a tight tensor fascia latae. Lastly, pain, clicking, or popping may indicate a hip labral tear (Nicholls 2004).

Hip External and Internal Rotation (Flexed and Extended Positions)

Equipment

Examination table, goniometer

Purpose

The purpose of these tests is to identify external or internal rotation deficits or imbalances between the right and left limbs.

Setup

External and internal rotation flexed hip: The athlete sits upright at the edge of the examination table (figure 2.2a).

External and internal rotation extended hip: The athlete lies prone on the examination table with their knees in 90 degrees of flexion (figure 2.2b).

In both scenarios, the stationary arm of a goniometer is aligned perpendicular to the floor. The goniometer movement is aligned parallel to the tibia's long axis, with the axis of rotation centered over the midpatella.

Procedure

With the athlete in position, the examiner moves the limb through its full range of motion, keeping the pelvis stable. This procedure will be performed on both legs.

Assessment

External and internal rotation are measured as the deviation from the zero starting point. Take note of each scenario's range, and identify significant differences between the right and left limbs and deficits within the limb. The typical range of motion for external rotation and internal rotation is up to 45 degrees, with internal rotation typically lower than external rotation (Cannon, Finn, and Yan 2018).

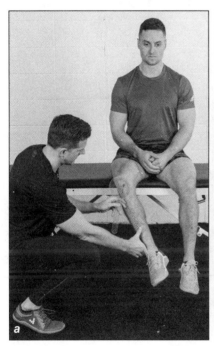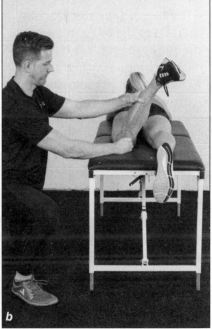

Figure 2.2　Hip external rotation: *(a)* flexed hip, *(b)* extended hip.

Craig's Test

Equipment

Examination table, goniometer

Purpose

The purpose of the Craig's test is to identify anteversion (inward twisting) of the femur. This test will determine the femur's natural position and guide training prescriptions. For example, if an athlete is positive for internal rotation of the femur (or anteversion), exercises that address hip external rotation strength and core and pelvis stability will help resolve the issue.

Setup

The athlete lies prone on the examination table with the knee of the limb in question placed at 90 degrees of flexion.

Procedure

The examiner rotates the hip into internal and external rotation to determine the hip position where the femur's greater trochanter is parallel to the table (figure 2.3). This procedure is performed on both legs.

Assessment

Once the femur's greater trochanter is parallel to the table, the examiner measures the hip's angle using a similar technique as hip internal and external rotation assessments. The normal range for this test is between 8 and 15 degrees of medial rotation. As with the previous range of motion tests, note asymmetries between limbs. If an asymmetry is present, exercise prescriptions can be made to minimize or eliminate it. For example, if one leg is excessively internally rotated and the other is normal, additional training of the hip external rotators on the affected limb might be required to balance the two sides.

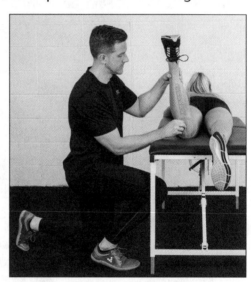

Figure 2.3   Craig's test.

Ankle Dorsiflexion

Equipment

Tape measure

Purpose

The purpose of measuring ankle dorsiflexion is twofold. First, ankle dorsiflexion deficits have been shown to negatively affect kinematics (movement) at the knee and hip joints. Second, since hockey is played in stiff skates, lack of dorsiflexion is a common concern in hockey players.

Setup

The athlete places their foot 4.9 inches (12.5 cm) from the wall and assumes a half-kneeling position.

Procedure

The athlete attempts to touch their knee to the wall (figure 2.4) while maintaining heel contact with the ground.

Assessment

This test is graded as a pass (if the knee touches the wall) or fail (if the knee does not contact the wall). A normal range of dorsiflexion is considered 4.9 inches (12.5 cm) or greater.

Figure 2.4   Ankle dorsiflexion.

Postural Assessment

Equipment

None

Purpose

The purpose of postural assessment is to obtain a qualitative glance into the natural state and tendencies of the athlete's upper and lower body.

Setup

The athlete stands relaxed with arms at their side.

Procedure

The examiner views the athlete in the frontal plane (front and back) and sagittal plane (from the side) (figure 2.5a, b).

Assessment

Analyze the position of the head and neck, shoulder girdle, rib cage, and pelvis. Two common abnormalities seen in the hockey player population are the upper-crossed and lower-crossed syndromes.

The upper-crossed syndrome consists of inhibited deep cervical flexors, lower trapezius, and serratus anterior, combined with tight upper trapezius, levator scapula, pectoralis, and sternocleidomastoid. These factors often lead to forward head position, internally rotated or rounded shoulders, and protracted scapulae, potentially leading to kyphosis of the thoracic spine (Moore 2004).

The lower-crossed syndrome consists of inhibited abdominal and gluteal muscles and tight rectus femoris, iliopsoas, and thoracolumbar extensors. The lower-crossed syndrome tilts the pelvis anteriorly, which can result in several lower-body pathologies such as sports hernia.

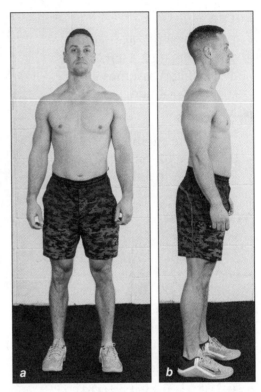

Figure 2.5   Postural assessment: *(a)* frontal view, *(b)* sagittal view.

Software Assessments

These assessments focus mainly on sensory qualities within the human systems. These sensors, in general, are governed by the nervous system and provide movement feedback. This information comes from sensors in the brain, nerves, joints, and muscles. The nervous system collects thousands of pieces of information that guide the hardware components on movement patterns. These qualities are often highly adaptable and can be modified in short periods of time.

Movement Screening

Equipment

Functional Movement Screen apparatus

Purpose

Movement screens are designed to highlight any movement deficits or deficiencies in specific movement patterns. The Functional Movement Screen is one example of many movement screens that exist. On one level, screening should be accomplished daily in the training environment; coaches must continually monitor the movement qualities and capabilities of athletes. However, formal movement screens provide some initial movement feedback in a safe and controlled fashion and are one tool in the coach's toolbox.

Setup

Measure the tibia length, which is the length from the ground to the tibial tuberosity. This distance determines the height of the hurdle step and spacing between the feet in the inline lunge. The hand length is also measured, from the wrist crease to the tip of the longest finger. Hand length is used for scoring the shoulder mobility portion of the test.

Procedure

The athlete completes seven movements: deep squat, hurdle step, in-line lunge, active straight-leg raise, trunk stability push-up, rotary stability, and shoulder mobility (Cook 2003).

Assessment

Each movement is scored on a scale of 0 to 3, in which 0 represents any pain in a specific pattern and 3 represents the pattern's completion without any compensation. The sum score is calculated. Typically, a score of 14 or less or the presence of asymmetries or 0 scores would require subsequent investigation into the individual's capabilities.

Star Excursion Balance Test

Equipment

Tape, tape measure

Purpose

The star excursion balance test is designed to assess postural control utilizing a unilateral stance (Robinson and Gribble 2008).

Setup

Place strips of tape that are approximately 7 feet (2 m) in length on a smooth and firm floor in the pattern outlined in figure 2.6.

Procedure

The athlete stands on one leg at the center of the star with their hands on their hips and reaches with the contralateral leg in eight different directions (figure 2.6). These include three anterior, two lateral, and three posterior positions. If the athlete cannot maintain the original foot position or heel contact with the floor on the balance leg, the trial must be redone. Perform this test on both legs.

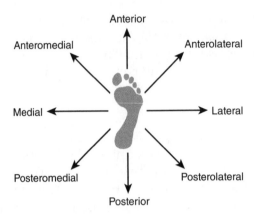

Figure 2.6   Star excursion balance test.

Assessment

The athlete reaches with the contralateral leg in each direction. The maximal reach for each position is measured. The tester notes any differences in measurement between the legs and subjectively identifies any deviations in hip, knee, and ankle stability and control.

ENERGY SYSTEMS ASSESSMENTS

Energy systems are divided into three broad categories: aerobic, anaerobic glycolytic, and anaerobic alactic. These systems are responsible for providing energy to support the game's demands and the other performance variables that have been outlined. The goal of an energy systems assessment is to measure these systems' capabilities and analyze the athlete's ability to perform the work required on the ice. This section will outline various laboratory and field tests that measure athletes' energy systems' capabilities and replicate the energy demands that support their physical performance on the ice.

Aerobic Capacity

Aerobic fitness and capacity provide the foundation on which all other energy systems are built. The measurement of aerobic capacity can be accomplished in many ways. These tests can be maximal or submaximal and done in the laboratory or on the field. In the context of the entire physical assessment battery, a submaximal test to estimate aerobic capacity might be the best choice, when applicable. The two tests that follow represent one submaximal effort laboratory test and one maximal effort field test. The field test can be used in populations that do not have the resources available to conduct laboratory testing.

PWC-150

Equipment

Cycle ergometer, heart rate monitor

Purpose

The purpose of the PWC-150 is to estimate the power output obtained on a cycle ergometer at a heart rate of 150 beats per minute (bpm). This test provides an estimate of the aerobic capabilities of the athlete at submaximal levels.

Setup

The test requires a cycle ergometer that can be calibrated and that provides power output feedback in terms of watts. The seat and handlebar heights are adjusted to a comfortable riding height. The athlete is required to wear a heart rate monitor to measure heart rate at specific intervals. The athlete should not consume caffeine or other stimulants before submaximal aerobic tests that are based on heart rate to ensure that the heart rate data is accurate.

Procedure

The athlete cycles at an initial workload of 50 watts and a cadence of 70 revolutions per minute (rpm). The workload is increased by 25 watts every 2 minutes until a heart rate of 150 bpm is achieved. Once a heart rate of 150 bpm is reached, the test is complete. Take note of the heart rate at every stage.

Assessment

The workload at the heart rate of 150 bpm is divided by the athlete's body weight in kilograms to give a score in watts per kilogram. Table 2.1 outlines the relative performance scores for the PWC-150 test.

Table 2.1 Relative Performance Scores in Watts per Kilogram for the PWC-150 Test

	Poor	Fair	Average	Good	Very good
Male	<1.50	1.50-1.99	2.00-2.49	2.50-3.00	>3.00
Female	<1.25	1.25-1.59	1.60-1.99	2.00-2.50	>2.50

20-Meter Multistage Fitness Test (Beep Test)

Equipment

Speaker or stereo, measuring tape, cones

Purpose

The 20-meter multistage fitness test estimates an athlete's maximal aerobic capacity. This test is continuous and progressive, with the running speeds gradually increased at specified intervals.

Setup

An audio recording of the test is required to guide the athletes through the various stages. Two lines are marked 20 meters (66 ft) apart from each other.

Procedure

The athletes line up at the starting line. The audio recording begins, signaling the athletes to commence running. They run to the line 20 meters (66 ft) away, arriving on or before the next audible beep. At the beep (and not before), the athletes return to the starting line. This process continues, with athletes maintaining pace with audible beeps. The beeps get progressively closer together, requiring athletes to run faster as the stages progress. The test is completed when the athlete can no longer run the distance before the beep two consecutive times.

Assessment

The athlete's score is the last completed shuttle level. Each level is associated with a running velocity. The running velocity can then be used to calculate an estimated $\dot{V}O_2$max (Flouris, Metsios, and Koutedakis 2005):

$$\dot{V}O2max = velocity \times 6.55 - 35.8$$

Anaerobic Capacity and Repeated Sprint Ability (Anaerobic Glycolytic System)

Anaerobic capacity or anaerobic work capacity is the total amount of energy available from anaerobic sources such as the ATP-CP (alactic system) and glycolysis (lactic acid system), with most of the energy produced by the latter. The anaerobic glycolytic system is responsible for most of the energy production for activities lasting 30 seconds to over 2 minutes. Anaerobic capacity is intimately related to the athlete's repeated sprint ability, which is the athlete's ability to maintain maximal effort during successive sprints with minimal recovery in between.

Anaerobic Work Capacity 2.5-Minute Bike Test

Equipment

Cycle ergometer, heart rate monitor

Purpose

The purpose of the anaerobic work capacity 2.5-minute bike test is to measure the overall capacity of the anaerobic energy system by measuring the total amount of work completed in 2.5 minutes.

Setup

This test requires a cycle ergometer that can be calibrated and set isokinetically to a specific cadence. This means that once the cadence in question is reached, the athlete cannot pedal any faster. Any additional effort will produce greater resistance (i.e., higher wattage) for the set cadence. The seat and handlebar heights are adjusted to a comfortable riding height. The athlete is required to wear a heart rate monitor, and the cycle ergometer will be connected to computer software that will measure power output in real time.

Procedure

The cycle ergometer is set to a maximum cadence of 80 rpm. The athlete is instructed to pedal as hard as possible for 2.5 minutes. After the test is complete, the athlete must sit upright in a chair for an additional 2 minutes; the heart rate is recorded at the 1- and 2-minute marks.

Assessment

The measured power throughout the 2.5-minute test can be used to calculate the specific energy requirements in kilojoules of the performance, where cycling at 1 watt for 1 second equals 1 joule. Therefore, average power multiplied by seconds riding will determine the amount of energy required to complete the test. The total joules are then divided by the athlete's body weight in kilograms to obtain a relative value. Note that the athlete must produce a maximal effort so they are completely exhausted by the end of the test to ensure accurate data; scores for this test range from 600 to 1100 joules per kilogram at the NHL level. In addition to the energy measurements, heart rate recovery is also measured.

Repeated High-Intensity Endurance Test (RHIET)

Equipment

Timing gates or stopwatch, tape measure, cones

Purpose

The purpose of the RHIET is to examine repeated sprint ability, which encompasses multiple aspects of the energy systems but anaerobic capacity in particular.

Setup

The test should be completed on a surface that provides adequate traction for the athletes (e.g., running track) because a change of direction is required to complete the test. A distance of 131 feet (40 m) is measured in a single lane, with cones placed at the startling line and 131 feet (40 m). Timing gates (or stopwatches) are placed at the 16 feet (5 m) and 115 feet (35 m) distances.

Procedure

The athlete begins at the starting line. They sprint as fast as possible to the 131-foot (40 m mark), stop, and return to the startling line, for a total of 262 feet (80 m), as quickly as possible. A total of six maximal repetitions are done, each starting at 30-second intervals (i.e., rep 1 at time 0, rep 2 at 30 seconds, rep 3 at 1 minute, etc.). Therefore, if the athlete completes the first repetition in 15 seconds, they will receive a 15-second recovery until the next repeat.

Assessment

Two times are recorded for each repetition, between 16 feet (5 m) and 115 feet (35 m), and between 115 feet (35 m) and 16 feet (5 m). These times are added together to obtain a total time for the repetition. With the resulting data, the coach receives information on the athlete's speed (i.e., the first repetition) and their ability to maintain this speed throughout the test. Both variables are important. If the athlete's first repetition is very fast but they drop off significantly throughout the assessment, this might represent deficits in anaerobic capacity. Conversely, if the athlete can maintain speed throughout the test but this speed is slow, this athlete might be underpowered. Of note is that the first repetition of the RHIET test is also a field test substitution for the 10-second Wingate test described later in the chapter.

Anaerobic Alactic (ATP-PCr) System

The anaerobic alactic system is responsible for providing most of the energy required for all-out bouts of work that are typically shorter than 10 seconds. In the sport of hockey, this system is vital in many scenarios, for example, when an athlete has a quick race to a puck or a goaltender is pushing quickly from post to post or sprints out to reach a loose puck.

10-Second Wingate Test

Equipment

Monark 894E (Anaerobic Wingate Ergometer)

Purpose

Traditionally, the Wingate test is performed over 30 seconds, with measurements of peak power, anaerobic capacity, and fatigue index. It is my opinion that the 30-second test is not an adequate duration to tax the anaerobic system completely; therefore, the tests described in the previous section are completed to accomplish that task. However, the 10-second Wingate test is designed to measure the anaerobic alactic (ATP-PCr) system's capabilities.

Setup

The 10-second Wingate test is typically performed on a Monark 894E (Anaerobic Wingate Ergometer) with its associated software. In recent years, other companies have designed cycle ergometers that can obtain the same measurements. The seat and handlebar heights are adjusted to a comfortable riding height. The cycle ergometer is connected to computer software that measures power output in real time.

Procedure

Two trials of the test will be conducted, and they are separated by a recovery period of 3 to 5 minutes. To start, the athlete pedals at 60 rpm for a lead-in time of 60 seconds at zero resistance. Once the 60-second lead-in is complete, the tester gives a verbal signal and drops the full load onto the bike. The athlete pedals as fast as possible for 10 seconds. The resistance can range from 0.17 to 2.9 pounds (0.075-1.3 kg) per 2.2 pounds (1 kg) of body weight. To ensure that the athlete is optimizing their power, the number of pedal revolutions is counted during the period the 5-second peak power is maximized. If the pedal revolutions are 11 to 13, the loading is adequate. If the pedal revolutions drop below 11, weight should be removed for the second trial. If the pedal revolutions exceed 13, additional weight can be added for the second trial.

Assessment

The computer software calculates the 5-second peak power over the 10-second duration. Typical values at the NHL level range between 14.0 and 21.0 watts per kilogram.

STRENGTH AND POWER ASSESSMENTS

Strength and power are essential performance variables in the sport of hockey. Most strength evaluations should be performed in the daily training environment. A system of tracking key performance indicators (KPIs) can be built directly into daily training plans. It is safe to assume that many of the exercises athletes perform within the gym setting are essential to their overall performance on the ice. That said, it is necessary to evaluate performance on these critical variables regularly.

Three general areas of concern should be measured in preseason testing: core strength and endurance, upper-body strength, and lower-body mechanical power (which, in theory, gives a good indication of lower-body strength).

Core Strength and Endurance Tests

As described in chapter 1, core strength and endurance (proximal stability) provide the foundation for many other performance variables. Therefore, it is imperative for hockey players to have adequate core strength and endurance to support other movements. Two tests to evaluate core muscular strength and endurance are the lateral musculature test (side plank) and the anterior abdominal test (front plank); these tests are guided by the work of Dr. Stuart McGill (McGill 2007).

Lateral Musculature Test (Side Plank)

Equipment

Exercise mat, stopwatch

Purpose

To evaluate the muscular strength and endurance of the lateral core musculature.

Setup

The athlete sets up in the side plank position, with legs fully extended and the top foot placed in front of the bottom foot. The athlete's top arm is held across the chest with the hand on the opposite shoulder.

Procedure

The athlete is instructed to raise the hips off the ground, creating a straight line from head to feet.

Assessment

The athlete holds this position until failure, meaning that posture cannot be maintained, or for 1 minute. This test is pass or fail.

Anterior Abdominal Test (Front Plank)

Equipment

Exercise mat, stopwatch

Purpose

To evaluate the muscular strength and endurance of the anterior core musculature.

Setup

The athlete sets up by lying prone on the floor with the elbows directly under the shoulders and with the feet together.

Procedure

The athlete elevates their body off the ground into a forearm plank, being sure to engage the gluteal muscles. A straight line from the shoulders to the feet should be observed.

Assessment

The athlete holds this position until failure, meaning that posture cannot be maintained, or for 2 minutes. This test is a pass or fail.

Upper-Body Strength and Endurance

Due to hockey's physicality, upper-body strength and endurance are essential pieces of the performance blueprint. Upper-body strength and endurance are critical for shooting, battling against opponents, and even skating through efficient arm and upper-body movement. In general, the pull-up is a good indicator of upper-body strength and endurance.

Pull-Up

Equipment

Pull-up bar

Purpose

Because hockey is a contact sport in which physical interactions with opposing players occur every shift, it is imperative for players to possess adequate upper-body strength and endurance to excel in these situations. A simple test to assess global upper-body strength is the pull-up.

Setup

A pull-up bar is set to a height that does not allow the athlete to touch the floor when in a fully extended position. The athlete grips the bar with an overhand grip and starts from a dead-hanging position with the arms and legs fully extended.

Procedure

The athlete performs as many complete pull-up repetitions as possible. The movement must be controlled with the arms fully extended in the lowered position and a straight line maintained from head to toe throughout the duration. The nose must break the bar's plane. Repetitions that do not satisfy all these requirements are not counted.

Assessment

Note the total number of repetitions completed. This data can then be referenced in subsequent testing to determine level of improvement. Table 2.2 outlines performance standards for both male and female players.

Table 2.2 Pull-Up Performance Standards

	Male	Female
Excellent	>16	>10
Good	10-15	6-9
Average	6-9	3-5
Fair	2-5	1-2
Poor	0 or 1	0

Lower-Body Power (Vertical Jump Testing)

When possible, vertical jump testing should be performed on bilateral force plates. This equipment provides multiple variables that pertain to jump performance and identify asymmetries between the right and left legs. Both the squat jump and countermovement jump should be performed.

Squat Jump

Equipment

Bilateral force plates, rope

Purpose

The primary purpose of the squat jump is to measure lower-body mechanical power from a static position. In theory, the static position eliminates any contribution from the stretch-shortening cycle and elastic energy.

Setup

Set the force plates on a firm, level surface, and ensure the force plates are level. Measure the distance of the superior border of the patella to the ground or force plate. A rope or stick is placed at the level measured. This device will guide the athlete to the appropriate squat depth for the trials.

Procedure

The athlete stands on the force plates with their hands on their hips. The athlete squats down to the level of the rope or stick and holds that position until stable (figure 2.7a). Once stable, they jump as high as possible (figure 2.7b) while keeping their hands on their hips. Four additional repetitions, for a total of five, are performed.

Assessment

Measurements of jump height, peak power, rate of force development, take-off velocity, and differences (kinetic asymmetries) between the right and left limbs are collected. The data from this test can track how the athlete is progressing throughout the year and make it possible to compare performance between athletes.

Figure 2.7 Squat jump: (a) squat and (b) jump.

Countermovement Jump

Equipment

Bilateral force plates

Purpose

The primary purpose of the countermovement jump is to measure lower-body mechanical power with contributions from the stretch-shortening cycle, elastic energy, and active state development.

Setup

Set the force plates on a firm, level surface, and ensure the force plates are level.

Procedure

The athlete stands on the force plates with their hands on their hips. On the tester's cue, the athlete descends as rapidly as possible, reverses direction at a level comfortable to the athlete, and subsequently jumps as high as possible (figure 2.8a-c). They land and reset, completing an additional four repetitions, for a total of five, in the same manner.

Figure 2.8 Countermovement jump: *(a)* starting position, *(b)* descent, and *(c)* jump.

Assessment

Measurements of jump height, peak power, rate of force development, reactive strength index, take-off velocity, and differences (kinetic asymmetries) between right and left limbs are collected. The data from this test can track how the athlete is progressing throughout the year and make it possible to compare performances between athletes.

NO TECHNOLOGY? NO PROBLEM

Although force plates are becoming more accessible to the average strength and conditioning coach, this technology is often out of reach at the game's lower levels. Even so, valuable information can be gained by measuring vertical jump height without force plates. Simply fix a tape measure to a wall, and have athletes jump as high as possible, touching the tape with their dominant hand. Athletes should perform this sequence for both the squat and countermovement jumps.

ACCELERATION ASSESSMENTS

As described in chapter 1, the ability to accelerate provides more value than top-end speed in hockey. Ideally, acceleration assessments should be completed on the ice to be as specific as possible, but often on-ice testing is prohibited or inaccessible. This section describes two tests, one on the ice and one off the ice, to assess the athlete's acceleration potential.

On-Ice Acceleration Test

Equipment

Timing gates or stopwatches

Purpose

The purpose of this test is to assess the athlete's ability to accelerate from a stationary position on the ice.

Setup

In a standard NHL-sized hockey rink, the distance between the two blue lines is 50 feet (15.24 m). These lines will serve as the start and finish lines. Timing gates (or stopwatches) will be set up at the start and finish lines.

Procedure

The athlete sets up in a comfortable stance with one foot on or behind the starting line, then accelerates as quickly as possible to the finish line. Three trials are completed, with 2 minutes of rest between trials.

Assessment

The trial times are recorded, with the fastest trial used for the assessment. If testing multiple players and the ice's quality is significantly diminished, the lane might need to be moved. The data from this test show how the athlete is progressing throughout the year and make it possible to compare performances between athletes.

30-Meter Off-Ice Acceleration Test

Equipment

Timing gates or stopwatches, tape measure

Purpose

The purpose of this test is to assess the athlete's ability to accelerate from a stationary position off the ice. The 30-meter (98 ft) distance off the ice has strong correlations to many on-ice performances, including acceleration, peak speed, and change of direction.

Setup

The test should be completed on a surface that provides adequate traction for the athletes (e.g., running track). A distance of 30 meters (98 ft) is measured and marked. Timing gates (or stopwatches) are set up at the starting line, 10 meters (33 ft), and 30 meters (98 ft).

Procedure

The athlete sets up at the starting line in a comfortable staggered stance, then accelerates as quickly as possible to the 30-meter (98 ft) mark. Three trials are completed, with 2 to 3 minutes of rest between trials.

Assessment

The trial times are recorded, with the fastest trial used for the assessment. Take note of both the 10-meter (33 ft) and 30-meter (98 ft) split times. The data from this test show how the athlete is progressing and make it possible to compare performances between athletes.

CHANGE-OF-DIRECTION AND REACTIVITY ASSESSMENTS

The ability to accelerate is essential; however, the game dynamics require split-second decision-making resulting in multiple changes of direction every shift. These direction changes vary in magnitude, but it is vital to possess the ability to change direction with an organized body and in a decisive manner. The two tests described in this section demonstrate how to assess change-of-direction capabilities both on and off the ice.

Off-Ice Pro Agility (5-10-5)

Equipment

Timing gates or stopwatches, tape measure, cones

Purpose

To evaluate change-of-direction capabilities off the ice.

Setup

The test should be completed on a surface that provides adequate traction for the athletes (e.g., running track) because a change of direction is required to complete the test. A distance of 10 meters (33 ft) is required for the test, with timing gates (or stopwatches) at the center line. Markers are placed 5 meters (16 ft) from the starting line to both sides (figure 2.9).

Procedure

The athlete sets up in a three-point position straddling the starting line. One hand must be in contact with the ground, and that hand determines the direction in which the athlete will run first. The athlete sprints as quickly as possible to the first line, changes direction (the foot and outside hand must touch the line), sprints as quickly as possible to the opposite line, changes direction again, and accelerates to the finish line (center line). Three trials in each direction are completed to obtain the best results, with each repetition separated by a rest period of 2 to 3 minutes.

Assessment

The time to completion is recorded in each direction. Take note of any significant differences between directions. The data from this test show how the athlete is progressing and make it possible to compare performances between athletes.

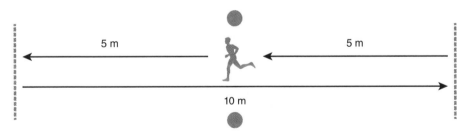

Figure 2.9   Off-ice pro agility (5-10-5).

On-Ice Pro Agility

Equipment

Timing gates or stopwatches, tape measure, cones

Purpose

To evaluate sport-specific change-of-direction capabilities while skating.

Setup

Timing gates (or stopwatches) are placed at the center ice (red) line. Markers are placed at the blue lines on either side, corresponding to a distance of 25 feet (7.6 m) from the red line (figure 2.10).

Procedure

The athlete straddles the center line. They skate as quickly as possible to one blue line, touch it with their skate, change direction, skate as quickly as possible to the opposite blue line, change direction again, and return to the center line. The athlete faces the same direction during all changes in direction (Delisle-Houde et al. 2019). After 2 to 3 minutes of rest, the test is repeated, starting in the opposite direction from the first trial.

Assessment

The time to completion is recorded in each direction. Take note of any significant differences in either direction. The data from this test show how the athlete is progressing and can make it possible to compare performances between athletes.

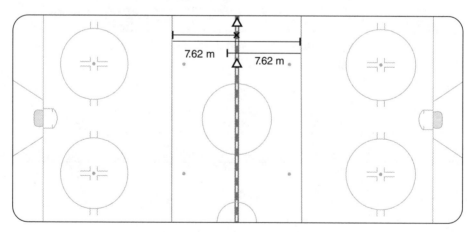

Figure 2.10   On-ice pro agility.

PROTOCOL DESIGN

Designing the assessment battery presents many challenges. Sport scientists and strength and conditioning coaches are often limited in time and structure. The testing battery must be standardized, with every athlete completing the tests in the same order, on the same surfaces, and in the same environment to ensure the protocol's validity and reliability. Additionally, the order in which the tests are performed is critical. The battery must be structured to minimize any potential negative effects that one test might have on another. For example, a maximum aerobic capacity test will negatively affect a lower-body power test. Organizing the battery so that a test might optimize performances in subsequent tests must also be considered. Following are two examples of testing batteries: one including laboratory tests and the other field tests. *Note:* Any on-ice testing should be completed on a separate day from these testing batteries due to the time constraints and logistics involved. Athletes are required to wear full equipment for the on-ice testing protocols.

Laboratory Testing Battery

1. Medical and orthopedic evaluations
2. Body composition evaluation
3. Submaximal aerobic testing
4. Movement screening
5. Vertical jump testing
6. 10-second Wingate testing
7. Strength testing
8. Anaerobic capacity assessments

Field Testing Battery

Morning

1. Medical and orthopedic evaluations
2. Body composition evaluation
3. Movement screening
4. Vertical jump testing
5. Strength testing
6. Linear sprint testing
7. Change-of-direction testing
8. Repeated sprint ability assessments

Afternoon

1. Maximal aerobic capacity assessments

ONGOING MONITORING

In the world of sports, particularly at the professional level, evaluating physical characteristics once or twice a year is not sufficient to assess the athletes' ongoing readiness and training loads to participate at the highest levels. Monitoring athletes' wellness and readiness must be completed at regular intervals throughout the season and off-season.

Readiness Monitoring

Part of the sport science and strength and conditioning staff's responsibilities are to assess athletes' daily readiness to compete or train. The training plans often need to be adjusted based on subjective and objective data regarding the athletes' well-being. This section describes two examples: one subjective (daily wellness and sleep questionnaire) and one objective (heart rate variability).

Daily Wellness and Sleep Questionnaires

Daily monitoring of athletes' subjective feelings provides valuable insights into their state of readiness. Traditionally, this has been accomplished through general conversations. However, a more sophisticated approach would be to devise a short, concise, and numerically coded daily questionnaire. Each question should be on a numerical scale (e.g., 1-5 or 1-10) and cover the athlete's overall feelings, muscle soreness, hours of sleep, quality of sleep, hydration status, nutritional status, stress, and body weight. An example questionnaire is presented in figure 2.11.

Name: _____

Date: _____

Body weight: _____

Total hours of sleep:_____

Rate each factor on a scale of 1 to 10, where 1 represents the worst and 10 represents the best outcome:

Overall feelings (1 = need recovery; 10 = ready to grind) _____

Muscle soreness (1 = extremely sore; 10 = no soreness) _____

Quality of sleep (1 = not rested; 10 = completely rested)_____

Hydration status (1 = dehydrated; 10 = fully hydrated)_____

Nutrition status (1 = poorly fueled; 10 = eating great) _____

Stress (1 = overwhelmed; 10 = in control) _____

Total score _____

Figure 2.11 Daily performance log.

Heart Rate Variability

Heart rate variability (HRV) is a measurement of the variation in time between each heartbeat. The autonomic nervous system (ANS) actively changes and adjusts for states of fatigue by regulating parasympathetic (fight or flight system) and sympathetic (rest and digest system) cardiovascular control mechanisms (Fogt et al. 2009). These adjustments can be measured through the analysis of HRV. When HRV is high, the parasympathetic and sympathetic nervous systems are in good balance. When HRV is low, these systems are out of balance, typically seen with sympathetic dominance. HRV measurement devices are becoming common in sports and are easily accessible for any individual. HRV provides insights into chronic fatigue and training readiness that can be utilized daily to individualize training plans as needed to avoid overtraining or chronic fatigue.

Workload Monitoring

Every training plan must be carefully periodized throughout a season and off-season. Structuring workloads safely and effectively to optimize performance should be a primary consideration of the sport science and strength and conditioning teams. That said, athletes will react differently to a given workload. These individual differences need to be monitored to ensure the appropriate balance between workload and recovery.

Session Rating of Perceived Exertion

Session rating of perceived exertion (S-RPE) is a simple yet effective tool to monitor the athlete's systemic workload (Haddad et al. 2017). The athlete rates the entire training session on a scale of 1 to 10, with 10 being the hardest possible exertion. This score is then multiplied by the session duration (minutes) to obtain the S-RPE score. The results can be plotted and tracked daily to ensure the athlete is experiencing the appropriate workload that matches the structure and training plan. S-RPE can be utilized for both off- and on-ice training or a combination of both.

On-Ice Internal and External Workload Monitoring

On-ice workload monitoring can be accomplished by measuring the body's internal response to training via heart rate monitoring (internal workload) or the work output (external workload). The internal workload is usually characterized by the training impulse (TRIMP) score. TRIMP considers three factors: session duration, the mean heart rate for the session, and a sex-dependent exponential coefficient that weights intensity (García-Ramos et al. 2015). External workload quantifies the amount of work performed. This can be quantified in many ways, such as distance traveled if using GPS or player load if using inertial movement analysis. If both internal and external workload monitoring are done simultaneously, the coach or sport scientist can then calculate the internal response for a given work output, also known as the training efficiency index (Delaney et al. 2018). The training efficiency index provides insight into how the athlete is adapting to the prescribed training.

Performance Monitoring

Performance monitoring throughout the season should also be considered. I recommend testing the countermovement vertical jump weekly, following the same protocol as preseason physical assessments. The data from the countermovement jump provide insights into how the central nervous system is responding to training and game workloads and how the athlete is adapting to training, and will highlight any asymmetries between the right and left legs that might be red flags for potential injury.

Body Composition Monitoring

Monitoring body composition throughout the season (e.g., every quarter) is an essential tool to highlight how the athlete's body adapts to the overall stress and is a good energy balance indicator. Measuring body composition at regular intervals allows for identifying fluctuations in overall body fat and lean tissue mass. These values can then be related to performance and wellness variables to paint a broader picture of how fat and lean tissue fluctuations affect the individual. There is no specific body fat percentage that can be applied across all hockey players; therefore, this data must be viewed in the context of the individual athlete's performance.

SUMMARY

In chapter 1, the physical demands of hockey were outlined. Through careful testing and monitoring throughout the season, coaches are able to

- understand the physical capabilities of the individual athletes,
- perform a physical demands needs analysis based on the physical assessments and ongoing monitoring for the individual in question,
- design appropriate training plans to address the needs analysis, and
- continually evaluate the athlete's readiness and physical capabilities and adjust the training plans accordingly.

The primary purpose of assessing and monitoring athletes is to collect data to make actionable changes. Time is a valuable commodity, and it must be optimized. If coaches feel they cannot make an actionable change on a specific variable or test, it must be reconsidered. Testing should not be done merely for the sake of testing. Coaches should start testing and monitoring simply and build as they become more comfortable with the process. They should highlight the areas that they deem most important and test those qualities, even if they can test only one variable. It is important to know what to measure in order to change what matters.

Chapter 3

Optimizing Movement Capacity

The capacity to move efficiently and with fluidity is a fundamental on which most areas of fitness are built. This fundamental often can be trained in conjunction with other performance characteristics, but it must be a significant focus of every training plan. Hockey players often add components of fitness (e.g., strength and power) without addressing their basic movement competencies. At best, this will not allow athletes to optimize their physical performance on the ice, and at worst, it might lead to injury. Inefficient movement is costly in terms of energy demands. If force generation cannot be optimized, the athlete will experience significant energy loss, which should be directed toward the task. Inefficient movement is also costly in mechanical demands, often creating excessive wear and tear on joint structures. That said, there might be many different movement strategies to accomplish a specific task, all with similar validity. Therefore, each athlete's movement patterns and competencies should be analyzed, and training guidelines should be tailored to the individual.

Chapter 2 highlighted various strategies to assess movement deficiencies. These focus on structural and neurological issues and are designed to identify potential roadblocks to more complex movements. The missing pieces in these assessments are movement at higher velocities and movement in different environments. As with every training scenario, competencies and skills must be progressively layered, both within a session and throughout an entire training program, to optimize movement capacity and skill.

This chapter will outline the following:

- Structures and function of the lumbopelvic-hip complex
- The kinetic chain and multijoint limb system
- Common pathologies and movement issues seen in hockey players
- The training sequence to optimize movement capacity
- Rebalancing techniques to offset the influence of the repetitive nature of skating mechanics

LUMBOPELVIC-HIP COMPLEX

Because skating is the primary action and mode of locomotion in hockey, the lumbopelvic-hip complex (LPHC) is of primary concern when analyzing hockey players' movement. It is also the area of most acute and insidious onset injuries that occur in hockey players. The LPHC, commonly called the *core*, consists of the structures responsible for spinal and pelvic stability that allow for efficient movement in the extremities (Chang et al. 2017). These include the lumbar spine, pelvis, femur, and associated ligaments and musculature. The LPHC has up to 35 muscles that attach to the lumbar spine or pelvis, a number that might feel overwhelming. However, we can simplify by focusing on movement patterns and the subsequent identification of why movement might not be optimal. We need to focus on the low-hanging fruit, such as broad muscle categories and their effects on pelvic positioning.

MULTIJOINT LIMB SYSTEM

Along with a focus on the LPHC, the athlete's kinetic chain (interrelated body segments) must be considered in its entirety. This sequence has often been termed the *joint-by-joint approach to training* (Boyle 2010). Movement or stability at each joint directly affects movement or stability at joints up or downstream in the kinetic chain. The joint-by-joint approach to training suggests that joints or body segments must alternate between mobility and stability (Boyle 2010). Beginning with ankle mobility, this alternating pattern requires knee stability, hip mobility, lumbar spine stability, thoracic spine mobility, scapular stability, and glenohumeral mobility. For example, the hip joint must possess mobility in several different motion planes, whereas the lumbar spine should be relatively stable during whole-body movements. The human body is a master of movement compensations. In general, the global movement task is executed by any means possible. Therefore, if a specific joint lacks mobility where mobility should be present, the joints or areas directly above or below this restriction ultimately express movement where there should be stability. For example, if the hip joint is experiencing limitations in extension, additional extension might be added by lumbar extension and subsequent anterior pelvic tilt. If patterns like this are repetitive over time, they might lead to specific overuse injuries or pain in the areas meant to be stable (e.g., lower back pain in the previous example). However, this theory is limited. Every joint or body segment should possess a certain degree of range of motion. Still, some areas are more on the spectrum of mobility and others stability when observing the system globally.

MOVEMENT PATHOLOGIES IN HOCKEY

The most common movement pathologies in hockey involve the hip joint and associated structures. The hip joint is a ball-and-socket joint with the ability to move in all three planes of motion (i.e., sagittal, frontal, and transverse).

The joint is formed between the acetabulum (socket) of the pelvis and the head of the femur (ball). The acetabulum is extended by a soft tissue structure known as the *acetabular labrum*. The labrum helps to minimize fluid expression from the joint space to protect the cartilage of the hip (Shindle, Domb, and Kelly 2007). Four of the most common pathologies seen in hockey players are femoroacetabular impingement (FAI), hip labral tear, groin or adductor strain, and sports hernia. These all share one significant risk factor in common: a low range of motion of the hip. Therefore, these four issues are intimately connected and not necessarily mutually exclusive.

Femoroacetabular Impingement and Hip Labral Tears

Two types of FAI are presented in the literature: cam and pincer (Shindle, Domb, and Kelly 2007). Cam impingement results from a bony outgrowth on the femoral head, and pincer impingement is due to abnormalities in the acetabulum. Lerebours et al. (2016) studied 130 elite hockey players from the NHL and their associated development teams. They noted that 69.4 percent of these players met radiographic imaging criteria for the cam deformity, with goalies having the highest prevalence at 93.8 percent. This type of deformity was also shown to limit the hip range of motion. When dealing with the ice hockey population, FAI is a primary concern even if the athlete is asymptomatic.

FAI typically results in injury to the acetabular labrum (hip labrum). These injuries might be to the labrum itself or cause fraying at the labrum–cartilage junction. A recent study suggests that 70 percent of hip and groin injuries in elite hockey players can be accounted for by hip labral tears (Epstein et al. 2013). The biomechanics of skating, a combination of hip extension and external rotation, is a specific risk factor for developing a tear to the hip labrum. Based on the data presented, it is safe to assume that due to the skating pattern's nature, most hockey players either have or are at risk of developing FAI, which can directly lead to the labrum's injury. This risk factor is one of the primary reasons a significant focus of training programs should be on movement in the LPHC.

Groin or Adductor Strain

Six muscles along the inner thigh accomplish the adduction of the hip. They originate from the pelvis and have insertion points along the inside of the femur. During push-off of the skating stride, the adductors shift from a decelerating contraction to a powerful accelerating contraction to accomplish stride recovery (Kuhn et al. 2016). The adductors also act with the lower abdominals to stabilize the pelvis. Kuhn et al. (2016) and Tibor and Sekiya (2008) suggest that adductor strain risk factors include FAI and labral tears, bilateral strength and power asymmetries, decreased hip range of motion, and asymmetrical adduction–abduction strength ratios.

Sports Hernia, or Athletic Pubalgia

Sports hernia, or athletic pubalgia, is another injury that can be the source of chronic groin and abdominal pain in hockey players. There has been some debate about the cause of the condition (Tibor and Sekiya 2008). In my experience, weakness or tearing of the rectus abdominis at its insertion on the pelvis is the definition of sports hernia that describes most of the cases observed in hockey. Athletes who cannot control and stabilize their LPHC during movement are at the highest risk of developing sports hernia. Repetitive oscillations of anterior and posterior pelvic tilting combined with rotation and hip adduction during high-velocity actions will stress the lower abdominal muscular and pubic symphysis and, over time, might develop into muscle weakness or injury. This weakness or injury will then result in further destabilization of the pelvis, creating a positive feedback loop, unless these actions are addressed.

SKATING MECHANICS

The mechanics of the skating stride in hockey must be considered when designing training plans for hockey athletes. The coach's goal is to minimize any roadblocks to movement that might affect the athlete's ability to perform. Athletes who cannot attain appropriate biomechanical positions off the ice will not be able to get into those positions on the ice either. That said, there are many aspects of skating skill that cannot be trained off the ice, but specific off-ice body positions must be attainable to minimize compensations during skating.

The skating stride is biphasic, consisting of support and swing phases, where the support phase is classified as either single or double support (Upjohn et al. 2008). Upjohn et al. (2008) demonstrated that high-caliber skaters had greater stride length and stride width than low-caliber skaters. The high-caliber skaters also possessed greater hip flexion at weight acceptance, knee extension and plantar flexion at propulsion, and knee and ankle–foot ranges of motion. These researchers also demonstrated that high-caliber skaters maintained deeper knee flexion until later in the stride's stance phase and larger lateral displacement range of motion of the lower limb segments (Upjohn et al. 2008). Although force and power development are vital contributors to skating speed, it is undeniable that mechanics and efficiency play a significant role in skating performance. The coach's job is to help athletes reach specific benchmarks in ranges of motion, both passively and weight-bearing, to minimize any potential blocks to skating performance once they are on the ice.

PREACTIVITY PREPARATION TO OPTIMIZE MOVEMENT CAPACITY

After close consideration of the factors outlined previously in this chapter, it is necessary to help athletes achieve movement capacities that maximize performance and potentially reduce injury risk. Before every training session, athletes should complete a series of tasks designed to prepare them for the specific patterns and movements required. These sessions can range from simple (e.g., strictly linear) to more complex (e.g., multidirectional). Each activity preparation session should follow a specific sequence of tasks designated by broad categories. The tasks within each category will vary depending on the type and complexity of movement to follow. The categories of activity preparation include the following:

- Inhibition of tight tissue
- Muscle length
- Joint mobilization
- Muscle activation
- Movement integration
- Structural and neural priming
- Movement strength and skill

Inhibition of Tight Tissue

Hockey players have specific areas of concern when it comes to tight muscle tissue. These areas directly contribute to many of the disadvantageous postural and joint positions described in this and the previous chapter (i.e., excessive anterior pelvic tilt and lower- and upper-crossed syndromes). When thinking pragmatically, muscle actions that contribute to these positions should guide exercise and drill prescriptions. Therefore, all approaches must be individualized to a degree; however, hockey players are a relatively homogenous group, with the majority requiring many of the same prescriptions.

Releasing tone and tightness from tissues can be accomplished by a skilled practitioner in manual therapy or by the athlete. In most cases, the athlete should assume this responsibility by using various self-myofascial release (SMR) techniques such as foam rolling, massage stick, or rolling on a lacrosse ball or softball. The specific modality will be dictated by the muscle or muscle group in question. Large muscle group SMR (e.g., quadriceps or hamstrings) can be accomplished with a foam roller, and smaller groups or more precise areas (e.g., hip flexors) might require a smaller ball. The technique of SMR is quite simple: identify the tissue or location of concern and apply pressure either continuously or intermittently by rolling over the muscle in a slow and controlled manner. If, for instance, any area of increased pain or a trigger point is found, hold pressure on that point for a more extended period. I generally recommend rolling on each site for up to 1 minute, while spending more time on specific areas of concern for the individual. Following are particular areas of concern for the hockey player.

Hip Flexors SMR

One of the most common areas of chronic tightness and tone in hockey players is the hip flexor complex. The hip flexors are a group of muscles responsible for hip flexion, as the name suggests. SMR of the hip flexors typically requires a lacrosse ball or softball to access the precise area of concern while you lie prone on the ground.

Tensor Fasciae Latae (TFL) SMR

The TFL is a small muscle located on the thigh's lateral aspect near the hip. It attaches to the iliotibial band. SMR of the TFL typically requires a lacrosse ball or softball to access the area of concern while you lie on the ground.

Iliotibial (IT) Band SMR

The IT band is a thick band of fascia on the lateral aspect of the thigh and is responsible for stabilizing the knee. SMR of the IT band can be accomplished using a foam roller while you lie on the ground.

Quadriceps SMR

The quadriceps muscle is a four-part muscle on the anterior portion of the thigh. It is responsible primarily for knee extension; however, one part of the quadriceps also contributes to hip flexion. SMR of the quadriceps can be accomplished by using a foam roller while you lie prone on the ground or by using a massage stick while in a seated position.

Adductors SMR

The adductors are a main area of trigger points for hockey players. Their primary action is the adduction of the femur, as the name suggests. SMR of the adductors should be done in various ways. First, when using a foam roller while lying prone on the ground, adduct and externally rotate the thigh. Second, while seated on a bench, adduct and internally rotate the thigh with a ball between the bench and the thigh.

Hamstrings SMR

The hamstrings are a group of muscles on the posterior thigh. They are primarily responsible for knee flexion and hip extension. SMR of the hamstrings is accomplished by using a foam roller while you sit on the ground.

Calf Muscles SMR

The calf muscles are located on the posterior aspect of the lower limb and are responsible for plantar flexion (pointing of the toes) of the foot and ankle. Since skates are typically rigid and hockey players often present with ankle dorsiflexion deficits, the calf muscles are of primary concern when joint mobilization of the ankle is considered. SMR of the calf muscles is accomplished by using a foam roller while you sit on the ground.

SMR for Other Areas of Concern

Along with the muscle groups already outlined, other areas of concern for hockey players include the pectoralis minor, upper trapezius, latissimus dorsi, and the spinal erectors. SMR of these areas is best performed with a softball or lacrosse ball.

Pectoralis Minor SMR

The pectoralis minor muscle is located on the chest cavity's front wall and is responsible for the shoulder blade's movement and stability. SMR of the pectoralis minor is accomplished by placing a lacrosse ball between the chest and a wall. Lean your body to generate more pressure and glide your body over the ball.

Upper Trapezius SMR

The trapezius muscle is located on the back of the body and extends from the base of the skull and spinal column out to the shoulder blades. The upper trapezius portion moves the shoulder blade up and to the middle, extends and laterally flexes the head and neck, and helps rotate the head. In SMR of the upper trapezius, lie on your back and place a lacrosse ball between the upper trapezius and the floor. Body weight can be used to generate more pressure if necessary. For more intensity, turn your head to the opposite side and tuck the chin.

Latissimus Dorsi SMR

The latissimus dorsi muscle spans the majority of the back and is responsible for arm internal rotation, adduction, and extension. In SMR of the latissimus dorsi muscle lie on your side with the arm closer to the floor extended overhead and with a foam roller or ball under the arm, just below the armpit. Gently roll back and forth on the muscle.

Spinal Erectors SMR

The spinal erector muscles extend along the spinal column from the base of the skull to the pelvis and are responsible for extending and laterally flexing the spine. In SMR of the spinal erectors lie on your back on a foam roller starting at the upper back level and slowly moving over the roller down to the lower back.

SPECIAL CONSIDERATIONS WITH SMR

Since muscle tissue is highly adaptable and changes from day to day depending on the athlete's training, SMR techniques and patterns should also be adapted to accommodate the changes in the muscle. The athlete should explore different areas and points of concern regarding the muscle or muscle group in question.

SMR is also a balancing act between too little and too much pressure. At first, athletes must be gentle and gradually increase pressure based on cues from the nervous system. If the pressure is too great initially, this might make the muscle contract further.

Muscle Length

Once muscle tone issues have been addressed, muscle lengthening drills should be performed to restore and maintain appropriate muscle length. Many methods can be used to lengthen muscle tissue, including static stretching, proprioceptive neuromuscular facilitation (PNF), and active isolated stretching (AIS).

When static stretching, the athlete simply holds a muscle or muscle group in a lengthened position for some time, usually up to 1 minute. During PNF stretching, also known as the *contract–relax method*, the muscle is extended to a specific position. The athlete then contracts that muscles, or presses against resistance, for approximately 5 seconds, followed by relaxation. The muscle is then lengthened to a greater degree and held. This process is repeated two to four times. AIS usually takes the same form as various static stretches but is dynamic. The muscle in question is stretched repeatedly, held at the end range for approximately 2 seconds, followed by a short relaxation period. This process is repeated for a set number of repetitions, usually 8 to 15. Regardless of the methods used, tissue-lengthening drills should be multiplanar. In this section, specific muscle-lengthening techniques for concern areas are outlined.

Hip Flexors

The hip flexors are a group of muscles that are responsible primarily for flexing the hip, but they also rotate and adduct the thigh. Maintenance and care of this group of muscles is essential in hockey due to the skating position. While skating, the hips are constantly in a flexed position, and over time they may become short and weak if they are neglected from a self-care standpoint. Stretching of these muscles can be performed before, during, and after training. The following exercises provide various hip flexor muscle-lengthening techniques.

Half-Kneeling Hip Flexor Static Stretch

Assume a half-kneeling position. While contracting the gluteal muscles on the same side as the down knee to maintain a neutral pelvic position, shift your weight forward until you reach your end range (figure 3.1). The lower abdominals should also be engaged while keeping the rib cage down to prevent the lumbar spine's extension. This position can be held for up to 1 minute. This stretch should be performed on both legs.

Figure 3.1 Half-kneeling hip flexor static stretch.

Supine Assisted PNF Hip Flexor Stretch

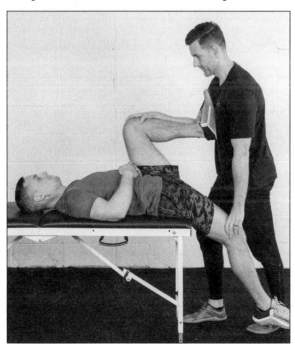

Lie on an examination table with the hip aligned to the edge of the table. The contralateral leg and hip are placed into flexion. The extended hip is moved to its end range by a coach or trainer (figure 3.2). Once the hip is fully extended, push against resistance for approximately 5 seconds, followed by relaxation and subsequent extension into the new end range. This process is repeated two to four times on both legs.

Figure 3.2 Supine assisted PNF hip flexor stretch.

Half-Kneeling Hip Flexor AIS

Assume a half-kneeling position. Like the half-kneeling hip flexor static stretch, the ipsilateral side's gluteal muscles are contracted to maintain a neutral pelvic position. Shift your weight forward until you reach your end range. This position is held for approximately 2 seconds, followed by a short relaxation period. This process can be repeated for up to 15 repetitions on each leg.

Quadriceps

The quadriceps muscles are a group of four muscles that are primarily responsible for leg extension, but one of the muscles, the rectus femoris, also plays a role in hip flexion. Since skating is a quadriceps-dominant movement, it is important to ensure that these muscles are healthy and supple. Stretching these muscles regularly before, during, and after training will ensure they have adequate length and range of motion.

Prone Quadriceps Static Stretch

Lie prone on the floor and place a band or stretching strap around the foot. While lying flat on the floor, grip the band or strap with the hand on the same side as the banded foot and pull the knee into full flexion (figure 3.3). This position is held for up to 1 minute on both legs.

Figure 3.3 Prone quadriceps static stretch.

Prone Quadriceps PNF Stretch

The setup is the same as the prone quadriceps static stretch, and the procedure is similar to the prone quadriceps static stretch. However, once the knee is fully flexed, push against the band's resistance, contracting the quadriceps as forcefully as possible for approximately 5 seconds. This sequence is followed by relaxation and subsequent extension into the new end range. This process is repeated two to four times on both legs.

Prone Quadriceps AIS

The setup is the same as the previous two quadriceps stretches, and the procedure is similar to the prone quadriceps PNF stretch. However, once the knee is fully flexed, hold this position approximately 2 seconds, followed by relaxation and full extension. This cycle is repeated for up to 15 repetitions on both legs.

HIP FLEXOR AND QUADRICEPS COMBINATION

The hip flexors and quadriceps often work in combination. Therefore, combining both patterns into one stretch is advised. The setup for all three methods of stretching is the same. Assume a half-kneeling position, and place the knee into full flexion by elevating the foot to a bench or box (figure 3.4). From this position, these muscle groups can be lengthened using static, PNF, and AIS techniques.

Figure 3.4   Stretching the hip flexor and quadriceps at the same time.

Adductors

The adductors are a group of muscles on the inside of the thigh and are responsible for bringing the thigh toward the midline of the body. The health of this muscle group is essential due to the skating stride's mechanics. When the leg is extended during the skating stride, the adductors are in a lengthened position; therefore, it is important to maintain adequate length in these muscles to minimize the risk of injury. Stretching these muscles regularly before, during, and after training will ensure they have adequate length and range of motion.

Quadruped Adductor Static Stretch

Assume the quadruped position, then extend one leg laterally with the knee straight and foot in line with the opposite knee (figure 3.5). Hold this position for up to 1 minute on each leg.

Figure 3.5 Quadruped adductor static stretch.

Butterfly Adductor PNF Stretch

While seated on the ground, assume the butterfly position, then place your hands on the ankles and elbows on the knees (figure 3.6). Apply pressure through the elbows onto the knees until the adductors reach their end range. At the end range, contract the adductors against the elbows for approximately 5 seconds, followed by a period of relaxation. This process is repeated two to four times.

Figure 3.6 Butterfly adductor PNF stretch.

Quadruped Adductor Rock Back

Assume the quadruped position, then extend one leg laterally with the knee straight and foot in line with the opposite knee (figure 3.7). Move forward and back, holding each position for approximately 2 seconds. This procedure is performed on both legs.

Figure 3.7   Quadruped adductor rock back: *(a)* forward and *(b)* back.

Hamstrings

The hamstrings are a group of muscles on the back of the thigh that are primarily responsible for flexing the knee and extending the hip. This muscle group's health is essential to minimize injury, particularly during sprint running in off-ice training. Maintaining adequate length and mobility in these muscles through various stretching forms is critical from performance and health standpoints. Stretching of the hamstrings should be performed during warm-ups, after training, and on recovery days.

Supine Hamstring Static Stretch

Lie supine on the floor, and place a band or strap around one foot. With that leg straightened, pull the hip into full flexion (figure 3.8). It is essential to push the contralateral heel into the floor to stabilize the pelvis. This position is held for up to 1 minute on each leg.

Figure 3.8   Supine hamstring static stretch.

Supine Hamstring PNF Stretch

Lie supine on the floor, and place a band or strap around one foot. With that leg straightened, pull the hip into full flexion. It is essential to push the contralateral heel into the floor to stabilize the pelvis. Then contract the hamstrings against the resistance for approximately 5 seconds, followed by a brief period of relaxation, at which point the new end range is found. The process is repeated two to four times on each leg.

Supine Hamstring AIS

The setup is the same as the previous two stretches. Raise your leg into full hip flexion. Once the active end range is found, apply additional force with the band or strap, and hold the stretch for approximately 2 seconds. Follow by relaxing and fully extending the hip to the initial starting point. This process is repeated for up to 15 repetitions on each leg.

Pectoralis

The pectoralis muscles are located on the front of the upper body and are also known as the *chest muscles*. These muscles are primarily responsible for arm adduction and internal rotation. The health of these muscles is critical for performance and reducing injury risk. If the pectoralis muscles are short and tight, the shoulder might be pulled forward in a disadvantageous position. Ensuring the pectoralis muscles have adequate length is important for posture and shoulder function. Stretching these muscles regularly before, during, and after training will ensure they have adequate length and range of range of motion.

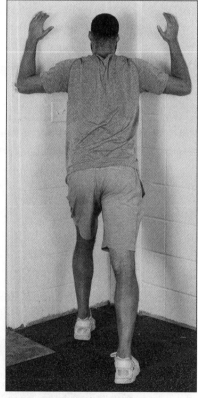

Corner Pec Static Stretch

Facing the corner of the room, place your hands on the wall with elbows at 90 degrees of flexion. From a split stance, gradually lean into the wall until a gentle stretch is felt in the pectoralis muscles (figure 3.9). Maintain abdominal activation with the rib cage down, and hold this position for up to 1 minute.

Figure 3.9   Corner pec static stretch.

Corner Pec PNF Stretch

Using the same setup as the static version, when at the end range, contract the pectoralis muscles forcefully against the wall for approximately 5 seconds. This sequence is followed by a short period of relaxation. This process is repeated two to four times.

Corner Pec AIS

Using the same setup as the previous two examples, gently lean into the wall, actively pulling the shoulder blades together. The end range position is held for approximately 2 seconds, followed by relaxation. Then return to the initial position. This process is repeated for up to 15 repetitions.

Upper Back and Shoulder

The muscles of the upper back and shoulder are important for both performance and health. Ensuring that these muscles possess adequate length will allow for optimal joint positioning and movement mechanics, which might reduce the risk of injury in these areas. Stretching these muscles regularly before, during, and after training will ensure adequate length and range of motion.

Banded Overhead Static Stretch

Attach a thick superband to a stable structure. Hook the band around the wrist of the arm being stretched, and externally rotate that arm. With a straight arm, push the hips back, lower the upper body toward the floor, and extend the leg on the same side back and medially (figure 3.10). This position is held for up to 1 minute on each side.

Figure 3.10 Banded overhead static stretch.

Banded Overhead PNF Stretch

Using the same setup as the previous stretch, contract the lats and depress the shoulder for approximately 5 seconds, followed by a short period of relaxation. This process is repeated two to four times on both sides.

Banded Overhead AIS

The setup is the same as the previous two stretches. However, the act of pushing the hips back, lowering the upper body toward the floor, and extending the leg on the same side back and medially is repeated continuously, holding the end range for approximately 2 seconds (figure 3.11). This process is completed up to 15 times on each side.

Figure 3.11   Banded overhead AIS.

STRETCHING AND POWER OUTPUT

It has been demonstrated that static and other stretching forms might decrease power output immediately following the stretch. This fact must be taken into consideration. Therefore, it is advised to follow the specific preactivity sequences outlined in this chapter to optimize power output for the tasks in question.

Joint Mobilization

After removing many of the barriers to joint movement by addressing muscular tone and length, the focus can be shifted to other aspects of joint mobilization, primarily removing joint restrictions. True joint mobility is the degree to which an articulation or joint surface can move in the absence of inhibition from surrounding structures and tissues. Careful observation of the multijoint limb system highlights four main areas that require higher degrees of mobility. These include the ankle, hip, thoracic spine, and glenohumeral (shoulder). In previous sections, muscle tone and length have been addressed. However, in this section, capsular mobility will be the focus.

Every synovial joint is surrounded by a joint capsule that maintains the joint's integrity and contains the fluid that keeps the joints lubricated (Mangus et al. 2002). Hypomobility is typically a result of a tight or restricted joint capsule. To modify or minimize these restrictions, space needs to be created within the joint. Removal of joint restriction can be accomplished by using three methods: joint distraction, distraction combined with joint glide, and joint glide.

The goal of method 1, joint distraction, is to create a greater degree of separation between the joint's articulating surfaces. This method will provide more space for the fluid in the joint and reduce joint friction.

Method 2, distraction combined with joint glide, is the combination of joint separation with joint movement in the appropriate plane of motion. The plane of motion will be dictated by the joint in question.

Method 3, joint glide, is merely moving the joint through its planes of motion, provided there is no capsular restriction.

These three methods can be used individually or in combination, and the individual restrictions will guide the method or methods of choice. The following sections outline how each of these methods can be self-administered for the ankle, hip, thoracic spine, and shoulder.

Ankle Joint Mobilization

Method 1: Ankle Distraction

Attach a band to a stable point. Sit on the floor, and loop the opposite end of the band to the foot. Create as much tension on the band as possible (figure 3.12a), and hold this position for 30 to 60 seconds. This procedure is performed on both sides.

Method 2: Ankle Distraction and Glide

Attach one end of a band around a stable point. Loop the opposite end around the front of the ankle, and assume a split-stance position facing away from the anchor point, with the ankle in question being the front leg. Create as much tension on the band as possible while the foot is in contact with the floor. Then move the ankle through its entire range of motion in the sagittal plane (figure 3.12*b*), holding each endpoint for approximately 2 seconds. Once completed, perform the same procedure on the other ankle.

Method 3: Ankle Glide

Assume a split-stance position, with the ankle in question being the front leg. Move the ankle through its entire range of motion in the sagittal plane (figure 3.12*c*), holding each endpoint for approximately 2 seconds. Once completed, perform the same procedure on the other ankle.

Figure 3.12 Ankle joint mobilization: *(a)* ankle distraction, *(b)* ankle distraction and glide, and *(c)* ankle glide.

Hip Joint Mobilization

Method 1: Hip Distraction

Attach one end of a band around a stable point. Lie supine on the floor, and loop the opposite end of the band around the foot. Place a foam roller under the thigh to put the hip in slight flexion, and adduct and externally rotate the hip slightly (figure 3.13). Create as much tension on the band as possible, and hold this position. Once completed, perform the same procedure on the other side.

Figure 3.13   Hip distraction.

Method 2: Hip Distraction and Glide

Attach a band around a stable point. Loop the band around the leg at the hip.

This pattern has two parts: anterior-posterior and medial-lateral. In the anterior-posterior position, assume a sprinter position with as much tension on the band as possible. Then oscillate the hip from side to side, holding each point for approximately 2 seconds (figure 3.14*a*). To add internal rotation bias, internally rotate the thigh, and perform the same pattern (figure 3.14*b*). Once completed, perform the same procedure on the other leg.

In the medial-lateral position, assume the same sprinter position, but the band force is perpendicular to the body. Perform the same motions as the anterior-posterior pattern (figure 3.14*c*). Additionally, in the medial-lateral position, you can introduce external rotation of the thigh (figure 3.14*d*). Once completed, perform the same procedure on the other leg.

Figure 3.14   Hip distraction and glide: anterior-posterior position *(a)* hip motion and *(b)* internal rotation; medial-lateral position *(c)* hip motion and *(d)* external rotation.

Method 3: Hip Rotations

Figure 3.15   Hip rotations.

Assume the quadruped position. Brace the core musculature, then flex the hip to the chest, followed by complete circumduction (rotation) of the hip at its end range until it is in extension (figure 3.15). This process should be completed in a slow and controlled manner that challenges the pattern's end ranges.

Thoracic Spine Joint Mobilization

Method 1: T-Spine Distraction

Distraction of the thoracic spine is often challenging to accomplish and generally looks quite different from the other joints covered. Space can

be created in the joints with the use of a foam roller. Simply lie supine on a foam roller at the level of the thoracic spine. Extend and expand the chest cavity by opening up the rib cage (figure 3.16). This process can be accomplished at various levels of the T-spine.

Figure 3.16　T-spine distraction.

Method 2: T-Spine Distraction and Glide

The setup is identical to the previous exercise. In this method, alternate between positions of flexion and extension (figure 3.17). This can be accomplished at various levels of the T-spine.

Figure 3.17　T-spine distraction and glide.

Method 3: T-Spine Glide

This method has two components: flexion-extension and rotation. To improve T-spine flexion-extension, sit on a bench with your hands behind your head. Alternate between full extension and flexion of the T-spine (figure 3.18a, b).

T-spine rotation can be accomplished by assuming the child's pose position with one hand behind the head. Rotate and open in the direction of that hand (figure 3.18c). Perform this procedure in both directions. These processes are repeated for multiple repetitions.

Figure 3.18 T-spine glide: *(a)* extension and *(b)* flexion from a seated position; *(c)* rotation from child's pose.

Shoulder Joint Mobilization

Method 1: Shoulder Distraction

Shoulder distraction is accomplished by performing the same pattern as the banded overhead static stretch described earlier. Attach a band to a stable structure. Hook the band around the wrist of the arm in question, and externally rotate that arm. With a straight arm, push the hips back, and lower the upper body toward the floor (figure 3.19). Perform this action on both sides.

Figure 3.19　Shoulder distraction.

Method 2: Shoulder Distraction and Glide

Assumes the same setup as shoulder distraction. Slowly move the shoulder joint between internal and external rotation, holding each position for approximately 2 seconds. This is repeated for a set number of repetitions on both sides.

Method 3: Shoulder Rotation

To start, stand with your arms at the side of your body. Elevate the arm in question with the thumb up until the arm is entirely overhead and the hand is internally rotated. The arm continues its path around while continuing to internally rotate until the arm reaches its endpoint at extension (figure 3.20). The motion is slow and controlled throughout the entire path, and the arm should be extended as far as possible. This cycle can be performed up to five times per side.

Figure 3.20　Shoulder rotation.

IF THERE IS PAIN, LOOK ABOVE AND BELOW

If the athlete is experiencing pain in a particular area, focus on mobilizing the joints and tissues both upstream and downstream from the pain site. For example, if knee pain is present, ensure that the ankle and hip have adequate range of motion.

Muscle Activation

All the activities to this point have focused on mobility and optimizing range of motion. To maximize this range of motion, muscles are inhibited and lengthened. For athletes, this is not an optimal state from a performance or dynamic movement perspective. Therefore, it is imperative to stimulate these muscles and, in a sense, reactivate them to the point at which the athlete can increase the complexity of movement efficiently with a stable LPHC. For hockey players required to perform on and off the ice, the main focal points should be the core musculature, gluteal muscles, adductors, and shoulder girdle.

Muscle activation is quite simple. Each specific area requires only one or two exercises before the athlete moves on to postural control and movement integration. To activate the core musculature, the athlete can simply perform the front and side planks for up to 1 minute. Gluteal muscle activation can be accomplished by glute bridging and miniband walking (both in linear and lateral directions) (figure 3.21a-c). The foam roller groin squeeze (figure 3.21d) can be used to activate the adductor muscles. A shoulder complex of prone Ys, Ts, and Ls (figure 3.21e-g) can stimulate the shoulder girdle muscles. The exercises listed should be progressed in complexity and intensity as the athlete adapts to the given stimulus. Table 3.1 provides a sample muscle activation sequence.

Figure 3.21 Muscle activation exercises: (a) glute bridge,

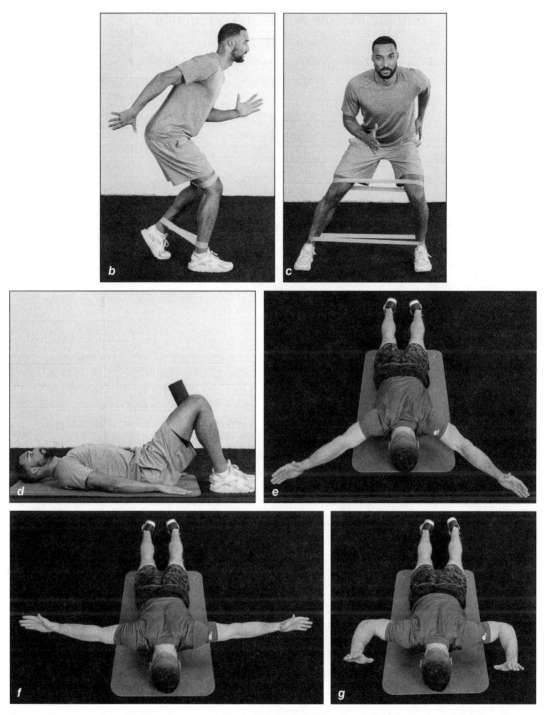

Figure 3.21 *continued (b)* linear miniband walk, *(c)* lateral miniband walk, *(d)* foam roller groin squeeze, *(e)* Ys, *(f)* Ts, and *(g)* Ls.

Table 3.1 Sample Muscle Activation Sequence

Exercise	Sets	Repetitions, time, or distance	Notes
Front plank	1	30 seconds	Engage glutes and abdominals
Side plank	1	30 seconds each side	
Glute bridge	1	12 repetitions	
Groin squeeze	1	20 seconds	
Shoulder complex: Ys, Ts, Ls	1	10 repetitions each exercise	
Linear miniband walk	1	33 ft (10 m)	Athletic position, forward, and backward
Lateral miniband walk	1	33 ft (10 m) each direction	Athletic position

Movement Integration

Postural control and movement integration techniques need to focus on the tasks the athlete is preparing to perform. For example, if an off-ice session's goal is to improve linear movement and speed, the movement integration should be biased in that linear direction. On the other hand, if the athlete is preparing for an on-ice practice or game, movement integration will include techniques and drills that are multiplanar. This preparation component should be progressive, with each task building on the previous one. In general, movements should follow these progressions: ground to standing, slow to fast, single joint to multijoint, simple to complex.

For example, consider a high knee run. The sequence leading up to the high knee run might include standing knee hug, static split squat, reverse lunge to hip lock, walking lunge, elbow to instep, linear march, linear skip, and then, finally, the high knee run. Each layer of this movement builds off the previous in terms of intensity and complexity. An athlete who cannot perform any of the tasks correctly for some reason needs to spend more time on those tasks. We cannot skip steps or bypass areas of concern to accomplish what is written on the training plan. This is where the art of coaching comes into play. Bypassing steps and checkpoints will result in dysfunction as time progresses.

Tables 3.2 and 3.3 provide two sample movement integration sections, one preparing for linear movement and speed off the ice (table 3.2) and one preparing for an on-ice practice (table 3.3).

Structural and Neural Priming

As the intensity and complexity of preparation continue to increase, so must the athlete's structural tissues and nervous system's capacity to withstand the demands of the training exercises to follow. This section includes a series of

Table 3.2 Sample Movement Integration for Linear Movement (Off Ice)

Exercise	Sets	Repetitions or distance	Description
Stationary knee hug	1	6 repetitions each leg	Stand with feet shoulder-width apart. Lift one knee toward the chest and pull it to the end range with the arms. Alternate sides.
Stationary quad pull	1	6 repetitions each leg	Stand with feet shoulder-width apart. Flex one knee, bringing the heel toward the glute. Pull it to end range with the hand. Alternate sides.
Reverse lunge to hip lock	1	6 repetitions each leg	See chapter 5.
Elbow to instep	1	5 repetitions each side	Stand with feet shoulder-width apart. Step forward with the right leg into a lunge position while keeping the left leg straight. Place the left hand on the floor underneath the left shoulder. Bring the right elbow down and inside the right knee as close to the floor and right ankle as possible, then return to the starting position. Perform this action on both sides.
Linear march	1	49 ft (15 m)	Stand with feet shoulder-width apart. Drive the right knee up toward the chest, and push into the floor with the left leg. As the right knee moves up, swing the left arm up to 90 degrees and right arm back. Return the right foot back to the ground. Repeat this pattern on the left side.
Linear skip	1	49 ft (15 m)	Begin with a low-level skipping pattern. Then transition to driving the right knee up to approximately 90 degrees, and drive the left leg back into the ground. Swing the arms while skipping in the opposite pattern from the legs.
Butt kicks	1	49 ft (15 m)	Begin slightly leaning forward and jogging lightly. Then transition to bringing the heels up toward the glutes. The arm action opposes the leg action.
High knee run	1	49 ft (15 m)	Begin slightly leaning forward and jogging lightly. Then transition to driving the knees up to 90 degrees similar to the linear march but with a rapid rate of turnover.
Stationary single-leg Romanian deadlift to hip lock	1	6 repetitions each leg	See chapter 5.

(continued)

Table 3.2 *(continued)*

Exercise	Sets	Repetitions or distance	Description
Straight-leg march	1	49 ft (15 m)	Perform the same way as the linear march; however, maintain a straight leg.
Straight-leg skip	1	49 ft (15 m)	Perform the same way as the linear skip; however, maintain a straight leg.
Backpedal	1	49 ft (15 m)	Start in an athletic position with feet shoulder-width apart. With short and quick steps, backpedal in the backward direction.
Backward run	1	49 ft (15 m)	Start with feet shoulder-width apart. Begin by pushing off the foot to move in the backward direction. At the same time, extend the opposite leg back. This pattern should mimic running forward but in the backward direction.

Table 3.3   Sample Movement Integration for On-Ice Practice

Exercise	Sets	Repetitions or distance	Description
Stationary knee hug	1	6 repetitions each leg	See table 3.2.
Stationary quad pull	1	6 repetitions each leg	See table 3.2.
Reverse lunge to hip lock	1	6 repetitions each leg	See table 3.2.
Lateral lunge	1	6 repetitions each direction	Start with feet shoulder-width apart, then take a step to the right about double shoulder width. Sit back and down into the right hip. Push with the right leg to return to the starting position. Alternate sides.
Rotational lunge	1	6 repetitions each direction	Start with feet shoulder-width apart, then take a step to back with the right foot and rotate the hips so the right foot plants perpendicular to the left. Push off with the right leg to return to the starting position. Alternate sides.
Drop lunge	1	6 repetitions each leg	Start with feet shoulder-width apart. Step back with the right foot and cross behind the left leg. The right foot will plant on the outside of the left shoulder. Weight bearing is primarily on the left leg. Drive off the left leg to return to the starting position. Alternate sides.

Exercise	Sets	Repetitions or distance	Description
Drop unders	1	6 repetitions each leg	Begin in a squat position with feet shoulder-width apart. Reach the right leg out to approximately double shoulder width while bearing weight on the left leg. While staying in the low position, shift the hips over to the right so now the right leg is weight bearing. Alternate sides.
Lateral march	1	49 ft (15 m) each direction	Same procedure as the linear march; however, movement is in the lateral direction.
Lateral skip	1	49 ft (15 m) each direction	Same procedure as the linear skip; however, movement is in the lateral direction.
Stationary single-leg RDL to hip lock	1	6 repetitions each leg	See chapter 5.
Drop step squat	1	6 repetitions each leg	Start with feet shoulder-width apart. Then lift the right leg, open the hips, and plant the right foot so it is heel to heel with the left foot but shoulder-width apart. Then perform a squat. Drive off the right foot to return to the starting position. Alternate sides.
Drop step skip	1	49 ft (15 m) each direction	Moving in a backward direction, perform the same pattern as the linear skip; however, at each step open the hips as with the drop step squat.
High knee carioca	1	49 ft (15 m) each direction	Moving laterally to the left, cross the right leg in front of the left. Once the right foot is planted, return the left to the starting position. Then cross the right leg behind the left. Once the right foot is planted, return the left leg to the starting position. Perform this pattern rapidly, bringing the knees high while crossing over. Perform in both directions.

priming drills focusing on both the lower and upper body. These drills prime the musculotendinous units and various factors controlled by the nervous system, such as the stretch-shortening cycle (SSC). In addition to priming, these types of drills directly contribute to the athlete's power-generating capabilities, which will be discussed in chapter 6. As with all training, these drills should progress in complexity and intensity at each step and should be done whether preparing for off-ice or on-ice training.

Table 3.4 represents a sample structural and neural priming sequence.

Table 3.4 Sample Structural and Neural Priming Sequence

Exercise	Sets	Repetitions or distance	Notes
Right and left disassociation	1	16 ft (5 m) each	Move the feet as quickly as possible.
Forward bilateral rudimentary linear hops	1	10 repetitions	Maintain flat foot contacts, soft knees and hips, and stiff ankles.
Backward bilateral rudimentary linear hops	1	10 repetitions	Maintain flat foot contacts, soft knees and hips, and stiff ankles.
Forward unilateral rudimentary linear hops	1	5 repetitions each	Maintain flat foot contacts, soft knees and hips, and stiff ankles.
Backward unilateral rudimentary linear hops	1	5 repetitions each	Maintain flat foot contacts, soft knees and hips, and stiff ankles.
Hurdle jump (noncountermovement)	2	6 repetitions	Use a 6-inch (15 cm) hurdle; stick and hold landing.
Medicine ball chest toss (kneeling)	1	5 repetitions	
Medicine ball overhead toss forward (kneeling)	1	5 repetitions	
Medicine ball perpendicular side toss (half-kneeling)	1	5 repetitions each	

Lower-Body Priming

When considering an end goal of high-velocity movement patterns, lower-body priming is a significant component to developing these capabilities. The following is a priming sequence for the lower body.

Right and Left Disassociation Drills

These drills serve two purposes: to provide very low-amplitude, quick ground contacts and to increase neural demand by using patterns not familiar to the athlete.

To execute these drills, move forward slowly for approximately 16 feet (5 m). One foot moves up and down. The other foot moves in and out as quickly as possible with low amplitude. The drills are performed for both sides of the body and in the forward and backward directions.

Rudimentary Hop Series

The rudimentary hop series is a regression from traditional plyometrics. These drills are designed to address stiffness in the musculotendinous units and to prime the SSC.

The series is completed using low-amplitude bilateral and unilateral hops in both linear and lateral directions. Foot contacts should be relatively flat, the ankle should be stiff, and the hips and knees should have a degree of softness. Complete up to 20 repetitions for the bilateral movements and 10 repetitions per leg for the unilateral actions.

Plyometric Hurdle Series

Although the name suggests this series is plyometric with short ground contact times, it does not begin in that manner. Progress from nonplyometric to plyometric jumps and hops as your tissues and skill adapt over time.

Typically, bilateral and unilateral jumps and hops are performed on different days, as are linear and lateral jumps and hops. For example, in a four-day training week, bilateral linear would be on Monday, bilateral lateral on Tuesday, unilateral linear on Thursday, and unilateral lateral on Friday. The sequence of jump progression for both bilateral and unilateral jump is as follows:

1. Noncountermovement jump
2. Countermovement jump
3. Double-contact countermovement
4. Continuous

Hockey players should use 6- to 12-inch (15-30 cm) hurdles.

Upper-Body Priming

The goals of upper-body priming are the same as for lower-body priming, just with an upper-body emphasis. The medicine ball priming series can be used to accomplish these goals.

Medicine Ball Priming Series

Three movement patterns are used in this series: perpendicular side toss, chest toss, and slam. These exercises are described in detail in chapter 6. The complexity and intensity of these variations should progress as you adapt to the training. These progressions include stance variations (ranging from kneeling to split stance to adding a jump with the toss) and progressing from static (no catch) to catch and release.

Movement Skill and Strength

Although movement technique and skill are observed and corrected throughout the entirety of preactivity preparation, the movement skill and strength section is where various aspects of movement are brought together into more complex and real-world movement applications. Once the athlete's joints, tissues, and physiological systems have been primed and optimized, movement patterns can be fine-tuned while adding velocity and complexity. That said, the skill level of the athlete must be taken into consideration. For younger and beginner populations, the drills in the movement integration section might be at the upper limits of their skill base. In that case, no additional skill work is required. Athletes need to learn to walk before they can run. Training must be structured and systematic, following a specific set of guidelines. This system allows for the identification of weak points within the athlete. If we do not follow a system, it will be impossible to gauge progress in specific movements. Far too often, young coaches start with the endpoint and bypass many steps and evaluations that should precede it. For example, coaches often have their athletes move as quickly as possible in multiple directions through a series of cones to train change of direction when their athletes cannot perform the linear skip or drop squat properly. In this scenario, the young athletes might improve their speed in this particular sequence of cones but lack the necessary skill to excel in real-world tasks down the road.

The movement skill and strength sequences are structured as follows.

Monday: Linear movement, skill

The main focus is on linear movement mechanics, emphasizing acceleration and progressing to adding deceleration.

Tuesday: Multidirectional movement, skill and strength, lateral stride focus

The main focus is on lateral skating stride mechanics, emphasizing deep knee and hip flexion while maintaining posture. Training progresses through slow and controlled strength movements to more dynamic bounding, lateral accelerations, and direction change. Table 3.5 outlines a sample multidirectional lateral stride focus sequence. The exercises are described in chapter 7.

Thursday: Linear movement, strength and skill

The main focus is on linear movement mechanics while emphasizing strength, acceleration, and progressing to deceleration techniques.

Friday: Multidirectional movement, strength and skill, cross-over, and drop-step

The main focus is on skating cross-over and drop-step mechanics, emphasizing deep knee and hip flexion while maintaining posture. Training progresses through slow and controlled strength movements to more dynamic bounding, cross-over accelerations, and direction change.

Note: As the skill level of the athlete progresses, so does the complexity of the movement skill demands, where linear and multidirectional skills begin to merge within each session. If the athlete is transitioning to on-ice training after the off-ice session, the coach should focus on the specific skills that were the theme off the ice. For example, if the off-ice session's theme was cross-over skill, this should also be a theme on ice to optimize skill transfer.

Table 3.5 Sample Multidirectional Lateral Stride Focus for Movement Skill and Strength

Exercise	Sets	Repetitions or distance	Notes
Lateral low skater stride (resisted)	2	49 ft (15 m) each	Partner resist with strap, low posture, 45-degree body lean
Side skate jump	2	33 ft (10 m) each	Low posture, single-leg stance, opposite knee at level of stance heel, low-amplitude jump
Resisted explosive lateral stride	2	49 ft (15 m) each	Resisted with band
Resisted explosive lateral stride, continuous	2	49 ft (15 m) each	Resisted with band
Half-kneeling lateral acceleration	4	33 ft (10 m) each	

PUTTING IT ALL TOGETHER

Designing preactivity movement optimization plans does not need to be complicated. Follow the system, and choose specific exercises and drills that (1) address the movement goals of the day and (2) address the particular needs of the athletes. There are multiple scenarios in which these sequences must be used, including before off-ice training and on-ice training or games, after off- or on-ice training or games, and on recovery and regeneration days. That said, these scenarios will differ in terms of content and focus. The following are the sequences to be conducted for each scenario.

Before Off-Ice Training

1. Inhibition of tight tissue
2. Muscle length
3. Joint mobilization
4. Muscle activation
5. Movement integration
6. Structural and neural priming
7. Movement strength and skill

Before On-Ice Training or Game

1. Inhibition of tight tissue
2. Muscle length
3. Joint mobilization
4. Muscle activation
5. Movement integration
6. Structural and neural priming

Rebalancing After Off- or On-Ice Training or Games and Recovery or Regeneration Days

1. Inhibition of tight tissue
2. Muscle length
3. Joint mobilization
4. Muscle activation

SUMMARY

Movement capacity training is often overlooked when designing training programs for hockey players; however, many other training variables cannot be optimized without the capacity to move efficiently. This type of training must be a program staple and performed almost daily. This chapter outlined how to prescribe movement capacity training in many different scenarios effectively. Moving with efficiency is paramount, but all human movement requires adequate energy to perform at the highest levels consistently. Chapter 4 will discuss how the human body generates this energy supply and how to train the human energy systems effectively.

Energy Systems Development

The conversion of energy within the body is fundamental to support optimal on-ice performance. Consider the following: you are a winger who just won a short 49-foot (15 m) race to a loose puck. You then move the puck to your center, who turns it over in the neutral zone, and your team gets hemmed in your defensive zone for the next 30 seconds. Not until your team regains possession and clears the puck can you go off the ice for a line change. This one shift has three distinct scenarios: (1) an explosive race to the puck, (2) a grueling period of work in your zone, and (3) recovery on the bench. For each of these scenarios, the energy requirements are met predominantly by three separate energy systems: the anaerobic alactic energy system, the anaerobic glycolytic energy system, and the aerobic energy system.

Energy is the most valuable commodity in the human body. Every aspect of human movement requires energy input, including skeletal muscle contractions and heartbeats. Even the pathways that produce our energy currency require energy input. This currency is known as adenosine triphosphate (ATP) and is produced by our energy systems. The three systems mentioned earlier vary in terms of the rate at which they can create energy and the overall amount.

Hockey is an intermittent skating sport, characterized by repeated sprints throughout a game. As a result, hockey players are often thought of as solely anaerobic athletes, but this could not be further from the truth. The pendulum has swung too far in the anaerobic direction. The reality is that all energy systems are always contributing but vary in degree depending on intensity and duration. The systems intricately support one another in the overall energy supply during a hockey game. Therefore, the development and optimization of all energy systems are paramount to developing a hockey player. The enhancement of these energy systems is the focus of this chapter.

ADENOSINE TRIPHOSPHATE (ATP)

The physical demands of hockey are complex. These demands require energy input to produce and maintain the movements required during training or competition. At the cellular level, ATP is the source of energy for all functions. ATP consists of an adenosine base (a form of sugar) with three phosphate molecules bonded to it. When the links between the second and third phosphate groups are broken off the base, energy is released.

This released energy can then be used for biological functions, such as muscle contractions and nerve firing. Muscle fibers have thick (myosin) and thin (actin) filaments. These filaments bind to each other, and through the pulling action of the thick filaments on the thin filaments, the muscle fibers shorten or contract. During this repeating pattern of muscle contraction, ATP serves the following functions (Dunn and Grider 2020):

1. ATP binds to the thick filament, and one of the phosphate (P) bonds is broken, creating a high-energy state, placing it in a cocked position.
2. Calcium ions are pumped against their concentration gradient. This calcium then binds to the thin filament, which exposes the thick filament's attachment site.
3. When the thick filament releases the broken ATP (ADP + P), it returns to its low-energy state, which in turn pulls on the thin filament to contract the muscle.
4. A new ATP molecule then binds to the thick filament, placing it back into its cocked position, and the cycle continues.

The ATP used for functions such as muscle contractions is generated from the breakdown and chemical conversion of the food we eat. ATP can be stored directly within the cell, but this capacity is limited to only a few seconds' worth of energy. Therefore, it must be produced continuously to sustain activity and movement for longer durations of time. The energy demands of hockey are remarkably high. The athlete's ability to resynthesize ATP dictates their ability to maintain elite performance levels in training and competition. The aerobic system manufactures most of this ATP, but ATP can also be created through anaerobic processes. These systems are outlined in the following sections.

AEROBIC (OXIDATIVE) ENERGY SYSTEM

Using the metaphor of an automobile, the aerobic energy system is responsible for refilling the gas tank. This system is often described as the long-term energy system responsible for providing most of the energy at submaximal workloads of long duration. The term *aerobic* means that the system breaks down carbohydrates and fat (and sometimes protein) in the presence of oxygen to produce energy. Historically, the aerobic system has been thought to contribute little to high-intensity exercise over short durations. However, this assumption has not gone unchallenged. For example, Kavanagh and Jacobs (1988) reported that the aerobic system contributed approximately 18.5 percent of the energy requirements during a 30-second all-out Wingate test. These data have been verified by several other scientific studies, suggesting that story is more complicated than initially thought. During repeated high-intensity sprints, such as in a hockey game or practice, the total energy contribution progressively relies more on the aerobic system as time goes on. Gaitanos et al. (1993) showed that aerobic energy's relative contributions increased significantly throughout 10 6-second maximal sprints, with the majority of the energy to support power output in the final sprint provided by the aerobic energy system. Ice hockey is highly aerobic, and possessing an adequate aerobic base and capacity offsets anaerobic energy demands within the game and optimizes recovery between shifts and periods. The three energy systems never turn off. They are always active and work together to provide the energy required to complete a given task regardless of duration and intensity.

When contemplating our aerobic exercise prescriptions, we must consider the factors and limitations responsible for the overall aerobic capacity. These factors include central adaptations in the heart, arteries, and blood and peripheral adaptations within the muscle cells.

Central Training Adaptations to Aerobic Exercise

Cardiac output (the amount of blood the heart pumps through the circulatory system per minute) matches the skeletal muscle's energy and metabolic demands during exercise (Hellsten and Nyberg 2015). It is the combination of heart rate and stroke volume (the amount of blood the heart pumps per beat). As the exercise intensity increases, the heart will beat progressively faster to match the cardiac output demands. However, the maximum heart rate changes little with exercise training. Therefore, structural and functional changes to the heart itself, such as increased heart wall thickness and ventricular size, contribute to a higher stroke volume to improve cardiac output due to aerobic training.

Along with the heart adaptations, aerobic training also affects other factors that influence cardiac output and circulation. For example, aerobic exercise increases the total blood volume within the body. Increases in blood volume are correlated to higher stroke volumes and, as a result, higher cardiac output. This added blood volume reduces the viscosity (thickness) of the blood, which lowers peripheral resistance and the workload on the heart itself (Hellsten and Nyberg 2015). Other adaptions also occur within the blood, including an increase in hemoglobin, which is a protein in the red blood cells responsible for carrying oxygen to cells and carbon dioxide away from cells. Lastly, aerobic training has also been shown to elicit adaptations within the arteries. Hellsten and Nyberg (2015) revealed that top-level athletes demonstrated training-induced enlargement of arteries within the heart and other conduit arteries. These factors can be influenced by aerobic training and directly affect aerobic capacity and power by improving cardiac output and oxygen delivery to the muscles.

Peripheral Training Adaptations to Aerobic Exercise

Central training adaptations improve the delivery of oxygen and nutrient-carrying blood to the muscle. However, if the muscle does not possess the appropriate machinery to utilize these resources, performance on the ice will not be optimized. Central adaptations will get you to the door, but peripheral adaptations are the key to unlocking the system's true potential. These peripheral training adaptations occur within the muscle. Some of these adaptations include increases in capillary number and utilization, mitochondrial density, aerobic enzyme activity, and myoglobin activity. Capillaries are small blood vessels that penetrate the muscle to allow the delivery of oxygen and nutrients and remove waste products. Mitochondria are tiny structures within the cell that produce ATP in the presence of oxygen with the help of aerobic enzymes. In comparison, myoglobin is a structure related to hemoglobin and is responsible for transporting oxygen into the muscle cells.

Peripheral adaptations to aerobic exercise contribute to oxygen kinetics (the rate at which oxygen is consumed). Typically, aerobic energy sources cannot supply 100 percent of the energy required to perform exercise at its onset due to a relatively slow climb in oxygen consumption and aerobic energy production. As a result, anaerobic energy sources must make up the cost of this energy demand discrepancy, which might contribute to an initial feeling of fatigue. This phenomenon is called oxygen deficit. Have you ever stepped onto the ice without an adequate warm-up and felt fatigued in the first few minutes until you gradually begin to feel normal? This feeling is a result of your oxygen kinetics and resulting oxygen deficit.

Sport scientists and strength and conditioning coaches need to understand how to manipulate factors associated with improving the aerobic energy system zones listed in table 4.1 through central and peripheral adaptations.

Table 4.1   Aerobic Energy Systems Training Zones

Zone	Intensity	Target heart rate (HR)	Primary effect
Aerobic capacity	Aerobic base	Max HR minus 50-65 beats per minute	Improve work capacity below anaerobic threshold
	Anaerobic threshold	Max HR minus 25-30 beats per minute	Improve the intensity at which anaerobic acidosis begins to occur, at which time lactate and hydrogen are being produced at a higher rate than it is removed
Aerobic power	$\dot{V}O_2$max	Max HR	Improve the maximal rate of oxygen consumption ($\dot{V}O_2$max)
Work capacity	Maximal or supramaximal*	N/A; all-out effort	Improve maximal energy contributions from both aerobic and anaerobic sources

*Supramaximal = outputs greater than $\dot{V}O_2$max.

These factors can combine in different degrees to obtain a similar output. Therefore, no one-size-fits-all approach exists when designing an athlete's aerobic training prescriptions. The assessment modalities in chapter 2 can help define the appropriate course of action for each athlete. Exercise prescriptions can range from traditional aerobic training to high-intensity interval training, improving the aerobic energy system when prescribed correctly. It should also be noted that there is significant overlap in the effects of specific exercise prescriptions. For example, anaerobic threshold training will also improve many variables responsible for aerobic base development and vice versa. Aerobic energy systems training is the primary focus of phase 1, the general preparatory phase (GPP), outlined later in this chapter.

ANAEROBIC GLYCOLYTIC ENERGY SYSTEM

As discussed in chapter 1, the anaerobic glycolytic system is like the gas tank for a hockey player. The size of this gas tank determines how long an athlete can sustain high-intensity work bouts before fatigue onset. Also, the gas tank's size determines the amount of work that can be performed in a given time. For example, if athlete A has a larger gas tank than athlete B, and all else is equal, athlete A can sustain a specific intensity above their anaerobic threshold longer than athlete B. If the duration of time is constant, athlete A will complete more work above their anaerobic threshold than athlete B in that given amount of time.

As the energy system's name implies, the anaerobic glycolytic system creates energy by breaking down glucose (a sugar that is the body's preferred fuel source) in the absence of oxygen. The glycolytic process takes one molecule of glucose and converts it to another molecule called pyruvate. If oxygen is present, pyruvate enters the aerobic energy system, resulting in 32 ATP molecules. If oxygen is not present, anaerobic glycolysis converts the pyruvate to lactate. The net ATP produced through anaerobic glycolysis is only two molecules. This difference in energy production between the aerobic energy system and anaerobic glycolysis is massive. Still, the benefit of anaerobic glycolysis lies in the rate at which it can produce ATP. Anaerobic glycolysis produces ATP at a rate 100 times faster than the aerobic system (Melkonian and Schury 2020). Therefore, during short, high-intensity efforts above the anaerobic threshold, the anaerobic glycolytic system is responsible for producing the majority of energy.

As with aerobic energy system training, training the anaerobic glycolytic system involves central and peripheral adaptations. There is an overlap between adaptions to aerobic and anaerobic exercise training, which highlights that both systems work in symphony and are intricately intertwined to improve the athlete's overall work capacity. When considering exercise prescriptions for this energy system, the goals are to increase the system's capacity and efficiency.

Central Adaptations to Anaerobic Exercise

Adaptations to anaerobic training include changes within the heart and blood, as noted with aerobic system training. Laursen and Jenkins (2002) highlighted that improvements in oxygen delivery occur due to increases in the heart's stroke volume and blood volume. These authors also suggest that exercise tolerance may improve due to an improvement in heat tolerance through increased blood flow to the skin and an increase in sweating. Lastly, Laursen and Jenkins (2002) suggested that there are adaptations within the nervous system, highlighting increases in the nervous system branch responsible for the fight or flight response.

Peripheral Adaptations to Anaerobic Exercise

As described previously, peripheral adaptations occur within the muscle. These include increased anaerobic (glycolytic) enzyme activity. This increase in enzyme activity enhances lactate production within the muscle. Contrary to popular belief, producing high amounts of lactate is a good thing. It signifies efficiency within the anaerobic glycolytic process, which in turn might lead to greater work output. However, when lactate is produced, it is associated with a hydrogen ion that creates an acidic environment within the muscle. This acid is evident when muscles begin to burn during high-intensity exercise. These hydrogen ions have been shown to inhibit the very enzymes that are responsible for creating them. Therefore, the body must have the ability to remove or neutralize these ions, known as buffering capacity. High-intensity anaerobic exercise increases your body's ability to deal with this acidic environment by repeatedly exposing it to acidic environments. This repeated exposure is an essential stimulus for the muscle's systems that remove the acid (Bishop, Girard, and Mendez-Villanueva 2011).

A sound understanding of how to manipulate factors associated with improving the following zones of the anaerobic glycolytic energy system (table 4.2) through central and peripheral adaptations is paramount when designing programs.

Table 4.2   Anaerobic Glycolytic Energy Systems Training Zones

Zone	Intensity	Target heart rate	Primary effect
Lactate capacity	Maximal	N/A; all-out effort	Improve the capacity of the anaerobic glycolytic system, buffering capacity
Lactate production	Supramaximal	N/A; all-out effort	Improve lactate production and flux through the anaerobic system, efficiency of lactate production

ANAEROBIC ALACTIC (ATP-PCR) ENERGY SYSTEM

The anaerobic alactic energy system can resynthesize ATP at a very high rate, allowing for large muscle power outputs. Continuing the automobile metaphor, this energy system is the horsepower of the engine. This energy is produced by removing phosphagens from creatine phosphate to regenerate ATP with no lactate produced, hence *alactic* in the name. Although this energy system can generate energy rapidly, its capacity is low and can only support these high-energy outputs for a few seconds. These short-burst, high-power outputs (table 4.3) are essential during a hockey game, and recovery from these short, high-intensity bouts is highly reliant on the aerobic system.

Table 4.3 Anaerobic Alactic Energy System Training Zone

Zone	Intensity	Primary effect
Speed	Supramaximal; all-out effort	Increase PCr stores or capacity and power

ENERGY SYSTEMS INTEGRATION IN HOCKEY

The three energy systems outlined are continuously operating; however, they contribute to energy production in different degrees depending on exercise intensity and duration. Figure 4.1 summarizes the relative energy contribution of each energy system as a factor of exercise duration.

Where does the hockey player fit into this model? The truth of the matter is that a hockey player requires the optimization of all energy systems. Figure 4.1 shows that a hockey player utilizes each of these energy systems to a high degree during a game. The alactic system is responsible for supporting the short bursts (e.g., races to pucks). The glycolytic system is accountable for supporting intense shifts of longer duration (e.g., when the team is hemmed in its zone on the penalty kill). The aerobic system aids in the recovery between these high-intensity bouts and provides more energy overall as the game progresses. Table 4.4 outlines the general breakdown of phases of energy systems training throughout the calendar year.

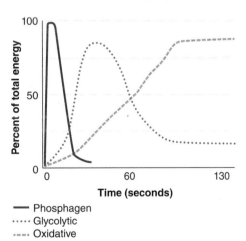

Figure 4.1 Relative energy contributions from the various energy systems depending on intensity and duration.

Table 4.4 Breakdown of Energy Systems Training Phases Throughout the Annual Training Plan

Phase		Zones	Intensity	Target HR	Duration
Phase 1	General preparatory: block 1	Aerobic capacity	Aerobic base	Max HR minus 50-65 beats per minute	3 weeks
			Anaerobic threshold	Max HR minus 25-30 beats per minute	
		Aerobic power	$\dot{V}O_2$max	Max HR	
	General preparatory: block 2	Aerobic capacity	Anaerobic threshold	Max HR minus 25-30 beats per minute	3 weeks
		Aerobic power	$\dot{V}O_2$max	Max HR	
		Work capacity	Maximal, supramaximal	N/A; all-out effort	
Phase 2	Anaerobic and aerobic power	Speed	Supramaximal	N/A; all-out effort	3-4 weeks
		Lactate production	Supramaximal	N/A; all-out effort	
		Aerobic power	$\dot{V}O_2$max	Max HR	
Phase 3	Anaerobic power and capacity	Speed	Supramaximal	N/A; all-out effort	3-4 weeks
		Lactate production	Supramaximal		
		Lactate capacity	Maximal		
Phase 4	Preseason and in-season	Speed	Supramaximal	N/A; all-out effort	Used selectively for the duration of the competitive season
		Lactate production	Supramaximal		
		Lactate capacity	Maximal		
		Aerobic power	$\dot{V}O_2$max	Max HR	
Phase 5	Postseason	Aerobic capacity	Aerobic base	Max HR minus 50-65 beats per minute	Used selectively for the duration of the postseason

Phase 1: General Preparation Phase, Block 1 (Weeks 1-3)

GPP block 1 aims to build the aerobic base and improve aerobic power and anaerobic threshold by specific central and peripheral adaptations to the exercise prescription.

- *Aerobic base.* The first task is to increase the work capacity below the anaerobic threshold. This work is typically accomplished by performing continuous aerobic base training at approximately 50 to 65 beats per minute below maximum heart rate for up to 45 minutes. The modality of exercise is not as important as the heart rate response.

- *Aerobic power.* The second task in block 1 is to improve maximum aerobic power. Increasing aerobic power is accomplished by performing shorter intervals of 2 to 5 minutes at the athlete's maximum heart rate. The modality of exercise is not as important as the heart rate response.

- *Anaerobic threshold.* The third task is to increase the exercise intensity at which the anaerobic threshold occurs, which signifies a delayed onset of fatigue at higher workloads. This improvement in anaerobic threshold can be accomplished by either performing continuous training or long intervals at 25 to 30 beats per minute below maximum heart rate. I typically prefer long intervals of 6 to 8 minutes for hockey players. As with the first two tasks, the modality of exercise can vary.

Block 1 can be performed using a three- or four-day model and is typically three weeks in duration. Table 4.5 represents the weekly breakdown of the process, and tables 4.6 and 4.7 outline potential parameters for each step in a three- and four-day model.

Table 4.5 Phase 1, Block 1 Weekly Energy Systems Training Variable Breakdown

Model	Three-day model	Four-day model
Day 1	Aerobic base	Aerobic base
Day 2	Aerobic power	Aerobic power
Day 3	Anaerobic threshold	Aerobic power
Day 4		Anaerobic threshold

Table 4.6 Three-Day Phase 1, Block 1 Training Variables and Parameters

Day	Monday	Tuesday	Wednesday	Thursday	Friday	Saturday	Sunday
Modification	Aerobic base		Aerobic power		Anaerobic threshold		
Intensity/HR zone	Max HR minus 50-65 beats per minute		Max HR		Max HR minus 25-30 beats per minute		
Sets	1		3-5		2-4		
Duration of interval	20-45 min		2-5 min		6-8 min		
Work-to-rest ratio	N/A		1:1		2:1		
Modality	Any		Any		Any		

Table 4.7 Four-Day Phase 1, Block 1 Training Variables and Parameters

Day	Monday	Tuesday	Wednesday	Thursday	Friday	Saturday	Sunday
Modification	Aerobic base	Aerobic power		Aerobic power	Anaerobic threshold		
Intensity/HR zone	Max HR minus 50-65 beats per minute	Max HR		Max HR	Max HR minus 25-30 beats per minute		
Sets	1	3-5		3	2-4		
Duration of interval	20-45 min	2-3 min		4-5 min	6-8 min		
Work-to-rest ratio	N/A	1:1		1:1	2:1		
Modality	Any	Any		Any	Any		

Phase 1: General Preparation Phase, Block 2 (Weeks 4-6)

The goal of GPP block 2 is to pull the central and peripheral adaptations together to work in synergy. The specific objectives are to increase the capillary number and utilization, mitochondrial density, aerobic enzyme activity, and myoglobin activity as described earlier. Aerobic power and anaerobic threshold training are still performed in block 2 with a fourth task: work capacity. Aerobic base training is not forgotten; however, it is maintained within the warm-up, movement training, and cooldowns.

- *Work capacity.* This training task is designed to increase the system's total work capacity by pulling all aerobic variables together. It is accomplished by performing short-duration intervals (10-60 seconds) at an all-out intensity. In addition to the peripheral adaptions, the athlete will acclimatize to maximal or supramaximal efforts. This type of interval can be performed on the ice, stationary bike, or by sprint running.

Block 2 is accomplished by using a three- or four-day model and is typically three weeks in duration. Table 4.8 represents the weekly breakdown of the process, and tables 4.9 and 4.10 outline potential parameters for each step in a three- and four-day model.

Table 4.8 Phase 1, Block 2 Weekly Energy Systems Training Variable Breakdown

Model	Three-day model	Four-day model
Day 1	Aerobic power	Aerobic power
Day 2	Work capacity	Work capacity
Day 3	Anaerobic threshold	Work capacity
Day 4		Anaerobic threshold

Table 4.9 Three-Day Phase 1, Block 2 Training Variables and Parameters

Day	Monday	Tuesday	Wednesday	Thursday	Friday	Saturday	Sunday
Modification	Aerobic power		Work capacity		Anaerobic threshold		
Intensity/HR zone	Max HR		N/A; maximal effort		Max HR minus 25-30 beats per minute		
Sets	5-10		6-12		3-5		
Duration of interval	2 min		10-60 sec		6-8 min		
Work-to-rest ratio	1:1		1:2 or 1:3		2:1		
Modality	Any		Skating, cycling, sprinting		Any		

Table 4.10 Four-Day Phase 1, Block 2 Training Variables and Parameters

Day	Monday	Tuesday	Wednesday	Thursday	Friday	Saturday	Sunday
Modification	Aerobic power	Work capacity		Work capacity	Anaerobic threshold		
Intensity/HR zone	Max HR	N/A; maximal effort		N/A; maximal effort	Max HR minus 25-30 beats per minute		
Sets	5-10	6-12		6-12	2-4		
Duration of interval	2 min	30-60 sec		10-30 sec	6-8 min		
Work-to-rest ratio	1:1	1:2		1:3	2:1		
Modality	Any	Skating, cycling, sprinting		Skating, cycling, sprinting	Any		

Phase 2: Anaerobic and Aerobic Power (Weeks 7-10 or 7-11)

Phase 2 aims to improve alactic power (speed) and lactate production while continuing to improve aerobic power.

• *Speed.* When considering alactic power (speed), the goal is to increase PCr stores in the muscle and the enzymes involved in the process of its energy conversion. This work is typically performed by conducting all-out efforts of 5 to 15 seconds. Speed training requires a significant amount of rest because the quality of work outweighs the volume. To improve this system's power (or enzyme activity), rest periods of 1 to 3 minutes are advised. Conversely, to improve capacity (amount of PCr in the muscle), rest periods of 45 to 90 seconds are recommended. Therefore, this phase's structure is paramount to ensure the athlete is in a good recovery state to perform this training. This type of exercise's ideal modality is skating, but it can also be accomplished through stationary cycling, sprint running, or resisted sprint running.

• *Lactate production.* During this phase, a transition to focusing on the efficiency of lactate production also occurs. Efficiency is improved by performing all-out maximal intervals of 15 to 30 seconds with rest intervals ranging from 30 to 90 seconds. The preferred modality for this type of exercise is skating with elements of change of direction. It can also be accomplished through sprint running with a change of direction (e.g., shuttle runs) or stationary cycling, for example.

Phase 2 can be accomplished by using a three- or four-day model and is typically three or four weeks in duration. Table 4.11 represents the weekly breakdown of the process, and tables 4.12 and 4.13 outline potential parameters for each step in a three- and four-day model.

Table 4.11 Phase 2 Weekly Energy Systems Training Variable Breakdown

Model	Three-day model	Four-day model
Day 1	Speed	Speed
Day 2	Lactate production	Lactate production
Day 3	Aerobic power	Speed
Day 4		Aerobic power

Table 4.12 Three-Day Phase 2 Training Variables and Parameters

Day	Monday	Tuesday	Wednesday	Thursday	Friday	Saturday	Sunday
Modification	Speed		Lactate production		Aerobic power		
Intensity/HR zone	N/A; maximal effort		N/A; maximal effort		Max HR		
Sets	10-30		4-8		5-10		
Duration of interval	5-10 sec		15-30 sec		2 min		
Rest or work-to-rest ratio	1-3 min		30-90 sec		1:1		
Modality	Skating, cycling, sprinting, resisted sprinting		Skating, cycling, sprinting		Any		

Table 4.13 Four-Day Phase 2 Training Variables and Parameters

Day	Monday	Tuesday	Wednesday	Thursday	Friday	Saturday	Sunday
Modification	Speed	Lactate production		Speed	Aerobic power		
Intensity/HR zone	N/A; maximal effort	N/A; maximal effort		N/A; maximal effort	Max HR		
Sets	10-20	4-8		10-30	5-10		
Duration of interval	5-10 sec	15-30 sec		10-15 sec	2 min		
Rest or work-to-rest ratio	1-3 min	30-90 sec		45-90 sec	1:1		
Modality	Skating, cycling, sprinting, resisted sprinting	Skating, cycling, sprinting		Skating, cycling, sprinting	Any		

Phase 3: Anaerobic Power and Capacity (Weeks 11-13 or 12-15)

Phase 3 aims to improve lactate production and capacity while continuing to enhance alactic power (speed). Alactic power (speed) and lactate production are described earlier.

• *Lactate capacity.* As the season draws closer, a greater emphasis is placed on lactate capacity training. This type of training is a grueling but necessary addition to the energy systems training workload. It improves the athlete's ability to tolerate fatigue by increasing buffering capacity and efficiency of the system. Lactate capacity intervals are between 30 seconds and 2 minutes at all-out efforts. The work-to-rest ratios range from 1:1 for the longer lactate capacity intervals to 1:4 for shorter duration intervals. This type of exercise's preferred modality is skating with elements of change of direction for the shorter duration intervals. It can also be accomplished through sprint running with a change of direction (e.g., shuttle runs), stationary cycling, and sled pushing.

Phase 3 can be accomplished by using a three- or four-day model and is typically three to four weeks in duration. Table 4.14 represents the weekly breakdown of the process, and tables 4.15 and 4.16 outline potential parameters for each step in a three- and four-day model.

Table 4.14 Phase 3 Weekly Energy Systems Training Variable Breakdown

Model	Three-day model	Four-day model
Day 1	Speed	Speed
Day 2	Lactate production	Lactate production
Day 3	Lactate capacity	Lactate production
Day 4		Lactate capacity

Table 4.15 Three-Day Phase 3 Training Variables and Parameters

Day	Monday	Tuesday	Wednesday	Thursday	Friday	Saturday	Sunday
Modification	Speed		Lactate production		Lactate capacity		
Intensity/HR zone	N/A; maximal effort		N/A; maximal effort		N/A; maximal effort		
Sets	10-30		4-8		4-8		
Duration of interval	5-15 sec		15-30 sec		30 sec-2 min		
Rest	1-3 min		30-90 sec		1-4 min		
Modality	Skating, cycling, sprinting, resisted sprinting		Skating (with change of direction [COD]), cycling, sprinting (with COD)		Skating (with COD), cycling, sprinting (with COD), sled pushing		

Table 4.16 Four-Day Phase 3 Training Variables and Parameters

Day	Monday	Tuesday	Wednesday	Thursday	Friday	Saturday	Sunday
Modification	Speed	Lactate production		Lactate production	Lactate capacity		
Intensity/HR zone	N/A; maximal effort	N/A; maximal effort		N/A; maximal effort	N/A; maximal effort		
Sets	10-20	4-8		4-8	4-8		
Duration of interval	5-10 sec	20-30 sec		15-20 sec	30 sec-2 min		
Rest	1-3 min	40 sec-2 min		30-60 sec	1-4 min		
Modality	Skating, cycling, sprinting, resisted sprinting	Skating (with COD), cycling, sprinting (with COD)		Skating (with COD), cycling, sprinting (with COD)	Skating (with COD), cycling, sprinting (with COD), sled pushing		

Phase 4: Preseason and In-Season (Duration of Competitive Season)

Transitioning from the off-season to the competitive season adds a significant amount of complexity, stress, and workload to the athletes. The addition of games, practices, travel, anxiety, and pressure all contribute to the ever-changing web of workload variables that must be navigated when prescribing in-season energy systems work for athletes. In general, high-minute players (i.e., 15 minutes or more per game) typically do not require any additional energy systems training on top of practices and games if the total practice and game schedule is more than four sessions in a week. Players who play fewer minutes (i.e., less than 15 minutes) might require additional energy systems training in the form of speed or lactate production. This extra work's volume and intensity are guided by the individual in question and their specific requirements. Athletes who do not play in games or are healthy-scratched should follow the outline in table 4.17, which describes the appropriate energy systems training in the absence of games. This training should be done on the game day itself, preferably on the ice. Again, the volumes and intensities are guided by the individual and the previous and upcoming schedules. For example, suppose the team played three games in four days previously and has an upcoming back-to-back scenario. In that case, the athlete might benefit from alactic speed work but should refrain from more metabolically demanding energy systems training in the event that they are required to play in the upcoming game.

Table 4.17   Energy Systems Training When the Athlete Does Not Participate in the Game

Days before next game	Intensity	Special considerations
2 or more	Aerobic power	Intervals longer than 1 minute completed off ice
	Lactate capacity	
1 or more	Lactate production	On-ice training
1 or more	Speed	On-ice training, 10-15 repetitions maximum
First game of back to back		

Phase 5: Duration of Postseason

The postseason is the time between the end of the season and the start of off-season training when the athletes can regenerate and recharge physically and mentally. After an initial period of complete rest (approximately 1-2 weeks), athletes should perform low-level aerobic base work most days of the week. This aerobic base work should not be viewed as training in the eyes of the athlete. It should be in the form of fun and unstructured activities (e.g., hiking or leisurely bike rides) to get them moving again. During this time, the athlete should also focus on their soft tissue by performing self-myofascial (SMR) techniques, stretching, and mobility work.

DOES MODALITY MATTER?

I often hear that hockey players should not ride the stationary bike in the off-season. The rationale behind this is that hockey players should be completing their energy systems training in an upright position, such as when running. An upright position is said to counteract the short and tight hip flexor muscles acquired from skating and cycling. There is some validity to the argument that the modality of running provides some benefits over cycling. However, I do not believe that hip flexion muscular factors are one of these benefits provided that the movement capacity plan is appropriate. Running can provide cardiovascular advantages such as an increased rate of oxygen consumption. However, cycling more closely mimics the local leg fatigue mechanisms of skating. Therefore, it is imperative to evaluate the individual athlete and their specific needs to adjust the program accordingly.

POSITION SPECIFICITY

Although the hockey positions vary in their roles on the ice, I believe all positions need to optimize the energy systems regardless of whether it is a skating position or a goalie. Each energy system is in the forefront providing energy at one point or another during a game. For example, a skating player might rely primarily on the anaerobic alactic system to win a race to a puck, whereas a goalie depends on the same system when moving post to post as quickly as possible. Conversely, skating positions and goalies rely heavily on the anaerobic glycolytic energy system when they get hemmed in their zone on the penalty kill. All players depend on the aerobic system to recover between shifts or zone play and between periods. The specificity lies in the modality of anaerobic alactic training. For example, goalies might benefit from adding short, lateral pushing intervals on a slide board.

SUMMARY

As the off-season progresses, it is imperative to build from the ground up with all forms of training. The duration of the phase and focus variables are guided by the individual assessments performed, outlined in chapter 2. As coaches, we cannot skip steps in the relatively long energy systems development and optimization process. Following the steps outlined in this chapter will give your athletes the energy systems support to perform on the ice while resisting fatigue within a game and throughout the long season.

Chapter 5

Systemic Strengthening

The ability to generate high amounts of force is one of the most critical performance characteristics required to excel in hockey. The human body's ability to produce force is known as *strength*, and it forms the base of support for many other performance characteristics, such as power development. Regardless of whether the athlete is a small, skilled forward or a big, stay-at-home defenseperson, strength development is a primary concern when programming to optimize their performance on the ice.

This chapter will outline various aspects of strength and its development, such as the length–tension relationship, the force–velocity relationship, types of muscle contractions, adaptations to strength training, and the inside-out approach to strength development, and will provide exercises in each category of movement.

LENGTH–TENSION RELATIONSHIP

The length–tension relationship is a vital characteristic of skeletal muscle. This relationship represents the force a muscle can generate at different lengths corresponding to various joint angles. The optimum muscle length is defined as the position at which maximum force is observed (Chang et al. 1999). If the muscle length is outside of this optimal range, force production will not be optimized. However, while playing hockey, athletes often find themselves in compromised positions, potentially outside of the optimal muscle length zone. The good news is that this zone can be modified and shifted as a result of carefully planned and structured strength training programs and exercises. For example, Brughelli and Cronin (2007) highlighted several studies that demonstrated a shift in this length–tension relationship after eccentric training, as described later in the chapter. Not all muscles are the same in terms of optimal length. When performing multijoint compound movements, one muscle might be optimal length and another too short or too long; therefore, it is imperative to perform strength training exercises in different ranges and positions to optimize force production.

FORCE–VELOCITY RELATIONSHIP

The force–velocity relationship is another critical characteristic of the muscle's force-generating capabilities and involves the muscle's dynamic properties. This relationship suggests that as the velocity of movement increases, force-producing abilities decrease and vice versa. Since hockey is often a high-velocity sport, generating force at these high speeds is essential. L.L. Andersen et al. (2005) demonstrated that resistance training elicited an immediate improvement in force production at slow and moderate velocities but saw no immediate changes in force production at higher rates. However, after a period of recovery, an increase in force production was observed during high-velocity movement. Studies like this highlight the impact of strength training on the athlete's ability to generate force at various velocities.

TYPES OF MUSCLE CONTRACTION

The three types of muscle contraction—isometric, eccentric, and concentric—are defined by the changes (or lack thereof) in muscle length during contraction:

- Isometric contractions are characterized by force generation in the absence of any changes in the muscle's length. For example, exerting force on an immovable object will result in force production from the muscle without the joint in question moving, resulting in no change in length of the muscle producing the force.

- Eccentric contractions are characterized by force generation while the muscle length is increasing. For example, during the lowering phase of a biceps curl, the muscles are generating significant force while lengthening.

- Concentric contractions are characterized by force generation while the muscle is shortening in length. For example, while raising the weight during a biceps curl, the muscles generate force while shortening.

Typically, isometric and eccentric force–generating capabilities are higher than concentric force–generating capabilities. These are essential programming variables to consider when designing strength training plans for athletes.

PHYSIOLOGICAL ADAPTATIONS TO STRENGTH TRAINING

The importance of strength training for hockey players cannot be understated. The improvement in force-generating capabilities from strength training directly improves the neuromuscular system's capacity through adaptations to many physiological variables. These variables include neurological adaptations, increases in muscle size (muscle hypertrophy), changes in muscle fiber type (fast- and slow-twitch muscles), and hormonal changes, to name a few.

Neurological Adaptations

It has been well established that adaptations within the nervous system (neurological adaptations) contribute to initial improvements in force production in the absence of muscle size changes. For example, Moritani and deVries (1979) demonstrated that neural factors accounted for most of the improvements in strength in the first four weeks of an eight-week strength training program. These adaptations are generally in the form of modifications in intra- and intermuscular coordination. Intramuscular coordination happens within the motor unit, which is the combination of the muscle fiber and nerve that makes it contract. These changes include the ability to contract different motor units simultaneously, recruitment of more motor units, and changes to the nerves' firing rate causing muscle contraction. Intermuscular coordination occurs between muscle groups. These adaptations include increased activation of muscle groups that directly contribute to the movement and decreased simultaneous contraction of muscle groups that act against the motion. For example, when extending the knee, the prime movers are the quadriceps muscles. If the hamstrings, which are primarily responsible for knee flexion, are overly active during knee extension, force will not be optimized. Strength training will improve the coordination between these two muscle groups by decreasing the hamstring muscles' contribution in this scenario. When considering youth hockey players, these are the primary mechanisms resulting in most improvements in strength.

Muscle Hypertrophy

Muscle hypertrophy refers to the increase in the whole muscle's size and the individual muscle fibers themselves. After the initial training period, during which neurological adaptations primarily contribute to increases in strength, increased muscle size will then account for a significant proportion of strength increases (Deschenes and Kraemer 2002). These authors suggest that the reason for this delay is that creating the contractile proteins in the muscle is a relatively slow process, whereas neurological adaptations happen quite rapidly.

Muscle Fiber Type

While muscle fibers exist on a spectrum, they are generally divided into three types: slow-twitch (type I) muscle fibers and two types of fast-twitch (type II) fibers. Slow-twitch fibers are typically small, produce force slowly with low magnitude, and primarily use aerobic energy mechanisms, making them more fatigue resistant than fast-twitch fibers. One type of fast-twitch fiber primarily uses aerobic energy sources, and the other uses mostly anaerobic energy sources. The fast-twitch muscle fibers are generally larger, produce force more rapidly than slow-twitch fibers, and fatigue more rapidly. The structure and type of strength training can elicit significant adaptations within each of these fiber types. Although a complete restructuring of muscle fiber type within a muscle is likely not possible, these fibers' properties can be changed. For example, J.L. Andersen and Aagaard (2010) demonstrated that exposing fast-twitch muscle fibers to large amounts of low-frequency electrical stimulation (similar to the type of stimulus received by slow-twitch muscle fibers) will induce changes in composition, transitioning their properties from fast to slow. Therefore, it is imperative to understand how loading, the velocity of movement, and exercise duration influence the different types of muscle fibers' performance.

Hormonal

Mechanical stress on muscular structure from resistance training has also been shown to influence hormonal profiles in both acute (immediately after exercise) and chronic resting levels within the blood (Deschenes and Kraemer 2002). Studies have shown an elevation in testosterone within the blood in males (McCall et al. 1999) and increased levels of growth hormone in females (Kraemer et al. 1998), which are likely the most potent gender-specific muscle-building hormones, respectively.

ABSOLUTE VERSUS RELATIVE STRENGTH

Absolute strength is the maximum amount of force produced regardless of body size and weight, whereas relative strength is the maximum amount of force produced in relation to body size. Both absolute and relative strength are fundamental in hockey. Absolute strength is required when battling against larger opponents, and relative strength is essential when generating movement. The higher the absolute strength, the higher the relative strength will be for a given body weight. Therefore, it is imperative that all hockey players, particularly younger athletes, attempt to increase their absolute strength during training.

INSIDE-OUT APPROACH TO STRENGTH TRAINING

The inside-out approach to strength training is designed to address the proximal stability for the distal force application concept discussed in chapter 1. Proximal stability is defined by the athlete's core (lumbopelvic hip complex) and shoulder girdle (rotator cuff) stability and strength. In contrast, distal force application is the expressed force throughout the athlete's moveable limbs. The core and rotator cuff musculature must possess adequate strength levels to optimize force production distally and resist forces imposed on the athlete's body. That is not to say that the athlete can only perform low-amplitude core and shoulder exercises for extended periods; in fact, these exercises should be performed in conjunction with more complex compound (multijoint) movements. However, the core and shoulder girdle are often the limiting factor. For example, an athlete who does not possess the appropriate core strength to perform a specific load on a barbell back squat has two options: One, reduce the weight until the core musculature can support the movement. Two, perform a variation of the exercise that places less demand on the core musculature. The remainder of this chapter will dive deeper into the inside-out approach concept and highlight various exercises athletes can use to gain the systemic strength required to perform at the highest levels on the ice.

Core Strength

To train specific groups of muscles, we must understand their function and then challenge their functional capacity. In essence, the musculature of the torso serves to perform eight functions. Four of these functions (flexion, extension, lateral flexion, and rotation) induce movement in the lumbar spine and pelvis. In contrast, the other four (antiextension, antiflexion, antilateral flexion, and antirotation) are antagonistic, preventing movement and generating stability and control within the lumbar spine and pelvis. The muscles that flex the lumbar spine are also responsible for antiextension. The muscles that extend the lumbar spine are also responsible for antiflexion. And the muscles that rotate the lumbar spine are also responsible for antirotation. The latter three stability (or antimovement) functions should be the primary concern for an athlete wanting to generate proximal stability.

Antiextension

Building anterior core strength to resist extension of the lumbar spine is imperative for hockey players from performance and injury perspectives. Antiextension exercises help enhance lumbopelvic stability, which in turn creates a larger base of support for force and power production and minimizes excessive movement, which can often lead to hip and groin injuries over time.

Front Plank

Difficulty

Beginner

Equipment

None

Purpose

The front plank strengthens the anterior core musculature.

Starting Position

Lie face down on the floor. Place your elbows directly under your shoulders with your forearms pointing forward. Feet should be close together to allow for greater glute muscle engagement.

Movement

Elevate your body off the ground. A straight line from your shoulders to feet should be observed, and your neck should be in a nicely packed position, with your chin tucked and eyes looking at the floor (figure 5.1). If you notice your lower back arching, make sure your abdominal and gluteal muscles are fully engaged, and do not let them relax for the exercise duration. If your hips begin to sag and you can no longer maintain form, it is time to end the exercise.

Figure 5.1   Front plank.

Stability Ball Rollout From Knees

Difficulty

Intermediate

Equipment

Stability ball, ab wheel, slide board or carpet sliders

Purpose

The stability ball rollout from the knees strengthens the anterior core musculature as the degree of difficulty changes throughout the movement.

Starting Position

Kneel on the floor with the stability ball in front of you. Place your hands on the ball with palms facing each other.

Movement

Press your hands into the ball and shift your weight, rolling the ball forward until your forearms are on the ball (figure 5.2). Maintain a straight body posture from knees to head for the duration of the movement. Use your abdominal musculature to return to the starting position. Adjust the size of the ball if needed. In general, the bigger the ball, the easier the exercise will be.

Figure 5.2   Stability ball rollout from knees.

Progressions and Variations

Stability Ball Rollout

Kneel on the floor with the stability ball in front of you. Place your forearms on the ball with your elbows directly under your shoulders and your forearms pointing forward. Your feet should be approximately shoulder-width apart.

Figure 5.3   Stability ball rollout.

Elevate your body off the ground to assume a plank position. While in the plank position on the ball, extend your arms forward as far as you can while maintaining posture (figure 5.3), and then return to the starting position.

Wheel Rollout

Kneel on the floor with the ab wheel in front of you. Engage your core musculature and extend your arms. Slowly roll the wheel forward until your body is parallel to the ground (figure 5.4). Return to the starting position.

Figure 5.4   Wheel rollout.

Body Saw

The starting position for the body saw is the same as the front plank; however, your feet are on a slide board or carpet sliders. Push through your forearms forward, sliding your entire body backward (figure 5.5). Return to the starting position by pulling your body forward again.

Figure 5.5   Body saw.

Antiflexion

Like the antiextension exercises, antiflexion exercises are designed to enhance stability in the lumbopelvic complex by building resistance to flexion of the lumbar spine. Lumbopelvic stability is essential from both performance and injury prevention points of view.

Glute Bridge

Difficulty

Beginner

Equipment

None

Purpose

Figure 5.6   Glute bridge.

The glute bridge strength-ens the gluteal musculature and improves the control of the pelvis.

Starting Position

Lie on your back with bent knees and feet flat on the ground, assuming what's called the hook-lying position.

Movement

Engage the gluteal musculature, and raise your hips off the floor into full hip extension. Create a straight line from the knees to the shoulders (figure 5.6). Be sure that the movement is generated through hip extension and not the extension of the lumbar spine. If this extension is observed, reset, engage the glute muscles and anterior core muscles, and rise again.

Progressions and Variations

Figure 5.7   Single-leg glute bridge.

Single-Leg Glute Bridge

Assume the hook-lying position and pull one knee to your chest with a bent knee. Engage the gluteal musculature, and raise your hips off the floor into full hip extension. Create a straight line from the knee to the shoulder (figure 5.7).

Stability Ball Back Extension Hold

Difficulty

Intermediate to advanced

Equipment

Stability ball

Purpose

The stability ball back extension hold strengthens the gluteal and spinal erector musculature.

Starting Position

While kneeling, place your feet against a wall or lock your heels under an immovable object. Position the stability ball under your hips and thighs.

Movement

Press your hips into the ball by engaging the gluteal and anterior core musculature. Maintain a straight line from the hips to the shoulders (figure 5.8). The spine and pelvis should be in a neutral position. Do not hyperextend your lumbar spine.

Figure 5.8   Stability ball back extension hold.

Antilateral Flexion

Due to the physical nature of hockey, lumbopelvic stability is an essential characteristic of performance and injury prevention. While competing against the opposition, it is crucial to have enough core strength to maintain stability in the lumbar spine and pelvis to effectively express power and force on the opponent and resist compromising body positions that could lead to injury. Antilateral flexion exercises build the core strength necessary to resist lateral (or side) flexion of the spine.

Side Plank

Difficulty

Beginner to intermediate

Equipment

Single-leg squat stand or bench for Copenhagen side plank

Purpose

The side plank strengthens multiple core and hip muscles that work to resist lateral flexion of the spine.

Starting Position

Set up in a side-lying position. Extend the legs and stack the feet, one on top of the other. Place your elbow directly under your shoulder with your forearm flat on the ground. Place your top hand on your opposite shoulder.

Movement

Raise your hips off the ground, creating a straight line from your head to your feet (figure 5.9). Make sure you are pushing your elbow into the ground to stabilize your shoulder. Avoid twisting your body forward or backward, staying as straight as possible. Engage glute muscles to maintain a neutral pelvic position. Your neck should be in a nicely packed position, with your chin tucked.

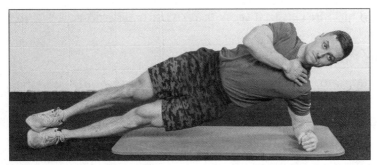

Figure 5.9   Side plank.

Progressions and Variations

Copenhagen Side Plank

This is an advanced progression designed to strengthen multiple core and hip muscles that work to resist lateral flexion of the spine. It places significant stress on the leg's adductor musculature. Set up in a side-lying position. Extend your legs, and place your top ankle on the stand or bench and your bottom leg underneath the stand. Place your elbow directly under the shoulder, keep the forearm flat on the ground, and put your top hand on your opposite shoulder. Raise your hips off the ground, creating a straight line from your head to your feet (figure 5.10). If proper alignment cannot be maintained, regress the exercise.

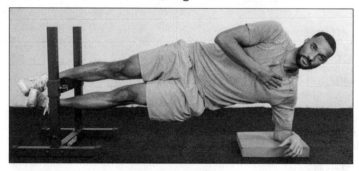

Figure 5.10   Copenhagen side plank.

Single-Arm Farmer's Carry

Difficulty

Intermediate

Equipment

Dumbbell or kettlebell

Purpose

The single-arm farmer's carry strengthens multiple core and hip muscles that work to resist lateral flexion of the spine.

Starting Position

While standing, pick up a weight with one arm, and hold the weight at your side.

Movement

Simply walk with the weight at your side, holding it slightly off your body (figure 5.11). Avoid excessive upper-body movement. If upper-body swaying cannot be avoided, decrease the weight or regress the exercise.

Figure 5.11   Single-arm farmer's carry.

Antirotation

As noted previously in this chapter, a common tenet for on-ice performance and injury reduction is lumbopelvic or core stability. The final category of core stability exercises is antirotation. These exercises are designed to build resistance to excessive rotation of the lumbar spine. The lumbar spine is designed to rotate to a degree; however, most of the rotation in many hockey-related activities, such as shooting the puck, is generated through the hip and upper back.

Half-Kneeling Pallof Press

Difficulty

Beginner

Equipment

Cable machine or resistance band

Purpose

The half-kneeling Pallof press strengthens multiple core muscles that work to resist the spine's rotation.

Starting Position

Begin in a tall half-kneeling position, with your inside knee forward and to the side of the cable machine or band

Figure 5.12   Half-kneeling Pallof press.

anchor. Tuck your chin to pack your neck. The cable or band should be placed at approximately chest and shoulder height. Begin by holding the cable to your chest with both hands.

Movement

While holding the cable handle with both hands, engage your contralateral glute muscles and core musculature. Press the cable away from your body until your arms are extended (figure 5.12). Return to the starting position.

Half-Kneeling Stability Chop

Difficulty

Intermediate

Equipment

Cable machine or resistance band, cable bar or rope attachment

Purpose

The half-kneeling stability chop strengthens multiple core muscles that work to resist rotation of the spine.

Starting Position

Assume a half-kneeling position, with the inside knee forward. Place your neck in a packed position, with your chin tucked. Place the cable at the highest setting. Hold the cable bar or rope attachment with palms down and arms in the extended position.

Movement

Pull the bar to your waist and press out with your inside hand (figure 5.13a). Resist the urge to rotate your hips, lumbar spine, and thoracic spine in the direction of the arm movement. If you are unsure what knee should be forward, look to where the cable is. If the cable is in the up position, the inside knee should be forward. The inside knee should mirror the cable. If the cable is in the down position, the inside knee should be down (see the half-kneeling stability lift variation).

Progressions and Variations

Half-Kneeling Stability Lift

Place the cable at the lowest setting. Assume a half-kneeling position, with the outside knee forward. Hold the cable bar or rope attachment with palms down and arms in the extended position. Pull the bar to your waist and press out with your inside hand (figure 5.13b). Resist the urge to rotate your hips, lumbar spine, and thoracic spine in the direction of the arm movement.

Figure 5.13   Half-kneeling stability chop and lift: *(a)* chop and *(b)* lift.

Antirotation Chop

Difficulty

Intermediate

Equipment

Cable machine or resistance band, cable bar or rope attachment

Purpose

The antirotation chop strengthens multiple core muscles that work to resist rotation of the spine.

Starting Position

Assume a wide stance, with your feet double shoulder-width apart, and with your side to the cable machine. Place the cable at shoulder height. Hold the cable bar or rope attachment with extended elbows and palms down close to the cable machine.

Movement

While maintaining a perfectly stable torso and extended elbows, move your arms across your body with the movement point being at the shoulders (figure 5.14). Return to the starting position. Resist rotation in the hips, lumbar spine, and thoracic spine in the direction of the arm movement. Be sure to maintain stability in these areas and move your arms around your body.

Figure 5.14   Antirotation chop.

Progressions and Variations

Split Stance Antirotation Chop

Assume a split stance with your inside knee forward. Hold the cable bar or rope attachment with your elbows extended and palms down close to the cable machine. While maintaining a perfectly stable torso and extended

elbows, move your arms across your body with the movement point being at the shoulders (figure 5.15). Return to the starting position.

Rotator Cuff Strength

The rotator cuff is composed of four muscles that act to stabilize the shoulder during upper-extremity movements. Shoulder stability is critical for injury prevention in hockey, because a stable shoulder is less prone to wear and tear from shooting and passing, and it adds protection to the shoulder joint during contact from an opposing player. The following exercises focus on strengthening the rotator cuff musculature.

Figure 5.15 Split stance antirotation chop.

Shoulder External Rotation

Difficulty

Beginner

Equipment

Cable machine or resistance band, pad or roller

Purpose

The shoulder external rotation strengthens the external rotators of the rotator cuff to aid in shoulder stabilization.

Starting Position

Stand with your side to the cable machine. Bend your elbow to 90 degrees, and set the cable to a height that lines up with your hand that is farthest from the cable machine. Place a pad or roller between your elbow and body to slightly abduct your upper arm.

Movement

Keeping your shoulder back, scapula stable, and elbow tight to the pad, externally rotate the shoulder to move your forearm across your body (figure 5.16). Return to the starting position. If you find yourself compensating and having difficulty maintaining stable positioning of your upper arm and shoulder, reduce the weight.

Figure 5.16 Shoulder external rotation.

Upward Cable X to Extension

Difficulty

Intermediate to advanced

Equipment

Two-pulley cable machine or resistance bands

Purpose

The upward cable X to extension strengthens the muscles of the rotator cuff to aid in shoulder stabilization.

Starting Position

Place the cables in the bottom position. Assume a kneeling position facing the cable machine. Hold the left cable handle in your right hand and the right cable handle in your left hand.

Movement

Begin with your arms crossed in front of your body. Pull your elbows up to your ears while maintaining bent elbows (figure 5.17a). Extend at your elbows to form a complete Y with your arms (figure 5.17b). Return to the starting position. Avoid upward flaring of the rib cage.

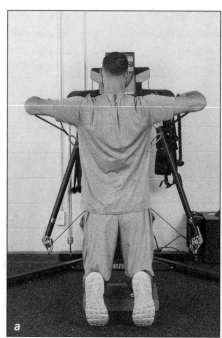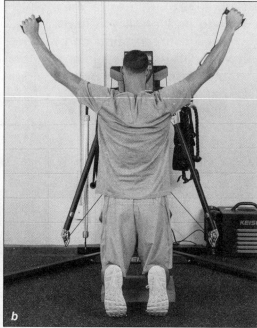

Figure 5.17   Upward cable X to extension: *(a)* pull bent elbows up and *(b)* straighten elbows to a Y position.

Downward Cable X to Extension

Difficulty

Intermediate to advanced

Equipment

Two-pulley cable machine or resistance bands

Purpose

The downward cable X to extension strengthens the muscles of the rotator cuff, upper back, and triceps to aid in shoulder stabilization.

Starting Position

Place the cables in the top position. Assume a kneeling position facing the cable machine. Hold the left cable handle in your right hand and the right cable handle in your left hand.

Movement

Begin with your arms crossed in front of your body. Pull your elbows down to your side while keeping your shoulders pulled back (figure 5.18*a*). Extend at your elbows with your arms at approximately 30 to 45 degrees from your body (figure 5.18*b*). Return to the starting position. Avoid upward flaring of the rib cage.

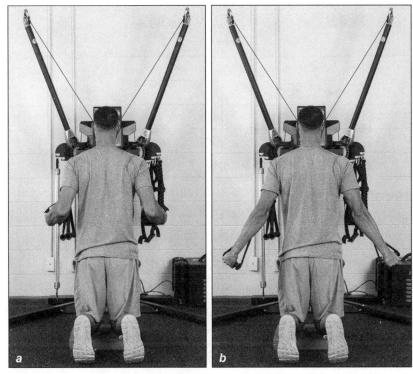

Figure 5.18 Downward cable X to extension: *(a)* pull elbows down and *(b)* straighten elbows to side.

Hip and Adductor Strength

Some of the most common injuries in hockey occur in the hip and adductors (groin). Scientific data suggest that increasing the strength in the hip and groin musculature decreases the risk of injury during the repetitive nature of skating. The following exercises focus on developing hip and adductor strength.

Groin Squeeze

Difficulty

Beginner

Equipment

Foam roller

Purpose

The groin squeeze activates and strengthens the adductor muscles.

Starting Position

Lie on your back with bent knees and feet flat on the ground, assuming the hook-lying position. Place a foam roller between your knees (figure 5.19).

Figure 5.19   Groin squeeze.

Movement

Engage your pelvic floor musculature, and squeeze the foam roller as hard as possible for the prescribed amount of time and repetitions.

Progressions and Variations

Glute Bridge Groin Squeeze

Add a glute bridge to the groin squeeze to increase the difficulty level.

Four-Way Cable Hip Series

Difficulty

Beginner to intermediate

Equipment

Cable machine or resistance band

Purpose

The four-way cable hip series strengthens the muscles responsible for stabilization and control of the hip and femur.

Starting Position

Place the cable machine at the lowest setting. Attach the cable to one ankle, and stand facing the machine. Lift the leg attached to the cable so you are standing on one leg.

Movement

Perform hip extension, keeping your spine stable (figure 5.20*a*). Rotate a quarter turn and perform hip adduction (figure 5.20*b*), bringing the feet together and then abducting your leg toward the cable machine. Rotate a quarter turn and perform hip flexion (figure 5.20*c*) by bringing your knee up and above the hip level. Rotate a quarter turn and perform hip abduction (figure 5.20*d*), bringing the leg from the midline away from the cable. Contrary to what you might expect, the stationary hip musculature should feel more fatigued due to its continuous stabilization demands.

Figure 5.20   Four-way cable hip series: *(a)* hip extension, *(b)* hip adduction, *(c)* hip flexion, and *(d)* hip abduction.

Cable-Resisted Slide Board Lateral Lunge

Difficulty

Advanced

Equipment

Cable machine or resistance band, slide board or carpet sliders

Purpose

The cable-resisted slide board lateral lunge is a closed-chain adductor exercise that places significant eccentric and concentric loading demands on the adductor musculature.

Starting Position

Place the cable machine at the lowest setting. Attach the cable to the inside ankle, and stand with your side approximately two or three steps away from the machine. The foot attached to the cable is on a slide board, and the stationary leg is on solid ground.

Movement

Perform a slide board lateral lunge, with the foot attached to the cable moving closer to the cable machine. Maintain a straight leg (figure 5.21). Pulling and pushing with the stationary leg, return to the starting position. If your form cannot be maintained, remove the cable and perform the exercise without external loading. Be sure to fully extend your hip and contract your glute muscles, avoiding an anterior tilt of the pelvis in the standing position.

Figure 5.21   Cable-resisted slide board lateral lunge.

Upper- and Lower-Body Disassociation

While playing hockey, players often find themselves in compromising positions in which they must reach in a direction different from where they are traveling. For example, if a puck is passed behind a player breaking down the wing, the player may have to reach behind while still traveling forward to retrieve the puck with minimal disruptions to skating. If the player has to turn their whole body to retrieve that same puck, their forward locomotion will be significantly compromised, potentially allowing the opposing team to track them down. Exercises can be performed to train the disassociation between the upper and lower body while still generating force.

Dowel Figure 8

Difficulty

Beginner

Equipment

Dowel or hockey stick

Purpose

The dowel figure 8 challenges your ability to disassociate your upper body from your lower body, improving your ability to reach with the stick in multiple directions while maintaining linear locomotion.

Starting Position

Stand in an athletic position with two hands on the dowel or stick.

Movement

While maintaining a forward-facing pelvis and base of support, reach as far behind yourself as possible with your stick while maintaining posture (figure 5.22). Loop around across your body, and reach as far behind on your other side using your backhand. Reach as far as possible but only as far as your posture will allow. If your pelvis begins to rotate, scale back the range.

Figure 5.22   Dowel figure 8.

Split Cable Reach to T

Difficulty

Intermediate to advanced

Equipment

Cable machine or resistance band

Purpose

The split cable reach to T challenges your ability to disassociate your upper body from your lower body when your base is compromised or unstable.

Starting Position

Set the cable in the middle position. Assume a low split position with your inside knee forward, approximately 3 to 7 feet (1-2 m) away from the cable column. Hold the cable with your outside hand.

Movement

While maintaining a stationary lower body, rotate your upper body and reach toward the cable as far as possible (figure 5.23a). Reverse the motion by pulling the cable back across your body and extending your arms out to a T position (figure 5.23b). If you cannot maintain your lower body posture, decrease the range of movement or load on the cable machine.

Figure 5.23　Split cable reach to T: *(a)* reach toward cable and *(b)* extend arms out to T.

Whole-Body Integration

The game of hockey is not played in a static environment in which specific muscle groups are isolated. Therefore, core and shoulder girdle exercises must be integrated to optimize these systems' global functioning. These are advanced exercises and might not be suitable for beginners.

Cable Single-Leg Squat Pallof Hold

Difficulty

Advanced

Equipment

Cable machine or resistance band

Purpose

The cable single-leg squat Pallof hold challenges many of the concepts discussed throughout this chapter by integrating them into a single exercise. The significant points of focus in this exercise are antirotation, shoulder stability, and hip stability.

Starting Position

Set the cable height just below your chest height. Stand on one leg (the leg closest to the cable) with your shoulders parallel to the cable (side facing). The outside leg should be in the hip lock position (hip flexed above 90 degrees). Hold the cable handle with two hands, and press it out in front of your body.

Movement

While maintaining the Pallof press, perform a single-leg squat (figure 5.24) and return to the starting position. Be sure to have adequate grip on your shoes. Otherwise, the force generated from your hip will cause your foot to rotate. If your posture cannot be maintained, reduce the load or change the exercise.

Figure 5.24 Cable single-leg squat Pallof hold.

Cable Single-Leg Romanian Deadlift (RDL) to Y

Difficulty

Advanced

Equipment

Cable machine or resistance band

Purpose

The cable single-leg RDL to Y challenges many of the concepts discussed throughout the chapter by integrating them into a single exercise. The significant points of focus in this exercise are antiflexion, shoulder stability, and hip stability.

Starting Position

Set the cable to approximately knee height. Face the cable, and hold it with one hand. Assume a single-leg stance on the opposite leg.

Movement

Perform a single-leg RDL by hinging at your hip and extending your leg straight back. At the same time, reach toward the machine with the arm holding the cable handle (figure 5.25a). Return to an upright single-leg stance with the opposite knee in the hip lock position. At the same time, extend the arm holding the cable handle overhead in the Y position (figure 5.25b). While performing the single-leg RDL, your swing foot should move in sequence with your shoulders, maintaining a straight line between the two. Think about pushing your back foot through the wall behind you.

Figure 5.25   Cable single-leg RDL to Y: (a) single-leg RDL and (b) upright stance with Y position.

Single-Leg Squat Roll to Back and Return

Difficulty

Advanced

Equipment

Approximately 12 to 24 inches (30-61 cm) of firm padding

Purpose

The single-leg squat roll to back and return challenges many of the concepts discussed throughout the chapter. The significant points of focus in this exercise are postural control and spatial awareness.

Starting Position

Stand on one leg facing away from the padding.

Movement

In one fluid motion, squat down to the padding, roll to your back and shoulders, and push your feet toward the ceiling (figure 5.26a). Reverse the action until you are in the single-leg hip lock stance (figure 5.26b).

Figure 5.26   Single-leg squat roll to back and return: (a) roll to back and shoulders and (b) return to single-leg hip lock stance.

Adjust the height of the padding to change this exercise's intensity. The lower the height, the more difficult this drill will be. The goal of this exercise is to move with control and fluidity.

MOVEMENT PATTERNS, NOT MUSCLES

A significant focus of the inside-out approach to training is generating stability and control in the lumbopelvic hip complex and shoulder girdle. As mentioned previously, this stability in the core allows the extremities to optimally express force either into the ground or onto objects, allowing for more forceful movement due to increased efficiency. The following section will focus on strengthening specific lower-body, upper-body, and combination movement patterns. It has often been said that movement patterns, not muscles, should be trained. When designing strength programs around specific movements, strengthening of the individual muscles will happen. Human locomotion is complex; therefore, the strength training program must build on steps to match this complexity to maximize its transfer to dynamic sporting actions. The majority of strength training should be in the form of compound movement patterns. These patterns involve multiple joints and large groups of muscles.

Lower-Body Movement Patterns

Two global patterns of lower-body movement must be addressed in training: the squat and the hinge. The squat pattern is more knee and quadriceps dominant, whereas the hinge emphasizes the hips and hamstrings.

Squat

The squat is one of the most fundamental patterns that hockey players must master. This compound movement involves most of the muscle groups that are essential in the skating stride. The squat is a demanding pattern and involves coordinating several moving parts, including the hip, knee, and ankle.

Bilateral Variations   These variations include exercises based on two legs.

Bodyweight Squat

Difficulty

Beginner

Equipment

Kettlebell for goblet squat variation; barbell and weights for front squat variation

Purpose

The bodyweight squat is a compound movement that provides many strength adaptations for hockey players. The major muscle groups involved in this movement include the quadriceps, glutes, adductors, hamstrings, calves, and spinal erectors.

Starting Position

Stand with feet approximately shoulder-width apart. Depending on your hip architecture, you might need to angle your toes out slightly. Stand as tall as possible, contract your glute muscles, engage your core musculature, and tuck your chin to align your head. Stabilize your shoulders and upper back by raising your arms to shoulder height and pulling your shoulder blades back.

Movement

Begin the movement by spreading the floor, in essence screwing your feet outwardly into the ground. Push your hips back and knees out to start descending to the lowered position while maintaining a stable spine (figure 5.27). While pushing your knees out, stand up out of the bottom position in the same manner you entered, and finish in the starting position.

Figure 5.27   Bodyweight squat.

Common Errors

Often, athletes will initiate the movement by driving their knees forward instead of their hips back. The main focus, in this case, should be cueing the first portion of the squat.

Another error is when the knees collapse to the middle and go into a valgus position. Focus on driving your knees out and spreading the floor.

A third error is the butt wink at the bottom of the squat. (The butt wink is when the pelvis tilts posteriorly near the bottom of the squat, causing the lower back to round.) This error can be fixed by maintaining a stable core throughout the pattern and decreasing the squat's depth.

Progressions and Variations

Goblet Squat

The goblet squat is an exercise for the beginner- to intermediate-level athlete and requires a dumbbell or kettlebell for loading. The initial setup and movement are the same as the bodyweight squat; however, a kettlebell or dumbbell is held in the goblet position (figure 5.28).

Figure 5.28   Goblet squat.

Front Squat

The front squat is an exercise for the intermediate- to advanced-level athlete and requires a barbell for loading. The front squat serves the same purpose as the bodyweight squat and goblet squat, but the front squat allows for significantly more loading than the previous two. The front squat has the same initial setup as the bodyweight squat and goblet squat; however, the barbell is held in the front racked position (figure 5.29). Grip the bar with your hands just outside of shoulder width, moving your arms underneath the bar, so your upper arm is parallel to the ground. Keep your elbows high, and maintain tension in your shoulders. The movement pattern is the same as the previous two squat exercises, but strive to keep your elbows high. In the front racked position, you must possess the appropriate wrist, shoulder, and thoracic spine mobility to maintain the bar in place. If this is not possible, you will need to work on your mobility in these areas.

Figure 5.29   Front squat.

Unilateral Variations   The squat can be performed with single-leg variations, which are critical squat patterns. A large portion of the skating movement and change-of-direction movements are performed on one leg, and the exercises listed target the quadriceps, glute, adductor, hamstrings, and calf muscles.

HIP LOCK

In several unilateral lower-body exercises, you will notice the use of the hip lock. In this position, the non-weight-bearing hip is flexed to a position above 90 degrees. This technique is used to protect the groin by stabilizing the pelvis during complex and high-velocity movements. Also, the cocontraction of muscles allows for a more forceful contraction of the glute on the stance leg. Therefore, many traditional single-leg stance exercises can incorporate the hip lock finish position to help protect the pelvis and surrounding musculature.

Split Squat

Difficulty

Beginner

Equipment

None (bodyweight only) or dumbbells or barbell, squat rack for barbell loading, single-leg squat stand or bench and pad for rear foot–elevated split squat

Purpose

The split squat, a single-leg squat variation, is essential for strength development in a sport in which a large portion of the game is spent on one leg.

Starting Position

Assume a split stance position with the back of your front foot approximately 3 feet (1 m) away from the front of your back foot, but maintain a stance approximately shoulder-width apart. If you are loading with dumbbells, hold them at your sides. If you are loading with a barbell, set the bar up in a squat rack at the appropriate height. Stand close to the bar with feet shoulder-width apart, and place your hands on the bar at an equal distance from the center, just outside of shoulder width. Set your body under the bar, and pull your shoulder blades together, creating a ledge on your upper back for the barbell. Lift the bar from the rack, and assume the split position. Brace your core to prevent movement of the spine throughout the movement.

Movement

Lower your back knee to the ground. Be sure not to hit your knee off the ground. Maintain an athletic position at the bottom with a positive shin

Figure 5.30   Split squat.

angle (figure 5.30), with most of the load received by the front leg. Finish the movement by returning to the starting position. Repeat this sequence on the opposite leg.

Common Errors

A common issue is when the front knee collapses to the middle (valgus). Be sure to drive the front knee laterally.

Another common error is when the torso flexes forward. Be sure to maintain proper core engagement and, if necessary, decrease the external load.

Progressions and Variations

Reverse Lunge to Hip Lock

Stand with your feet shoulder-width apart. Elevate the moving leg into the hip locked position (flexed hip above 90 degrees of flexion). Step back approximately 3 feet (1 m) with the moving leg. Lower your back knee to the ground; be sure not to hit your knee on the ground. Like the split squat, assume an athletic position at the bottom with a positive shin angle, with most of the load received by the front leg. Reverse the movement, bringing the swing leg up to the hip locked position (figure 5.31). Elongate at the top position by engaging the stance leg's glute muscles and core musculature. Once all repetitions are completed, switch legs.

Figure 5.31   Reverse lunge to hip lock.

Figure 5.32 Rear foot–elevated split squat.

Figure 5.33 Skater squat to hip lock.

Rear Foot–Elevated Split Squat

Assume the split stance position similar to the split squat; however, your back foot will be elevated. Lower your back knee to a pad (figure 5.32). Finish the movement by returning to the starting position. Once all repetitions are completed, switch legs.

Skater Squat to Hip Lock

Start with your feet shoulder-width apart, approximately 2 inches (5 cm) in front of a pad. Elevate the moving leg into the hip locked position (flexed hip above 90 degrees of flexion). Like the bilateral squat, begin by pushing your hips back and knee forward to start descending to the lowered position while maintaining a stable spine. Swing the moving leg back and, while keeping a bent knee, touch your knee to the pad. Simultaneously, move your hands forward, bending at the elbows to provide a counterbalanced load (figure 5.33). While pushing your knee out, stand up out of the bottom position in the same manner you entered, and finish in the starting position. Once all repetitions are completed, switch legs. The most common issue for hockey players in this exercise is performing the full range of motion without compensation or dropping to the pad in the lower portions of the exercise. This can be fixed by adding a second pad to limit the range of motion.

Skater Squat—Half Repetition

Start with your feet shoulder-width apart, approximately 2 inches (5 cm) in front of a pad. Assume a single-leg half-squat position to start. Descend and touch the non-weight-bearing knee to the pad. While pushing your

Figure 5.34 Skater squat—half repetition.

knee out, stand up out of the bottom position in the same manner you entered, and finish in the starting position, only halfway up (figure 5.34). Once all repetitions are completed, switch legs.

Hinge

The hinge is another fundamental pattern that hockey players must master. During the hinge, the athlete bends at the hips while maintaining a neutral spine. This movement involves the muscle groups primarily responsible for hip extension, the glutes and hamstrings, and the spinal erectors. The hinge is a demanding pattern and involves coordinated movement of the hip.

Bilateral Variations These variations include exercises based on two legs.

Hip Thrust

Difficulty

Beginner to intermediate (beginners perform the exercise without any external loading)

Equipment

Bodyweight (if no external load), barbell, or dumbbell; 12- to 16-inch (30-41 cm) box or bench; pad for the bar to minimize discomfort on the hip

Purpose

The hip thrust is a hip extension exercise that focuses primarily on the glute and hamstring musculature. Hip extension is an essential pattern for developing strength throughout the skating stride.

Starting Position

Sit on the ground with your shoulders in contact with the box or bench. If using a barbell, roll the bar onto your lap to the position of your hip crease. If you are using a dumbbell, place it in the same position. Place your feet shoulder-width apart and in a position so that your shins are relatively vertical when your hips are extended. Your chin should be tucked so your head and neck are in a neutral position.

Movement

Engage your pelvic floor, core, and glute musculature. Push the bar up by driving with your glutes and hamstring muscles. Push your knees outward, as with previous exercises, to maintain proper glute engagement. Think of tucking your hips under the bar and contracting your anterior core muscles at the top of the movement (figure 5.35). Maintain a neutral spine throughout the movement, moving only through your hips. Descend to the starting position. Maintain a flat foot position throughout the pattern.

Figure 5.35 Hip thrust.

Common Errors

The main issue observed with this exercise is the extension of the lumbar spine. Be sure to cue proper glute activation and pelvic movement.

Another error is shifting the distribution at the top of the movement to the toes. This issue can be fixed by a simple cue or by changing foot position.

Romanian Deadlift (RDL)

Difficulty

Beginner to intermediate

Equipment

Bodyweight only (beginner), dumbbells or barbell

Purpose

The RDL focuses primarily on the muscles responsible for hip extension. These include the hamstring and glute musculature.

Starting Position

If using external loading, pick up the weights in a controlled and safe manner. Stand with feet approximately shoulder-width apart, with feet pointing forward. Engage your glute and hip musculature by externally rotating your thighs or screwing your feet into the floor. Set your shoulders by pulling them back, and tuck your chin, placing your head and neck into a neutral position (figure 5.36a).

Movement

Start the movement by pushing your hips back and knees out while maintaining a soft knee bend. Move your upper body and torso forward while bending at the hips until your torso is close to parallel to the ground (or the point before you can no longer maintain a neutral spine) (figure 5.36b). Your knees should not bend more than the starting knee position. All motion is centered around the hips. Return to the starting position by pulling with your glutes and hamstrings. Your hips should be fully extended, with the glutes maximally contracted at the top position.

Figure 5.36 Romanian deadlift: *(a)* starting position and *(b)* torso near parallel.

Common Errors

If you cannot coordinate the hinge pattern, flexion at the lumbar spine instead of the hip will likely occur. In this case, simple cueing (without load) to teach the pattern might be required. However, lack of hamstring flexibility can prevent a proper hinge pattern. In this case, these flexibility issues must be resolved before performing this exercise and its single-leg variations.

Trap Bar Deadlift

Difficulty

Beginner, intermediate, advanced

Equipment

Trap bar

Purpose

The trap bar deadlift is a modification of the conventional deadlift that is less technically demanding and potentially places less stress on the lower back. This exercise is a hybrid between the squat and deadlift exercises, and it focuses on the glute, hamstring, and quadriceps musculature.

Starting Position

Step inside the trap bar. Your feet should be shoulder-width apart and facing forward. While standing, engage your hip and glute musculature by externally rotating the thighs or screwing your feet into the floor, and brace your core. Lower your hips by pushing them back and bending your knees. Maintain a neutral spine. In the lowered position, grab the handles of the bar.

Figure 5.37   Trap bar deadlift.

Movement

Without lifting the bar, place tension on it by contracting your leg and hip musculature and setting your shoulders back. Engage your pelvic floor muscles, drive your knees out, and push through the mid to heel of your feet, lifting the weight off the floor. Your hips and the weight should move in sequence; do not raise your hips before lifting the weight. Continue to externally rotate your thighs by screwing your feet into the floor for the movement's duration. At the top, fully extend your hips by maximally contracting your glute musculature. Keep your rib cage down (figure 5.37). Reverse the pattern in the same manner as your setup.

Common Errors

A common error with the trap bar deadlift is allowing your spine to flex or round during the movement. This fault primarily occurs due to using too much load on the bar. Remove weight and repeat.

If your knees collapse inward, be sure to focus on driving them outward for the entirety of the movement. Adding a miniband around your knees can help fire the muscles responsible for pushing your knees out.

Unilateral Variations   These variations include exercises based on one leg.

Single-Leg Hip Thrust

Difficulty

Intermediate

Equipment

Bodyweight, barbell, or dumbbell; 12- to 18-inch (30-46 cm) box or bench; pad for the bar to minimize discomfort on the hip

Purpose

The single-leg hip thrust is a hip extension exercise that focuses primarily on the glute and hamstring musculature. Transition to one leg increases the demand for coordination by decreasing stability.

Starting Position

Sit on the ground with your shoulders in contact with the box or bench. If using a barbell, roll the bar onto your lap to the position of your hip crease. If you are using a dumbbell, place it in the same position. Place your feet such that your shins are relatively vertical when your hips are extended. Then lift one leg off the ground. This non-weight-bearing leg should be flexed to 90 degrees at the hip. Tuck your chin so your head and neck are in a neutral position.

Movement

Engage your pelvic floor, core, and glute musculature. Push the weight up by driving with your glutes and hamstring muscles. Push your knee outward, as with previous exercises, to maintain proper glute engagement. Think of tucking your hips under the bar and contracting your anterior core muscles at the top of the movement (figure 5.38). Maintain a neutral spine throughout the movement, moving only through your hips. Complete this exercise on both legs.

Figure 5.38   Single-leg hip thrust.

Single-Leg Romanian Deadlift to Hip Lock

Difficulty

Intermediate to advanced

Equipment

Bodyweight (beginners), dumbbells, or kettlebells

Purpose

The single-leg RDL to hip lock focuses primarily on the muscles responsible for hip extension. These include the hamstring and glute musculature. The single-leg stance increases the demand for balance and coordination.

Starting Position

Stand on one leg with toes pointed forward. The opposite leg should be in the hip lock position. If you are using dumbbells or kettlebells to load the movement, hold them at your side in the starting position. Set your shoulders by pulling them back, and tuck your chin, placing your head and neck into a neutral position.

Movement

Start the movement by pushing your hips back and out while maintaining a soft knee bend. Simultaneously, the non-weight-bearing leg should swing back in a fully extended position (figure 5.39). Think about pushing through the back wall with the heel of your non-weight-bearing leg. This action will contract the contralateral glute musculature and stabilize the pelvis. Move your upper body and torso forward while bending at the hip until your torso is close to parallel to the ground (or the point before you can no longer maintain a neutral spine). If you are loading the movement with dumbbells or kettlebells, move them from your side to directly in front of your stance leg, and lower them toward the ground. Your knees should not bend more than the starting knee position; all motion is centered around the hips. Return to the starting position by pulling with your glutes and hamstrings. Your hips should be extended, with glutes maximally contracted at the top position. Repeat this sequence on the opposite leg.

Figure 5.39   Single-leg Romanian deadlift to hip lock.

Common Errors

A common issue is rotating the shoulders forward and reaching at the bottom position. Ensure your shoulders maintain their position pulled back and down.

Another error is when the swing leg does not move in sequence with the torso and shoulders and does not fully extend in the bottom position. Simply drive your leg back, and attempt to push it toward the back wall.

Other Lower-Body Isolation Exercises

The majority of exercises used in the training program should be compound movements that involve more than one joint, because they provide the most bang for your buck in terms of athletic performance. However, to build a robust program covering all training bases, isolation or single-joint exercises often need to be utilized. These exercises are essential in developing hip and leg musculature.

Stability Ball Leg Curl

Difficulty

Beginner to intermediate

Equipment

Stability ball

Purpose

The stability ball leg curl develops the hamstring and glute musculature with an emphasis on knee flexion rather than hip extension.

Starting Position

Lie on your back, and place your heels on the stability ball. Contract your glutes and hamstrings to raise your hips off the floor. Brace your core, and keep your rib cage down.

Movement

While maintaining the extended hip position, pull your heels toward your glutes (figure 5.40), and then reverse the pattern. Keep a neutral spine throughout. To increase difficulty, switch to a single-leg stability ball curl or swap the stability ball for a slide board.

Figure 5.40   Stability ball leg curl.

Common Errors

A frequent error is to not maintain full hip extension throughout the movement pattern. Be sure to keep your glute muscles engaged.

Another mistake is lumbar hyperextension and rib cage flaring in the top position. Keeping your glutes and anterior core musculature engaged at all times will minimize the risk of this error.

Nordic Hamstring Curl

Difficulty

Advanced

Equipment

Pad for knees, stable structure or partner to hold your heels in place

Purpose

This isolation exercise primarily develops the hamstring musculature with an emphasis on knee flexion rather than hip extension. It provides a significant eccentric hamstring load, which can aid in the prevention of hamstring injuries.

Starting Position

Assume a tall kneeling position on the pad with your heels anchored, and cross your arms over your chest.

Movement

Lower your body to the ground by extending at the knees (figure 5.41). Maintain fully extended hips, if possible. When you can no longer maintain control while lowering, use your arms to lessen the load, and push yourself back to the starting position.

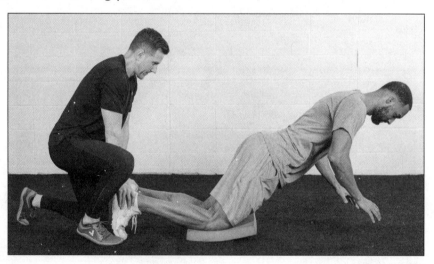

Figure 5.41   Nordic hamstring curl.

Common Errors

The most common error with the Nordic hamstring curl is too much bending at the hips. This fault is likely a result of not enough strength in the hamstrings to maintain the position. Focus on the eccentric portion of the movement with slow lowering, and push yourself back to the starting position with your arms.

Bottom-Up

One modification to make with hockey players during off-season training is to use a bottom-up approach instead of a top-down approach for several single-leg exercises (e.g., rear foot–elevated split squat and skater squat). The bottom-up approach means the athlete starts and finishes the exercise at the bottom rather than beginning and ending in a standing position. The rationale is that the athlete must generate force out of the hole without the active muscle state or elastic energy developed during the eccentric or lowering portion of the movement. Data suggest that the fastest and most efficient skaters typically have a higher squat jump power–to–countermovement jump power ratio compared to slower skaters. This suggests that the best skaters can generate force to a higher degree out of the hole without preload than weak skaters.

Upper-Body Movement Patterns

The two major upper-body movement patterns are the push and pull. The push is classified by the actions of extending the elbow joint and flexing the shoulder. The prime movers for pushing are typically the chest, shoulder, and triceps musculature. The pull is classified by the actions of flexing the elbow and extending the shoulder. The prime movers for pulling are typically the upper back, posterior shoulder, and biceps musculature. These actions can further be divided into horizontal and vertical push and pull.

Horizontal Push

The horizontal push is defined by pressing your arms in front of your body away from your chest. These movements are essential for shooting, passing, and battling with opposing players.

Push-Up

Difficulty

Beginner, intermediate, advanced

Equipment

Dumbbells for the dumbbell bench press variation, gymnastics rings for the rings variation

Purpose

Because hockey is a contact sport that often involves pushing off opponents, developing strength in the push-up pattern is essential. During shooting and passing, your bottom hand on your stick performs this pressing action. The push-up is one of the most fundamental horizontal push patterns for hockey players of all ages.

Starting Position

Set up in the quadruped position with your hands approximately shoulder-width apart and fingers pointing forward. Extend your legs back, and bring your feet together. Contract your glute muscles. Externally rotate your arms or screw your hands into the floor to stabilize your shoulders.

Figure 5.42   Push-up.

Movement

Lower your body toward the ground, keeping your forearms vertical and glutes and abdominals contracted (figure 5.42). While continuing to screw your hands into the floor, push your body away from the floor. Maintain a neutral spine and neck position throughout the movement.

Common Errors

A typical error during the push-up is a sagging abdomen resulting from anterior pelvic tilt and lower back extension. Be sure to engage your glutes and anterior abdominal muscles throughout the movement to prevent this. If necessary, start with your hands elevated on a box or a bench to reduce the load.

The second most common error during the push-up is flaring out the elbows and moving the shoulders forward as the body is lowered to the ground. This flaring might be due to a poor initial setup or lack of shoulder range of motion.

Figure 5.43   Dumbbell bench press.

Progressions and Variations

Dumbbell Bench Press

Sit upright on a flat bench with the dumbbells resting on your thighs. Lie down flat on the bench, using your knees to help elevate the dumbbells over your chest. Place your feet flat on the ground with your shins vertical, and screw your feet into the ground to stabilize your pelvis. Externally rotate your hands and set your shoulder blades to stabilize your shoulders. Initiate the movement by pulling the weight toward your body, keeping your shoulder blades pulled back (figure 5.43). Maintain vertical forearms throughout the motion.

The most common error with the dumbbell bench press is flaring out the elbows. Think about externally rotating your hands and keeping your elbows tighter to your body. If this does not work, you might need to work on the mobility of your shoulders, chest, and thoracic spine.

Rings Push-Up

Place the rings approximately shoulder-width apart. Kneel on the ground in front of the rings and grip them. Move your feet back to assume the push-up position, and contract your glutes. Externally rotate your hands to create stable shoulders. Lower your body while maintaining a strong core and contracted glute muscles (figure 5.44). Maintain externally rotated hands, vertical forearms, contracted glutes, and a neutral spine throughout the movement. Push your hands away from your body to return to the starting position.

A typical error seen during the rings push-up is a sagging abdomen resulting from anterior pelvic tilt and lower back extension. Be sure to engage your glutes and anterior abdominal muscles throughout the movement to prevent this. If necessary, regress to a less challenging exercise.

Figure 5.44　Rings push-up.

Vertical Push

The vertical push is defined by pressing the arms overhead. These movements are essential for shooting, passing, and battling with opposing players.

Half-Kneeling Landmine Press

Difficulty

Beginner to intermediate

Equipment

Barbell, pad or mat, landmine stand or wall corner; dumbbells for the dumbbell overhead press variation

Purpose

The half-kneeling landmine press is a hybrid press, meaning it is a mix between a vertical and horizontal press. This exercise is excellent for hockey players who have had previous shoulder injuries or lack overhead shoulder mobility.

Starting Position

Set up a barbell in a landmine barbell holder or a corner. Assume a half-kneeling position in front of the bar. Hold the bar with the hand on the same side as the knee that is down. Contract the glute muscles on that side to stabilize your pelvis and externally rotate your hand to stabilize your shoulder. Tuck your chin to create a neutral head and neck position.

Movement

While maintaining a stable pelvis and core, press the weight up. Attempt to move your shoulder blade on your rib cage, slightly shrugging at the top of the pattern (figure 5.45). As you lower the weight, pull your shoulder blade and shoulder back down to minimize the chance of your shoulder rolling forward.

Figure 5.45   Half-kneeling landmine press.

Common Errors

The most common error seen in this exercise is the shoulder moving forward as the weight is lowered. Be sure to actively pull your shoulder back and down as you lower the weight.

Progressions and Variations

Dumbbell Overhead Press

Stand with your feet shoulder-width apart. Contract your glutes and anterior core to stabilize your pelvis and spine. Hold a dumbbell in each hand and raise them to shoulder height with palms facing forward. Keeping your palms forward, press the weight over your head (figure 5.46). Continue to contract your glutes and core throughout the motion. As the weight is overhead, position your armpits forward to maximize stability in the shoulders. Lower the dumbbells in a controlled manner back to the starting position.

One of the most common errors seen with the overhead press is excessive arching and extension of the spine at the top of the pattern. Maintain contracted glutes and core throughout the movement. If this does not fix the issue, additional mobility work on the thoracic spine and lats might be necessary.

Figure 5.46 Dumbbell overhead press.

Horizontal Pull

The horizontal pull is defined by pulling the arms toward the body from straight out in front. These movements are essential for shooting, passing, and battling with opposing players.

Rings Row

Difficulty

Beginner, intermediate, advanced

Equipment

Gymnastics rings or suspension trainer; dumbbells for the staggered stance single-arm dumbbell row variation

Purpose

The rings row is a compound pulling movement that strengthens the upper back, posterior shoulder, and biceps musculature.

Starting Position

Grip the rings in both hands. Place your feet approximately shoulder-width apart at a spot determined by skill level. For the beginner athlete, feet

should be farther away from the point of attachment to create a more vertical body position (figure 5.47a). This position decreases the load on the body. As you improve your strength levels, place your foot closer to the attachment point, creating a more horizontal body position (figure 5.47b). Fully extend your arms so the straps are tight and your body is leaning back. Engage your glute and core musculature, and set your shoulders back for stability. Tuck your chin to place your head and neck in a neutral position.

Movement

Begin the movement by pulling your shoulders back and pulling the rings toward your body (figure 5.47c). As your elbows pass your body, allow for space between your body and elbows. Maintain a straight body posture throughout the movement pattern. Reverse the pattern to return to the starting point.

Figure 5.47 Rings row: (a) starting position for beginner with feet farther from point of attachment, (b) starting position for more advanced athlete with feet closer to point of attachment, and (c) pull rings toward body.

Common Errors

A typical error with the rings row is letting your hips drop during the movement. Maintain glute and core engagement throughout the pattern.

Another common error is not maintaining shoulder stability. Do not let your shoulders roll forward at any point throughout.

Progressions and Variations

Staggered Stance Single-Arm Dumbbell Row

Stand with feet shoulder-width apart, approximately 1 to 2 feet (0.3-0.6 m) away from a bench. Hinge at your hips, place one hand on the bench, and step back with the foot on the working arm side. Tuck your chin so your head and neck are in a neutral position. Engage your core musculature, and pick up the weight from the floor. Set your shoulder back for stability. To increase the demand for advanced athletes, simply remove the support from the nonworking arm. Begin the movement by pulling your shoulders back and pulling the weight toward your body (figure 5.48). As your elbow passes your body, allow for space between your body and elbow. Reverse the pattern to return to the starting point.

The most common error with this exercise is not pulling the shoulder blades and shoulder back during the pulling motion. This fault will result in your shoulder rolling forward, placing stress on the anterior portion of the shoulder.

Figure 5.48   Staggered stance single-arm dumbbell row.

Vertical Pull

The vertical pull is defined by pulling the arms down toward the body from an overhead position. These movements are essential for shooting, passing, and battling with opposing players.

Kneeling Cable Pull-Down

Difficulty

Beginner to intermediate

Equipment

Cable machine or resistance band, pad or mat for knee comfort, pull-up bar

Purpose

The kneeling cable pull-down is a compound pulling movement that strengthens the upper back, posterior shoulder, and biceps musculature.

Starting Position

Place the cables at the highest position, and grip the handles with your hands. Assume a half-kneeling position underneath the cables. Engage the glute musculature on the side with the knee down. Tuck your chin to maintain a neutral head and neck position.

Movement

Begin the movement by pulling your shoulder blades back and down. Pull the cables toward your body (figure 5.49). As your elbows pass your body, allow for space between your elbow and body. Reverse the pattern in the same manner to the starting position.

Common Errors

The most common error with this exercise is not pulling your shoulders back and down during the pulling motion. This fault will result in your shoulders rolling forward, placing stress on the anterior portion of the shoulders.

Figure 5.49   Kneeling cable pull-down.

Progressions and Variations

Chin-Up or Pull-Up

Set a box or bench close to the pull-up bar so you can reach the bar safely. Stand on the box directly underneath the bar. Grab the bar with both hands. For the chin-up, your palms should be facing your body (figure 5.50a). For the pull-up, your palms should be facing away from your body (figure 5.50b). While gripping the bar, externally rotate your arms to generate stability in your shoulders. Allow your arms to take the weight of your body by lifting your feet off the box. Engage your glute and core musculature. Keeping your glutes and core engaged, pull yourself up to the bar. Reverse the pattern while maintaining the same glute and core engagement.

Avoid flaring your rib cage at the beginning of the motion. If this cannot be controlled, regress the exercise until you possess the appropriate strength to perform the chin-up or pull-up correctly.

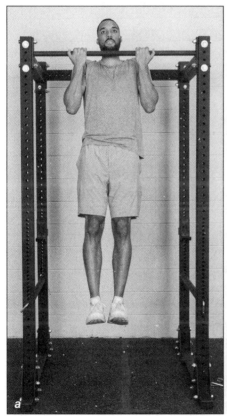

Figure 5.50 *(a)* Chin-up and *(b)* pull-up.

Combination Patterns

In combination patterns, both lower- and upper-body movement patterns are combined into one exercise. These are advanced exercises that significantly increase functionality and demand for whole-body coordination and strength. With these exercises, you can get creative with your combinations of movement patterns; there are no rules. One such exercise is the cable single-leg RDL to row.

Cable Single-Leg RDL to Row

Difficulty

Advanced

Equipment

Cable machine or band

Purpose

The cable single-leg RDL to row combines a lower- and upper-body movement pattern into one exercise, significantly increasing the demand for whole-body coordination.

Starting Position

Set the cable handle to approximately knee level. Grip the handle with one hand, and step a few feet away from the cable column. Assume a single-leg stance on the leg opposite the cable machine. Engage your glute and core musculature, and tuck your chin to set a neutral head and neck position.

Movement

Start the movement by pushing your hips back and out while maintaining a soft knee bend. Simultaneously, the non-weight-bearing leg should swing back in a fully extended position. Think about pushing through the back wall with the heel of your non-weight-bearing leg. This action will contract the contralateral glute musculature and stabilize the pelvis. Move your upper body and torso forward while bending at the hip until your torso is close to parallel to the ground (or the point before you can no longer maintain a neutral spine). The hand holding the cable reaches toward the column (figure 5.51). Your knees should not bend more than the starting knee position; all motion is centered around the hips. As you reverse the RDL, pull the cable toward your body with your elbow passing by your side; the row portion follows the same principles as the rowing variations outlined earlier. Your hips should be extended, with glutes maximally contracted at the top position. Repeat this sequence on the opposite leg.

Figure 5.51 Cable single-leg RDL to row.

COMPLEXES AND FINISHERS

Complexes and finishers are typically a series of exercises performed in rapid succession with the primary goal of building work capacity and muscle endurance. Complexes are often performed at the beginning of a training session, and finishers are performed at the end of the training session. Following are examples of complexes and a finisher.

Dumbbell Complex

The dumbbell complex is a series of exercises performed in rapid succession. The exercises, which are outlined in this book, include the RDL, reverse lunge to hip lock, and continuous jump squat. Suppose the recommendation is to perform three sets of five repetitions for each movement. In that case, you will perform five RDLs, five reverse lunges to hip lock on each leg, then five continuous jump squats with each repetition performed as quickly as possible. That entire sequence will then be performed again for sets two and three.

Kettlebell Complex

The kettlebell complex, like the dumbbell complex, is a series of exercises performed in rapid succession. The exercises, which are outlined in this book, include the staggered stance single-arm kettlebell row, RDL, goblet squat, and continuous jump squat. This sequence of exercises will be performed in the same fashion as the dumbbell complex.

Slide Board Finisher—Isometric Hold

Difficulty

Beginner, intermediate, advanced

Equipment

8-foot (2 m) slide board, slide board booties

Purpose

The purpose of the slide board finisher—isometric hold is to build work capacity and muscle endurance in the lower body.

Starting Position

Begin by assuming a low split squat stance, with your front foot on the slide board at the end against the slide board's wedge.

Movement

The low split squat stance is held for 10 seconds. Once the 10 seconds is completed, perform five lateral pushes over and back on the board (figure 5.52). After five lateral pushes, assume the low split squat stance on your opposite leg. This position is held for 10 seconds. Immediately upon completion of the 10-second hold, perform five more pushes over and back. This sequence is performed two times on each leg for each set.

Figure 5.52   Slide board finisher.

ADDING COMPLEXITY

Only select exercises have been listed in this chapter; however, the possibilities are endless. If you find exercises not challenging for your current skill level, you can make several modifications to increase complexity and physical demand on the movement pattern. These include but are not limited to increasing the load or weight, adding uneven weight distribution by using single-arm loading or water bag loading, increasing velocity, and adding torsional force to your body. Torsional force is accomplished by adding additional rotational demand on your torso with the aid of a strap or band. These additions need to be evaluated; structure your program accordingly based on your current skill level.

SUMMARY

This chapter outlined the inside-out approach to strength training. Core and rotator cuff strength provides a foundation to optimize force production at the extremities. A stable core will minimize so-called energy leaks in the system, allowing for efficient force production to maximize performance in the basic movement patterns, including the squat, hinge, push, and pull. Building systemic strength through the exercises listed in this chapter sets the foundation for developing functional power, which is the focus of the next chapter. All these factors are intimately intertwined. Proximal (core) strength sets the stage for distal (extremity) strength, and this strength provides the groundwork for functional power development.

Chapter 6

Training for Functional Power

Players and coaches hear the term *powerful* frequently, but what does it mean, and how does it relate to improved performance on the ice? This chapter will answer these questions. Power is the rate at which force is produced. In a highly dynamic sport such as hockey, possessing high absolute strength levels is essential but only tells a portion of the story because maximal strength or force development is not rate dependent. The ability to generate force faster than one's opponent is the characteristic that will set one apart from the pack. To be powerful in a meaningful way, one must also express power in multiple directions and often from compromising positions. This chapter will outline many concepts and associated exercises that address power-producing capabilities for hockey players.

FORCE–VELOCITY AND POWER OPTIMIZATION

In chapter 5 we discussed the force–velocity relationship. This relationship suggests that force production and the velocity of movement are intricately intertwined. The ability to produce force is greatest at low velocity and vice versa. For example, when one attempts to toss a 50-pound (23 kg) medicine ball, one's movement's velocity will be much slower than when one throws a 10-pound (5 kg) ball. This relationship causally relates to one's power output because it is a product of force and velocity. The force and velocity must be in an appropriate range to optimize power production. If force is too high and velocity too low, the result is low power output. If velocity is too high and force too low, the product is also low power output. The sweet spot is approximately in the middle of this range, corresponding to 30 to 80 percent of the maximum amount of weight you can lift. This is highlighted by observing the power curve with the force–velocity curve.

STRENGTH FIRST, THEN POWER

The name of the game in hockey is power output. However, power is dependent on the ability to generate force, which is the athlete's strength. Athletes who do not possess adequate strength levels (particularly youth and beginners) must work on their strength at lower velocities before performing high-velocity power movements. The reality is that improving strength levels alone will result in enhanced power output because power is a product of force and velocity. Skipping strength development will lower an athlete's power production ceiling as training progresses.

FACTORS THAT CONTRIBUTE TO POWER DEVELOPMENT

Because the athlete's strength levels provide the foundation for power production, many of the factors associated with increases in strength, outlined in chapter 5, also have a significant influence on power development. These factors include neurological, muscle size, and muscle fiber type adaptations. But developing maximal force alone is not necessarily rate dependent. However, the ability to modify the force–velocity relationship will significantly affect the athlete's power. If one can move the same amount of weight in less time (higher velocity), power will increase. In contrast, during the skating stride, the key is to maximize force production in relation to time; this is known as *impulse*. In addition to impulse, factors such as the stretch-shortening cycle (SSC) and elastic energy also contribute to power production in hockey.

Impulse

In contrast to sprint running, the impulse during the skating stride is much larger. This fact is related to the difference in ground or ice contact times between the two. During skating, ground contact times are up to four times longer than during sprint running. Since force production is not constant throughout the skating stride, impulse might be the best metric in determining performance. However, Taber et al. (2016) suggest that the duration of time in which forces are applied is only slightly modifiable; therefore, the total force must be increased during the action to improve impulse. Methods to improve impulse are described later in this chapter.

Stretch-Shortening Cycle

The stretch-shortening cycle (SSC) is characterized by a rapid cycle of eccentric muscle contraction and a short transition period to concentric muscle contraction. Imagine a countermovement jump, where there is a quick transition between the lowering and propulsion phases. The SSC is a significant contributor to performance in this movement. During the lowering phase, the muscle is stretched rapidly and quickly shortens to produce the power required to jump. There are three primary mechanisms responsible for the SSC. These include neurological mechanisms in the muscle, elastic energy, and the development of active state.

Neurological Mechanisms

Within the muscle, receptors analyze the rate of stretch on the muscle and the magnitude of the tendon's stretch. These receptors are known as the muscle spindles and Golgi tendon organs, respectively. The reality is that these receptors act to protect the muscle from being overstretched, which could result in injury. However, they will also act in conjunction to generate a more forceful concentric contraction. When a muscle stretches rapidly, the spindles sense this rate and interact with the nervous system to create a reflex that causes the muscle to contract involuntarily. An example of this is when a doctor strikes the tendon in one's knee with a rubber mallet. This procedure induces a rapid stretch in the quadriceps, inducing a kicking reflex. This stretch reflex also applies to sports performance when landing from a jump or running to generate rapid force production. If the Golgi tendon organs perceive too much stretch, they will force the muscle to shut down. Proper training can enhance the effects of muscle spindles and minimize the Golgi tendon organs' effects.

Elastic Energy

The best way to describe elastic energy is to think about a rubber band. When a rubber band is stretched, it begins to store energy passively, which is known as potential energy. This stored energy is then converted to kinetic energy (energy in motion) when the elastic is released, and the band will rapidly return to its initial state. Think of tendons as rubber bands. When one lands from a jump, one's tendons are stretched, storing energy that can then be used to contribute to rapid force production.

Active State Development

Active state is characterized by the formation of cross bridges within the muscle fibers. These cross bridges are where muscle contraction occurs at the most basic level and are the points at which the thick and thin filaments of the muscle fibers attach. It has been shown that active state is enhanced during the eccentric (or lowering) portions of a movement (e.g., during the lowering phase of a countermovement jump). The more cross bridges that are formed, the more force that can be generated.

FUNCTIONAL POWER TRAINING

Traditional power training methods are typically linear. However, since hockey is a multidimensional sport, power training must match these demands. The reality is that all power production is functional. Still, the ability to express power in multiple planes and from compromised positions will add elements to the athlete's game that many players lack.

QUALITY OVER QUANTITY

When training for power development, the focus must be on the quality and execution of the movements. Power exercises are usually high-velocity skills that are technically demanding. Therefore, rather than focusing on quantity and volume, the quality of action and intent to perform each repetition as rapidly as possible should be the desired training characteristics.

Non-SSC Power Development

The best skaters in hockey can generate force rapidly in the absence of the SSC. When examining the skating stride, this fact should be evident. For example, Behm et al. (2005) suggest that skating in hockey does not involve a significant SSC component but instead relies on impulse to a greater degree due to the relatively long foot contact times on the ice. Therefore, developing lower-body power in the absence of a preloading or countermovement phase to minimize the SSC's contributions should be a primary focus of the training plan early on. Also, performing various exercises from disadvantageous positions (e.g., below 90 degrees knee flexion) should be performed to maximize the impulse generated throughout the movements. To highlight this, Upjohn et al. (2008) showed that high-caliber skaters possessed greater hip flexion at the beginning of the stride and maintained deeper knee flexion until later in the stride's stance phase compared to low-caliber skaters. The exercise selection should also be multiplanar and focus on generating force rapidly in various planes and directions. Following are sample exercises, ranging in skill level, to develop impulse without the SSC's aid.

Noncountermovement Jump

Difficulty

Beginner

Equipment

Plyometric box

Purpose

The purpose of the noncountermovement jump is to train lower-body power and impulse development in the absence of SSC contributions.

Starting Position

Stand with your feet approximately shoulder-width apart, with your toes pointing forward. Lower into a squat position while screwing your feet into the ground (right foot clockwise and left foot counterclockwise), spreading

the floor, and driving your knees outward. Bring your arms back to your sides, internally rotating your hands (figure 6.1*a*).

Movement

From a static position on the ground, swing your arms forward and up while extending your hips and knees as rapidly as possible to jump off the ground (figure 6.1*b*). As you return to the ground or land on the box, drive your knees out, screw your feet into the floor, and land in the initial squat position (figure 6.1*c*).

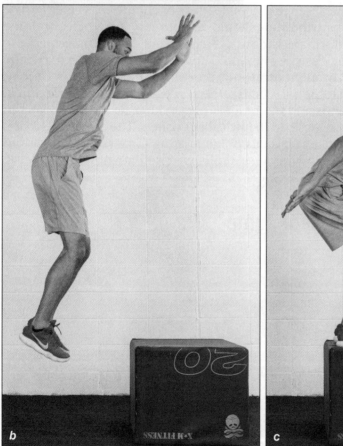

Figure 6.1 Noncountermovement jump: *(a)* starting position, *(b)* jump, and *(c)* landing.

Common Errors

The most common error seen during the jump is that triple extension (full extension of the hip, knee, and ankle) is not accomplished. Focus on extending in all of these areas to maximize impulse. A second error commonly seen is during the landing of the jump. Your hips, knees, and ankles should work in sequence when absorbing the load. If these joints are not working together, the load on the individual joints might be significantly higher, increasing the injury risk.

Progressions and Variations

Progressions to the noncountermovement jump are designed to add complexity and increase the jump's physical demands. They include lateral displacement, rotation, and single-leg stability.

Lateral Noncountermovement Jump

The lateral noncountermovement jump is performed in the same manner as the noncountermovement jump. However, instead of jumping straight up or forward to a box, you jump laterally 1 to 2 feet (0.3-0.6 m) (figure 6.2).

Rotational Noncountermovement Jump

The rotational noncountermovement jump is performed in the same manner as the noncountermovement jump. However, while in the air, perform 90 degrees of rotation (figure 6.3).

Figure 6.2 Lateral non-countermovement jump.

Figure 6.3 Rotational non-countermovement jump.

Figure 6.4 Single-leg noncounter-movement hop.

Single-Leg Variations

The noncountermovement jump and its lateral and rotational variations can also be performed on one leg. The difficulty level of these types of hops is intermediate. The same initial steps are taken, but you are now in a single-leg stance, with your free leg behind you. At takeoff, swing your free leg through and up into the hip lock position (figure 6.4). After landing, swing the free leg back to its initial starting point.

Bottom-Up Rear Foot–Elevated Jump

Difficulty

Intermediate

Equipment

Single-leg squat stand or bench, pad or mat

Purpose

The purpose of the bottom-up rear foot–elevated jump is to train lower-body power and impulse development in the absence of SSC contributions from a disadvantageous position.

Starting Position

Stand in front of the pad with your feet approximately shoulder-width apart and your toes pointing forward. Place one foot on the single-leg squat stand or bench. Lower your back knee down to the pad. Drive your primary weight-bearing knee out, resulting in a positive shin angle. Your arms then assume the standard running position (figure 6.5a). In the bottom position, your front leg should bear most of the load.

Movement

From the bottom position, extend your front hip and knee as quickly as possible while maintaining stand or bench contact with your back leg to jump off the ground (figure 6.5b). At the same time, swing one arm forward and the other back. As you return to the ground, drive your knee out, and land in the same initial position. Reset after each repetition to minimize contributions from the SSC.

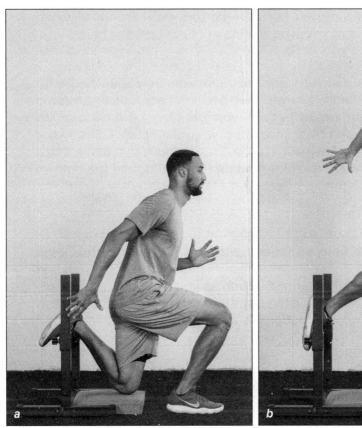

Figure 6.5　Bottom-up rear foot–elevated jump: *(a)* back knee on pad and arms in running position and *(b)* jump.

Common Errors

The most common error seen during this drill is the front knee collapsing to the middle on takeoff and landing. Be sure to drive it outward at all times while your front foot is on the ground.

Bottom-Up Skater Jump

Difficulty

Advanced

Equipment

Pad or mat

Purpose

The bottom-up skater jump trains lower-body power and impulse development in the absence of SSC contributions from a disadvantageous position. This is a progression from the bottom-up rear foot–elevated jump in that you will be removing one point of contact: the back foot.

Starting Position

Stand in front of the pad with your feet approximately shoulder-width apart and your toes pointing forward. Step back with one foot, and assume a half-kneeling position on the pad. Lift your back foot off the ground to make your front foot and back knee the only contact points. Drive your primary weight-bearing knee out, resulting in a positive shin angle. Place your arms in the standard running position (figure 6.6a). In the bottom position, your front leg should bear most of the load.

Movement

From the bottom position, extend your front hip and knee as quickly as possible. At the same time, swing one arm forward and the other back as you would while running. At takeoff, swing your free leg through and up into the hip lock position (figure 6.6b). As you return to the ground, drive your knee out, and land in the same initial position. Reset after each repetition to minimize contributions from the SSC.

Common Errors

Because this exercise is highly demanding, athletes often have difficulty getting out of the hole at the bottom position. As a result, the body often shifts forward, with the hips elevating before knee extension. This compensation can be eliminated by adding a pad to reduce the range of motion until you have the requisite strength to perform the exercise from the weakest position. If elevating the back knee does not solve this problem, regress the exercise.

Figure 6.6 Bottom-up skater jump: *(a)* starting position, *(b)* jump.

Half-Kneeling Lateral Bound

Difficulty

Advanced

Equipment

Pad or mat

Purpose

The half-kneeling lateral bound trains lower-body power and impulse development in the absence of SSC contributions from a disadvantageous position. This exercise is a progression from the bottom-up skater jump in that you generate impulse in the frontal plane (lateral) instead of the sagittal plane.

Starting Position

The starting point is the same as the bottom-up skater jump. Stand in front of the pad with your feet approximately shoulder-width apart and your toes pointing forward. Step back with one foot, and assume a half-kneeling position on the pad. Lift your back foot off the ground to make your front foot and back knee the only contact points. Drive your primary weight-bearing knee out, resulting in a positive shin angle. Place your arms in the standard running position (figure 6.7a). In the bottom position, your front leg should bear most of the load.

Movement

From the bottom position, extend your front hip and knee as quickly as possible in the frontal plane to push your body laterally. At the same time, swing one arm forward and the other back as you would while running. At takeoff, swing your free leg through and up (figure 6.7b). You will travel laterally in the air. As you return to the ground, land on the leading leg in a single-leg stance. Drive your knee out, and land in an athletic position. Return to the pad, and perform the exercise for the prescribed number of repetitions.

Figure 6.7   Half-kneeling lateral bound: *(a)* starting position, *(b)* bound.

Progressions and Variations

Noncountermovement Lateral Bound

The noncountermovement lateral bound is a variation of the half-kneeling lateral bound that decreases the strength requirements. The initial setup and movement are to begin standing on one leg and perform a quarter to half squat. Extend your hip, knee, and ankle as rapidly as possible, and bound laterally (figure 6.8). The landing is the same as the half-kneeling lateral bound.

Figure 6.8   Noncountermovement lateral bound.

Half-Kneeling Rotational Bound

Difficulty

Advanced

Equipment

Pad or mat

Purpose

The half-kneeling rotational bound trains lower-body power and impulse development in the absence of contributions from the SSC from a disadvantageous position. This exercise is a progression from the bottom-up skater jump and half-kneeling lateral bound. You will generate impulse in the frontal plane (lateral), then add a 90-degree rotation in the air.

Starting Position

The starting point is the same as the bottom-up skater jump and half-kneeling lateral bound. Stand in front of the pad with your feet approximately shoulder-width apart and your toes pointing forward. Step back with one foot and assume a half-kneeling position on the pad. Lift your back foot off the ground to make your front foot and back knee the only contact points. Drive your primary weight-bearing knee out, resulting in a positive shin angle. Place your arms in the standard running position (figure 6.9a). In the bottom position, your front leg should bear most of the load.

Movement

From the bottom position, extend your front hip and knee as quickly as possible in the frontal plane to push laterally. At takeoff, swing your free leg through and up and rotate 90 degrees in the air (figure 6.9b). At the same time, swing one arm forward and the other back as you would while running. When you return to the ground, land on the leading leg in a single-leg stance. Drive your knee out, and land in an athletic position. Return to the pad, and perform the exercise for the prescribed number of repetitions.

Figure 6.9   Half-kneeling rotational bound: *(a)* starting position and *(b)* bound and rotate.

Progressions and Variations

Rotational Bound

The rotational bound is a variation of the half-kneeling rotational bound that decreases the strength requirements. The initial setup and movement are to begin standing on one leg and perform a quarter to half squat. Extend your hip, knee, and ankle as rapidly as possible to bound laterally, and rotate 90 degrees in the air (figure 6.10). The landing is the same as the half-kneeling rotational bound.

Figure 6.10   Rotational bound.

Plyometric Power Development

Plyometric training is a category of exercise that exploits the SSC to increase power. During this type of activity, the muscle undergoes rapid lengthening (eccentric contraction), immediately transitioning to rapid shortening (concentric contraction). As described earlier, this quick stretch on the muscle induces the SSC to augment the force-generating capabilities during muscle shortening. Previously, impulse was outlined as an essential variable for skating performance. However, the ability to change directions on a dime is also critical in hockey. Therefore, training the SSC through plyometrics is paramount in developing this on-ice skill.

Plyometric exercises have three specific phases: the landing, amortization, and takeoff. The landing phase begins with the eccentric contraction of the muscle, which activates the SSC. The amortization phase is the time spent on the ground and represents the transition from landing to subsequent takeoff. The takeoff phase is the concentric muscle contraction following landing (Sandler 2005).

Plyometric training is highly demanding. Athletes must possess adequate strength levels to perform this type of training safely and effectively. As a result, plyometric training should be viewed on a continuum ranging from beginner to advanced levels in the movement's intensity and complexity (figure 6.11). On the beginner end of the continuum, these exercises are not truly plyometric because they might not involve all three phases. However, these steps need to be taken to ensure the athlete's safety and progression to plyometric exercises.

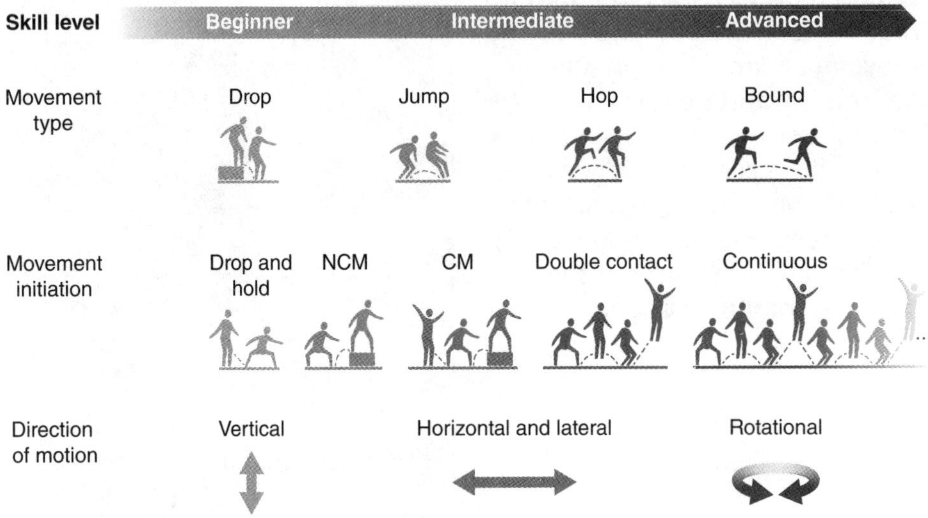

Figure 6.11   Plyometric training continuum.

The plyometric continuum is categorized by intensity and complexity of muscle action phases during plyometric exercise, type of movement initiation, motion direction, and movement type. These are the specific sequences that must be mastered before introducing true plyometric training into the plan. It is not prudent to skip steps.

The continuum has four types of movement: drop, jump, hop, and bound. The drop is characterized by starting in a standing position and rapidly descending into the landing position. A jump is classified by bilateral (double-leg) takeoff and landing, whereas a hop is characterized by unilateral (single-leg) takeoff and landing. Lastly, a bound is unilateral takeoff and landing on the opposite foot.

The continuum has three progressions: absorption (eccentric muscle action), propulsion (concentric muscle action), and true plyometric (a combination of absorption, amortization, and propulsion). In the early stages of development, beginners must possess the ability to absorb the forces on their bodies adequately. This feat is accomplished by performing only the eccentric portion of the movement (e.g., drop). As the athlete progresses, the focus can shift to the concentric phase of the jump. Once these two qualities have been mastered, the athlete can then transition to true plyometric exercises that combine absorption and propulsion.

Further breakdown of this continuum outlines the initial movement method, including drop and hold, noncountermovement, countermovement, double-contact, continuous, and drop jump.

Drop and Hold

This type of movement initiation addresses the absorption phase of the jumping pattern. The drop squat is an exercise that develops the drop and hold.

Drop Squat

Difficulty

Beginner

Equipment

None

Purpose

The drop squat develops the appropriate eccentric strength and mechanics, which allows for progression to countermovement variations and landing.

Starting Position

Stand with your feet shoulder-width apart and toes pointed forward. Raise your arms directly over your head and get as tall as possible (figure 6.12a).

Movement

Descend as rapidly as possible into an athletic squat position (figure 6.12b). As you descend, drive your knees outward. Focus on the

Figure 6.12 Drop squat: (a) starting position and (b) squat.

mechanics of your movement, with your hips and knees moving in sequence and arms swinging back. Hold the bottom position for 1 or 2 seconds until stable. Repeat this movement for the prescribed number of repetitions.

Progressions

Progress the exercise by performing it on one leg (single-leg drop squat). Begin on two legs in the same starting position as the drop squat (figure 6.13a), and rapidly descend to a single-leg athletic squat position (figure 6.13b).

Figure 6.13 Single-leg drop squat: *(a)* starting position and *(b)* end position.

Noncountermovement

This movement initiation is also for the beginner athlete and addresses the jumping pattern's propulsion phase. The noncountermovement jump and its variations and progressions were outlined earlier in the chapter.

Countermovement

This movement initiation addresses both the absorption and propulsion phases of the jumping pattern while using the SSC. Following are specific examples of countermovement exercises.

Countermovement Jump to Box

Difficulty

Intermediate

Equipment

12-inch (30 cm) box or bench

Purpose

The countermovement jump to box addresses both the absorption and propulsion phases of the jumping pattern while using the SSC.

Starting Position

Stand approximately 12 inches (30 cm) away from the box with your feet shoulder-width apart and toes pointed forward.

Movement

Rapidly descend into an athletic squat position (figure 6.14a) and immediately ascend, jumping off the ground as high as possible (figure 6.14b). Fully extend your hips, knees, and ankles. Land on the box, absorbing the forces with your ankles, knees, and hips working in harmony.

Figure 6.14 Countermovement jump to box: (a) squat and (b) jump.

Common Errors

The most common error with this exercise is the knees collapsing to the middle during descent and landing. Focus on driving them out during the movement.

Progressions

Countermovement Hop to Box

This exercise can be progressed by performing it on one leg, following the same steps as the countermovement jump to box (figure 6.14a-b). Begin by standing on one leg (figure 6.15a), then rapidly descend into an athletic single-leg squat position and immediately ascend, jumping off the ground as high as possible (figure 6.15b). Fully extend the hip, knee, and ankle of the working leg, and swing the free leg forward and up into a flexed position. Perform a single-leg landing on the box with the same leg that performed the jump, absorbing the forces with your ankle, knee, and hip working in harmony. Perform this movement on both legs.

Figure 6.15 Countermovement hop to box: (a) starting position and (b) jump.

Countermovement Jump or Hop

Remove the box, and land on the ground. This progression will increase the landing intensity and can be performed on two legs or one leg.

Lateral or Rotational Countermovement Jump

Perform the same sequences as the countermovement jump to box, but jump laterally (to the side) (figure 6.16a-b) or add a rotational component (figure 6.17a-b).

Figure 6.16   Lateral countermovement jump: *(a)* squat and *(b)* jump laterally.

Figure 6.17 Rotational countermovement jump: *(a)* squat and *(b)* jump and rotate.

Lateral Countermovement Hop

Perform the same sequences as the countermovement hop to box, but hop laterally and land on the ground instead of a box (figure 6.18*a-b*). If you are hopping to the right, perform the hop on the right leg. If you are hopping to the left, perform the hop on the left leg.

Countermovement Lateral Bound

Begin by standing on one leg, then rapidly descend into an athletic single-leg squat position (figure 6.19*a*). From the bottom position, extend your front hip and knee as quickly as possible in the frontal plane to push your body laterally. At the same time, swing one arm forward and the other back as you would while running. At takeoff, swing your free leg through and up (figure 6.19*b*). You will travel laterally in the air. As you return to the ground, land on the leading leg in a single-leg stance. Drive your knee out and land in an athletic position. Perform this sequence for the prescribed number of repetitions on each leg in an alternating fashion.

Figure 6.18   Lateral countermovement hop: *(a)* single-leg squat and *(b)* hop laterally.

Figure 6.19   Countermovement lateral bound: *(a)* single-leg squat and *(b)* bound.

Countermovement Rotational Bound

The countermovement rotational bound is a progression to the rotational bound. Begin by standing on one leg, then rapidly descend into an athletic single-leg squat position (figure 6.20a). Extend your hip, knee, and ankle as rapidly as possible to bound laterally and rotate 90 degrees in the air (figure 6.20b). As you return to the ground, land on the leading leg in a single-leg stance.

Figure 6.20　Countermovement rotational bound: *(a)* single-leg squat and *(b)* bound.

Double-Contact

This movement initiation addresses both the absorption and propulsion phases of the jumping pattern but with a more dynamic ground contact before executing the propulsion phase. Following are examples of double-contact exercises.

Double-Contact Jump

Difficulty

Intermediate

Equipment

None

Purpose

The double-contact jump is an intermediate step between the counter-movement and continuous jumps. The focus remains on the jumping pattern's absorption and propulsion phases while utilizing the SSC; however, the ground contact is more dynamic immediately before takeoff.

Starting Position

Assume the squat position with your feet approximately shoulder-width apart and toes pointed forward.

Movement

While maintaining this squat position, pop off the ground approximately 1 to 2 inches (3-5 cm), and immediately drive into the ground to initiate propulsion. Jump as high as possible. Fully extend your hips, knees, and ankles. Upon landing, absorb the forces with your ankles, knees, and hips working in harmony. During your initial pop off the ground, maintain your squat position to perform the takeoff's rapid concentric motion. If you stand too tall during this phase, it will be challenging to maximize power production.

Progressions

Double-Contact Hop

Perform the same task on one leg. The jump and the landing should be performed on the same leg, and the same leg should be used throughout the entire sequence. Perform this exercise on both legs.

Lateral and Rotational Double-Contact Jump or Hop

Perform both the double- and single-leg versions with lateral and rotational displacement.

Continuous Double-Contact Jump or Hop

Perform the same tasks in a continuous manner. Immediately upon landing, perform the short pop off the ground and repeat the cycle.

Double-Contact Lateral Bound

Begin by standing on one leg in a half-squat position. While maintaining this squat position, pop off the ground approximately 1 to 2 inches

(3-5 cm), and immediately drive into the ground to initiate propulsion. Extend your front hip and knee as quickly as possible in the frontal plane to push your body laterally. At the same time, swing one arm forward and the other back as you would while running. At takeoff, swing your free leg through and up. You will travel laterally in the air. As you return to the ground, land on the leading leg in a single-leg stance. Drive your knee out, and land in an athletic position. Perform this sequence for the prescribed number of repetitions on each leg in an alternating fashion.

Continuous

This movement initiation addresses both the absorption and propulsion phases of the jumping pattern. However, these are continuous, and the athlete should spend as little time on the ground as possible. Following are examples of continuous exercises.

Continuous Jump

Difficulty

Advanced

Equipment

None

Purpose

The continuous jump focuses on the absorption and propulsion phases of the jumping pattern while using the SSC; however, the ground contact times are short and physically demanding.

Starting Position

Stand with your feet approximately shoulder-width apart and toes pointed forward.

Movement

Rapidly descend into an athletic squat position, and immediately ascend, jumping off the ground as high as possible. Fully extend your hips, knees, and ankles at takeoff. Upon landing, absorb the forces with your ankles, knees, and hips working in harmony, spending as little time on the ground as possible and immediately ascending again into another jump.

Common Errors

The most common error with this exercise is the knees collapsing to the middle during the descent and landing. Focus on driving them out during the movement.

Progressions

Continuous Hop

Perform the same task on one leg.

Lateral and Rotational Jump or Hop

Perform both the double- and single-leg versions with lateral and rotational displacement.

Continuous Lateral Bound

Begin by standing on one leg, then rapidly descend into an athletic single-leg squat position. From the bottom position, extend your front hip and knee as quickly as possible in the frontal plane to push your body laterally. At the same time, swing one arm forward and the other back as you would while running. At takeoff, swing your free leg through and up. You will travel laterally in the air. As you return to the ground, land on the leading leg in a single-leg stance. Upon landing, immediately reverse your motion, and perform a lateral bound in the opposite direction. Spend as little time on the ground as possible. Perform this sequence for the prescribed number of repetitions on each leg in an alternating fashion.

Drop Jump

The drop jump is the most physically demanding type of movement initiation. It addresses both the absorption and propulsion phases of the jumping pattern.

Drop Jump

Difficulty

Advanced

Equipment

Plyometric box or bench

Purpose

With the drop jump, the eccentric demand of the jumping pattern is significantly increased because the athlete drops from an elevated box or bench.

Starting Position

Begin by standing at the edge of the plyometric box or bench.

Movement

Other than dropping from a higher level, the movement is the same as the countermovement jump (figure 6.21 *a, b*). There are no progressions to the drop jump, because I do not recommend performing this variation on a single leg for hockey players.

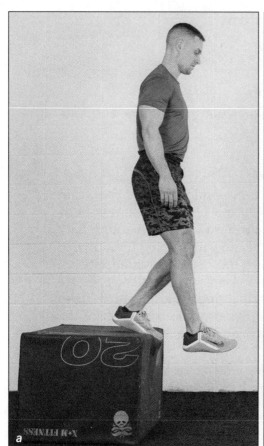

Figure 6.21   Drop jump: *(a)* drop and *(b)* jump.

Loaded Power Development

Going back to the force–velocity and power curves, it is evident that an optimal relationship between force production and velocity of movement must be observed to maximize power output. While performing jumps under load, err on the side of caution and begin with loads ranging from 10 to 30 percent repetition maximum (RM). If high-force, high-velocity movements are performed without jumping, loads of up to 80 percent RM can be used to optimize power. Loaded power development results in a larger impulse, which is important during the skating stride. If these exercises are performed with countermovement or are continuous, the SSC will also play a significant role in power development. Typically, this type of exercise is for intermediate or advanced athletes. However, technical aspects of these movements can be trained, using very light loads.

Loaded power development progressions fall on the same continuum as plyometrics (figure 6.11). The progressions include double- to single-leg, noncountermovement to continuous, linear to multidirectional. Following are exercises on the loaded power continuum.

Noncountermovement Trap Bar Jump

Difficulty

Intermediate to advanced

Equipment

Trap bar and weights

Purpose

The noncountermovement trap bar jump is a loaded jumping variation that focuses on generating impulse from a low position without the aid of the SSC.

Starting Position

Step inside the trap bar. Your feet should be shoulder-width apart and facing forward. While standing, engage your hip and glute musculature by externally rotating thighs (screwing your feet into the floor), and brace your core. Lower your hips by pushing them back and bending your knees. Maintain a neutral spine. In the lowered position, grab the handles of the bar (figure 6.22a).

Movement

Without lifting the bar, place tension on it by contracting your leg and hip musculature and setting your shoulders back. Engage your pelvic floor muscles, drive your knees outward, and rapidly push the ground away, jumping in the air (figure 6.22b). Extend fully at the hip, knee, and ankle. Your hips and the weight should move in sequence; do not raise your hips before lifting the weight. Upon landing, externally rotate your thighs by screwing your feet into the floor and driving your knees outward. Pause and reset at the bottom before completing your next repetition.

Common Errors

A common error with the noncountermovement trap bar jump is allowing your spine to flex or round during the movement. This fault primarily occurs due to using too much load on the bar. Remove weight and repeat.

If your knees collapse inward, be sure to focus on driving them outward for the entirety of the movement. Adding a miniband around your knees can help fire the muscles responsible for pushing your knees outward.

Athletes often do a short, rapid countermovement at the bottom to induce the SSC at initiation of the movement. Be sure to explode out of the hole without dipping in the hips or knees before movement initiation.

Figure 6.22   Noncountermovement trap bar jump: *(a)* starting position and *(b)* jump.

Progressions

Countermovement Trap Bar Jump

Perform the movement in the same manner; however, start from a standing position. Rapidly descend to the lowered position, and immediately reverse the action into a jump to induce the SSC. Reset after each repetition.

Continuous Trap Bar Jump

This progression is performed in the same manner as the countermovement trap bar jump; however, the movement is continuous with no reset after each repetition. Spend as little time on the ground as possible.

Noncountermovement Jump Squat

Difficulty

Intermediate to advanced

Equipment

Squat rack; barbell and weights; other apparatus such as medicine ball, kettlebells, or dumbbells

Purpose

The noncountermovement jump squat is a loaded jumping variation (with the load situated higher on the body) that focuses on generating impulse from a low position without the aid of the SSC.

Starting Position

Stand in front of the barbell in the squat rack with your feet approximately shoulder-width apart and toes pointed forward. Grip the barbell with your hands approximately shoulder-width apart. Step under the barbell, and place it on your upper back (trapezius muscles) below the cervical spine. Stand up and remove the weight from the rack.

Movement

Squat to a comfortable level (approximately 90 degrees of knee flexion) (figure 6.23a). Engage your pelvic floor muscles, brace your core, drive your knees outward, and rapidly push the ground away, jumping in the air (figure 6.23b). Upon land-

Figure 6.23   Noncountermovement jump squat: *(a)* squat and *(b)* jump.

ing, externally rotate your thighs by screwing your feet into the floor and driving your knees outward. Pause and reset at the bottom before completing your next repetition.

Common Errors

If your knees collapse inward, be sure to focus on driving them outward for the entirety of the movement. Adding a miniband around your knees can help fire the muscles responsible for pushing your knees outward.

Athletes often do a short, rapid countermovement at the bottom to induce the SSC upon initiation of the movement. Be sure to explode out of the hole without dipping in the hips or knees before movement initiation.

Progressions

Countermovement Jump Squat

Perform the movement in the same manner; however, start from a standing position. Then, rapidly descend to the lowered position, and immediately reverse the action into a jump to induce the SSC. Reset after each repetition.

Continuous Jump Squat

This progression will be performed in the same manner as the countermovement squat jump; however, the movement will be continuous with no reset after each repetition. Spend as little time on the ground as possible.

Rear Foot–Elevated Jump

Difficulty

Intermediate

Equipment

Single-leg squat stand or bench, dumbbells

Purpose

The purpose of the rear foot–elevated jump is to train lower-body power and impulse development.

Starting Position

Stand in front of the pad with your feet approximately shoulder-width apart and your toes pointing forward while holding dumbbells at your sides. Place one foot on the single-leg squat stand or bench.

Movement

Descend rapidly from the starting position (figure 6.24a), then reverse the motion by extending your front hip and knee as quickly as possible while maintaining stand or bench contact with your back leg to jump off the ground (figure 6.24b). As you return to the ground, drive your knee out, and land in the same initial position. Perform this movement in a continuous fashion. Switch legs after the prescribed number of repetitions has been performed.

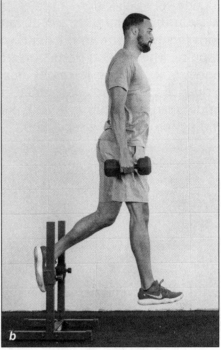

Figure 6.24   Rear foot–elevated jump: *(a)* squat and *(b)* jump.

Noncountermovement Resisted Lateral Bound

Difficulty

Intermediate to advanced

Equipment

Cable machine or band, waist belt

Purpose

The noncountermovement resisted lateral bound is a loaded jumping variation that focuses on generating impulse in the frontal plane (lateral direction), using a hip abduction pattern from a low position without the aid of the SSC.

Starting Position

Place the waist belt or band around your waist at the hip level. If a band is being used, it should be anchored securely to a squat rack or another stable anchor point. Stand on one leg (the leg closest to the cable column), and squat down to approximately 90 degrees of knee flexion.

Movement

Engage your pelvic floor muscles, brace your core, and push the ground away in the lateral direction as rapidly as possible to take off from the floor (figure 6.25a). Fully extend your hip, knee, and ankle to maximize impulse. The landing occurs on the opposite leg (figure 6.25b). Upon landing, absorb the forces by flexing at your hip, knee, and ankle in sequence to assume a half-squat position. Once you are stable on the landing leg, stand up and walk back toward the cable column to reset and perform the next repetition.

Figure 6.25 Noncountermovement resisted lateral bound: *(a)* bound and *(b)* landing.

Common Errors

Athletes often do a short, rapid countermovement at the bottom to induce the SSC on initiation of the movement. Be sure to explode out of the hole without dipping in the hips or knees before movement initiation.

Progressions

Countermovement Resisted Lateral Bound

Perform the movement in the same manner; however, you will start from a standing position. Rapidly descend to the lowered position, and immediately reverse the action into a jump to induce the SSC. Reset after each repetition.

Continuous Resisted Lateral Bound

This progression will be performed in the same manner as the counter-movement resisted lateral bound; however, the movement will be continuous. Immediately on landing, bound back toward the cable column to complete the next repetition. Spend as little time on the ground as possible.

Resisted Crossover Bound

Difficulty

Intermediate to advanced

Equipment

Cable machine or band, waist belt

Purpose

The resisted crossover bound is a loaded jumping variation that focuses on generating impulse in the frontal plane (lateral direction), using a hip adduction pattern from a low position without the aid of the SSC.

Starting Position

Place the waist belt or band around your waist at the hip level. If a band is being used, it should be anchored securely to a squat rack or another stable anchor point. Stand with feet approximately shoulder-width apart in an athletic stance, then load the leg that is farthest away from the cable column by leaning slightly in that direction (figure 6.26a).

Movement

Engage your pelvic floor muscles, brace your core, and push the ground away with your outside leg crossing under as rapidly as possible to take off from the floor. Simultaneously, the leg closest to the cable crosses over the push leg (figure 6.26b). Fully extend your hip, knee, and ankle to maximize impulse. The landing will occur by touching down with both legs at the same time. Upon landing, absorb the forces by flexing at your hip, knee, and ankle in sequence to assume a half-squat position. Once you are stable, stand up and walk back toward the cable column to reset and perform the next repetition.

Common Errors

The most common error in this exercise is not fully extending the hip, knee, and ankle on the pushing leg. Focus on maximizing this range of motion to optimize impulse.

Figure 6.26   Resisted crossover bound: *(a)* starting position and *(b)* bound.

Progressions

Continuous Resisted Crossover Bound

This progression is performed in the same manner as above; however, the movement is continuous. Immediately on landing, cross over back toward the cable column to complete the next repetition. Spend as little time on the ground as possible.

Olympic Weightlifting

The use of Olympic weightlifting in power training for hockey players is a highly debated topic. The reasons for this debate primarily focus on the mastery of the Olympic weightlifting movements. This type of exercise is technically demanding and can take years of practice to execute the lifts properly. As with any activity, the rewards must outweigh the risks to justify their placement into the training program. It is recommended to work with a qualified trainer or strength and conditioning coach to determine if Olympic weightlifting fits into a training program and, if so, to learn the proper lifting techniques.

That said, adding this type of exercise into training offers several benefits. The main benefit is whole-body coordination and integration. The entire body is taxed when moving a weight from the floor or hang position to overhead. For the majority of intermediate- and advanced-level hockey players, I recommend the single-arm dumbbell snatch.

Single-Arm Dumbbell Snatch

Difficulty

Intermediate to advanced

Equipment

Dumbbell

Purpose

The single-arm dumbbell snatch develops whole-body power and coordination.

Starting Position

Holding a dumbbell in one hand, stand with your feet approximately shoulder-width apart. Move your hips back, and bend your knees slightly while keeping a neutral spine. Reach the dumbbell between your legs, with your shoulders back and down (figure 6.27a).

Movement

Initiate the movement by rapidly extending your hips, knees, and ankles and pulling the dumbbell upward as close to your body as possible. Shrug your shoulder, and bring your elbow up high and back with the dumbbell traveling straight up. When the dumbbell is at its highest point, drop under the weight so your arm is fully overhead. Finish the movement in a half-squat position with your arm and the weight stabilized overhead (figure 6.27b).

Figure 6.27 Single-arm dumbbell snatch: *(a)* starting position and *(b)* finish position.

Common Errors

The most common error seen with hockey players during this exercise is not reaching full hip, knee, and ankle extension before dropping under the weight. One of the goals of this exercise is to generate a maximal impulse; therefore, do not cut your movement short.

Rotational Power

Hockey is a rotational sport. The acts of shooting, passing, and changing directions all involve rotation of the body at high velocities. Therefore, it is imperative to develop rotational power to maximize the effectiveness of these actions. Rotational power is typically generated through the athlete's entire body, with most of the force applied through the legs and hips. Contrary to what one might think, the rotation should generally occur at the hips and upper spine, with the torso remaining relatively stable. Many of the progressions listed previously in this chapter address rotational qualities at the lower-body level, but it is critical to integrate those movements into whole-body patterns. This section will outline exercises that develop whole-body rotational power.

Medicine Ball Perpendicular Toss

Difficulty

Beginner, intermediate, advanced

Equipment

Medicine ball, wall against which to throw the ball

Purpose

The medicine ball perpendicular toss mimics the rotational power aspects of shooting under additional load.

Starting Position

Begin by standing with your feet just outside of shoulder-width apart and your shoulders perpendicular to the wall. Hold the medicine ball in both hands.

Movement

Begin by loading the leg furthest away from the wall and holding the medicine ball on that side. Initiate the movement by driving through the loaded leg and rotating your hips toward the wall, transferring your weight to the lead leg. At the same time, swing the medicine ball across your body, and toss it to the wall as rapidly as possible. Your hips and shoulders should face the wall at the point of release, and your weight should be primarily on your lead leg (figure 6.28).

Figure 6.28   Medicine ball perpendicular toss.

Common Errors

The most common error observed with the medicine ball perpendicular toss is when athletes generate power only through upper-body rotation while keeping their hips stable. Focus on driving through your lower body, and rotate your hips throughout the movement to maximize power.

Progressions

Forward Step Medicine Ball Perpendicular Toss

Perform the exercise in the same manner as described earlier; however, open your hips and step forward with the lead leg (figure 6.29a).

Single-Leg Medicine Ball Perpendicular Toss

While performing this progression, load the leg furthest from the wall in a single-leg stance (figure 6.29b). Then rapidly drive off that leg into a rotational bound toward the wall. The upper-body motion will be the same as in the previous examples.

Butterfly Medicine Ball Perpendicular Toss for Goalies

Goalies can begin this drill in a butterfly position (figure 6.29c). Then rapidly stand and complete the same steps as the forward step medicine ball perpendicular toss.

Figure 6.29   Progressions for the medicine ball perpendicular toss: (a) forward step medicine ball perpendicular toss; (b) single-leg medicine ball perpendicular toss; (c) butterfly medicine ball perpendicular toss for goalies.

Horizontal Cable Chop

Difficulty

Beginner, intermediate, advanced

Equipment

Cable machine or band, cable bar or rope attachment

Purpose

Like the medicine ball perpendicular toss, the horizontal cable chop mimics shooting's rotational power aspects under additional load.

Starting Position

Begin by standing with your feet just outside of shoulder-width apart and your shoulders perpendicular to the cable column. Grip the cable bar with an alternating grip, like you would your hockey stick.

Movement

Begin by loading the leg closest to the cable column and extending your arms toward the column (figure 6.30a). Initiate the movement by driving through the loaded leg and rotating your hips away from the cable column, transferring your weight to the lead leg. At the same time, pull the bar across your body. As the bar passes your body, pull the end in with your lead hand, and press the other end of the bar out with your trailing hand (figure 6.30b). Perform this movement as rapidly as possible.

Figure 6.30　Horizontal cable chop: *(a)* load leg and extend arms

Figure 6.30 *(continued)* Horizontal cable chop: *(b)* rotate hips and pull bar.

Progressions

Forward Step Horizontal Cable Chop

Perform the exercise in the same manner as the horizontal cable chop; however, open your hips, and step forward with the lead leg (figure 6.31).

Figure 6.31 Forward step horizontal cable chop.

Upper-Body Power

A well-rounded hockey player must develop upper-body power because it is essential in many areas of the game, such as shooting and battling with an opposing player. Various exercises can be used to develop this quality. Like lower-body power development, these exercises can be performed with and without contributions from the SSC.

Medicine Ball Chest Toss

Difficulty

Beginner, intermediate, advanced

Equipment

Medicine ball, wall against which to throw the ball

Purpose

The medicine ball chest toss develops upper-body pressing and pushing power.

Starting Position

Stand facing the wall with your feet approximately shoulder-width apart. Squat down into an athletic half-squat position, and hold the ball on its sides with your hands at your chest.

Movement

Initiate the movement by pressing the ball as rapidly as possible toward the wall, fully extending your arms out in front of you (figure 6.32). Release the ball from your hands at full extension of your arms. Reset and perform the next repetition.

Figure 6.32   Medicine ball chest toss.

Progressions

Countermovement Medicine Ball Chest Toss

This progression adds a countermovement to the medicine ball chest toss to induce the SSC. Instead of beginning with your hands at your chest, start with your arms fully extended in front of you. Rapidly pull your hands toward your chest, and immediately reverse the motion to toss the ball against the wall.

Continuous Medicine Ball Chest Toss

Use a rubber medicine ball that will bounce off the wall rapidly. Perform the medicine ball chest toss in the same manner as outlined earlier; however, the repetitions are performed continuously.

Single-Arm Medicine Ball Chest Toss

Perform the same movements outlined earlier; however, use one arm at a time instead of two.

Medicine Ball Slam

Difficulty

Beginner, intermediate, advanced

Equipment

Medicine ball

Purpose

The medicine ball slam develops upper-body pulling power in the vertical direction.

Starting Position

Stand with your feet approximately shoulder-width apart and toes pointing forward. Hold the ball, raise your arms directly overhead, get as tall as possible, and engage your core.

Movement

Figure 6.33   Medicine ball slam.

Push your hips back, and slightly bend your knees. At the same time, keeping your core braced, rapidly use your arms to slam the medicine ball to the floor between your feet as forcefully as possible (figure 6.33). Repeat this process for the prescribed number of repetitions.

Progressions

Countermovement Medicine Ball Slam

This progression adds a countermovement to the exercise to induce the SSC. Instead of beginning with your arms overhead, start with the ball at waist level. Rapidly bring your arms overhead, and immediately reverse the motion to slam the ball to the ground.

Single-Arm Explosive Cable Row

Difficulty

Intermediate to advanced

Equipment

Cable machine or band

Purpose

The explosive cable row develops upper-body pulling power in the horizontal direction.

Starting Position

Stand facing the cable column with your feet approximately shoulder-width apart. Assume an athletic half-squat position, and grip the cable handle or band with one hand and reach toward the column.

Movement

Begin the movement by pulling your shoulders back and down. Pull the weight toward your body as rapidly as possible. As your elbow passes your body, allow for space between your body and elbow (figure 6.34).

Figure 6.34   Single-arm explosive cable row.

Common Errors

This exercise's most common error is not pulling the shoulder blades and shoulder back during the pulling motion. This fault will result in your shoulder rolling forward, placing stress on the anterior portion of the shoulder.

Progressions

Countermovement Single-Arm Explosive Cable Row

This progression adds a countermovement to the exercise to induce the SSC. Instead of beginning with your arm in the extended position, start with the cable at your body. Rapidly move your arm toward the column, and immediately reverse the motion.

Continuous Single-Arm Explosive Cable Row

Perform the exercise in the same manner; however, perform it continuously and as rapidly as possible.

Power Endurance

Muscle fatigue plays a significant role in the muscle's ability to generate power. For example, Beelen and Sargeant (1991) demonstrated that muscular fatigue reduced maximal power output, particularly at high velocities. During the game of hockey, it is rare that a player is not tired, and as a result, maximal power development might be reduced. Traditionally, it has been thought that power training should occur at the beginning of each workout to maximize output and quality of execution. However, adding exercises that focus on velocity and power output at the end of the training session while the athlete is fatigued might help train power endurance and sustainability.

While performing these exercises in a fatigued state, the general characteristics remain the same. The focus should be on the quality of execution. This particular placement of power exercises at the end of the training session should only be done for advanced-level athletes.

SUMMARY

The exercises described in this chapter are merely a snapshot of the vast array of possibilities. The critical takeaways are the concepts of developing a good strength base before performing high-velocity power movements, the importance of maximizing impulse for the skating stride, and training the SSC's contributions to power output in hockey. In terms of exercise selection, the individual athlete's needs must be assessed and addressed.

Chapter 7

Training for Acceleration and Speed

In the sport of hockey, the speed of the game is continuously increasing. Speed is the physical quality that many coaches and managers view as the most important characteristic in the physical realm. However, in hockey, top-end speed or maximum velocity is rarely realized due to the game's nature. Therefore, when coaches and managers refer to speed, they are most likely referring to the player's ability to accelerate.

Acceleration is defined as the rate at which a body changes its velocity or speed. Many physical qualities contribute to an athlete's ability to accelerate. These qualities include aspects of force production and biomechanics of the skating stride, which are discussed in this chapter. This chapter also highlights accelerations and speed considerations for youth and developing athletes.

FORCE PRODUCTION AND ACCELERATION

The mathematical equation for acceleration is as follows:

$$Acceleration = Force / Mass$$

Therefore, if body mass or weight remains constant, acceleration will occur in proportion to the applied force. The previous two chapters focused primarily on this quality: first, on the amount of force that can be applied, and second, on the force's application rate. Absolute strength is necessary, but the amount of force that can be employed per unit of body weight (relative strength) is likely more important. However, focusing primarily on force production does not paint the entire picture. Acceleration is rate dependent. Therefore, to be fast, the athlete needs to train fast because as speed increases, the time to produce force decreases.

YOUTH ACCELERATION TRAINING CONSIDERATIONS

Far too often, young athletes train acceleration and speed using many field-based exercises but neglect one of the most critical components of the acceleration equation: force production. With all else being equal, the athlete who can put more force into the ground or ice will demonstrate better acceleration capabilities. Therefore, when considering youth development, a primary focus should be placed on strength training and the application of force (mechanics). An adequately structured strength training program will significantly affect a young athlete's ability to accelerate because increases in strength undoubtedly will equate to acceleration increases.

BIOMECHANICS AND ACCELERATION

Force production qualities are only a piece of the acceleration and speed puzzle, and the biomechanics of the skating stride completes the puzzle. Biomechanics is the analysis of human movement mechanics and pertains to the application and efficiency of movement. The relevance of force production is decreased if the biomechanics of the skating movement is not optimized. Several scientific studies have outlined the biomechanical differences between high-caliber and low-caliber skaters. For example, Robbins, Renaud, and Pearsall (2018) demonstrated that high-caliber skaters had greater ankle range of motion throughout the stride, knee extension and external rotation at push-off, hip flexion during glide, and quicker stride recovery rate. Similarly, Upjohn et al. (2008) demonstrated that high-caliber skaters expressed greater stride length and width, hip flexion at weight acceptance, knee extension and ankle range of motion at push-off, lateral displacement of the limb, hip flexion throughout the stride, and rate of abduction and extension during the stride. Of note, the stride rates were not significantly different between high- and low-caliber skaters, suggesting stride length and total range of motion might be more important. These data indicate that high-caliber skaters might use force and impulse production more effectively than low-caliber skaters due to more efficient skating mechanics.

YOUTH DEVELOPMENT SPEED WINDOWS

In chapter 1, the long-term player development model was outlined. This model has two potential windows of opportunity where speed training can be maximized. Ford et al. (2011) suggest that these windows coincide with the athlete's age. The first window occurs between the ages of 7 and 9 for both boys and girls, and the second window occurs between 11 and 13 for girls and 13 and 15 for boys. The first window of opportunity is associated with developing the central nervous system and coordination. In contrast, the second window seems to be related to hormone-dependent increases in fast-twitch muscle fibers (Ford et al. 2011). Philippaerts et al. (2006) highlighted that youth attained their most significant improvements in speed around the time they reached their fastest growth in terms of height but experienced declines in speed in the 12 months before the point of their fastest growth. This decline might be related to changes in coordination as a result of the rapid growth. Therefore, when training acceleration and speed in youth, patience is a virtue, and a significant emphasis needs to be placed on the individual and their corresponding stage of physical development.

ACCELERATION AND SPEED EXERCISES

The exercises that follow primarily focus on the mechanics of movement, which optimize the force-producing capabilities throughout the skating and running strides. It is essential to understand the athlete's developmental stage and follow the guiding principle of slow to fast progressions.

SLOW IS SMOOTH, AND SMOOTH IS FAST

The U.S. Navy SEALS train under the philosophy "Slow is smooth, and smooth is fast." This has many implications. Primarily, by rushing movements, fundamental elements could be missed and ultimately hinder immediate and long-term development. We can apply this philosophy to acceleration and speed training. Do not start at the end goal of high-velocity movements. Begin by slowly training the mechanics of specific actions and gradually increasing the velocity as the athlete becomes more competent in the skill. If the athlete cannot attain efficient mechanics at slow speeds, it will be next to impossible to achieve these same mechanics during a maximum effort.

Off-Ice Acceleration Exercises

The off-ice exercises are designed to train mechanics and efficiency in various planes of motion, allowing force output to be optimized.

Stationary Skater Stride

Difficulty

Beginner to intermediate

Equipment

Long strap or heavy band, stable structure to attach the strap

Purpose

The stationary skater stride trains lateral stride mechanics, emphasizing full hip, knee, and ankle extension while applying force throughout the entire motion.

Starting Position

Attach the strap to a stable structure such as a squat rack at approximately waist height. Place the strap around your waist, and make sure it is taut. Grip the strap with the free hand closest to the point of attachment. Lean away from and move your inside foot closer to the point of attachment to achieve approximately 45 degrees of body lean. To finish the setup, brace your core, squat down on the inside leg, and lower your torso (figure 7.1a).

Movement

Fully extend your stance leg in a slow and controlled manner from your lowered position, applying force in the lateral direction throughout the movement. At the same time, your non-weight-bearing leg moves from an extended to a flexed hip position (figure 7.1b). To change the difficulty, move your weight-bearing foot closer to the point of attachment to increase the intensity or away from the point of attachment to decrease the intensity.

Common Errors

The most common error is rushing this movement. Focus on getting as low as possible in the stride and performing the pattern with control.

Figure 7.1 Stationary skater stride: (a) squat and (b) movement.

Speed Skater Stride

Difficulty

Beginner

Equipment

None

Purpose

The speed skater stride trains lateral stride mechanics, emphasizing full hip, knee, and ankle extension.

Starting Position

Begin by assuming a low athletic position. Lift your right leg, so all of your weight is now on the left leg.

Movement

Begin the movement by extending your right leg laterally as far as possible (figure 7.2a). Once you reach your endpoint laterally, arc your leg back until it is directly behind and in line with your hip (figure 7.2b). Finish the movement by returning your leg to the starting position. Maintain a low position throughout the movement, and do not touch your right foot to the ground.

Figure 7.2 Speed skater stride: (a) extend right leg laterally and (b) bring leg behind and in line with hip.

Perform this action on both legs for the prescribed number of repetitions.

Low Skater Lateral Stride

Difficulty

Beginner to intermediate

Equipment

Long strap or heavy band, partner to provide resistance to the strap

Purpose

The purpose of the low skater lateral stride is the same as the stationary skater stride; however, the addition of motion increases the demands on stability and coordination.

Starting Position

Secure the strap around your waist. Your partner holds the other end of the strap and provides resistance. Lean away from and move your inside foot closer to the point of attachment to achieve approximately 45 degrees of body lean. To finish the setup, brace your core, squat down on the inside leg, and lower your torso (figure 7.3a).

Movement

Fully extend your stance leg in a slow and controlled manner from the lowered position, applying force in the lateral direction throughout the movement. At the same time, your non-weight-bearing leg moves from an extended to a flexed hip position, then reaches and touches down on the ground (figure 7.3b). Transfer weight to the lead leg. Reset to the initial starting position to perform the next repetition. To change the difficulty of this exercise, modify your range of motion. The partner has a lot of responsibility to move with the working athlete to maintain appropriate resistance. This technique might take some practice.

Figure 7.3   Low skater lateral stride: (a) starting position and (b) movement.

Common Errors

The most common tendency is rushing this movement, which could create slack in the strap, causing it to be unstable. Focus on getting as low as possible in the stride and performing the pattern with control.

Side Skate Jumps

Difficulty

Beginner, intermediate, advanced

Equipment

None

Purpose

Side skate jumps train range of motion and stability on a single leg in a low position.

Starting Position

Stand on a single leg, and squat down until the knee of your non-weight-bearing leg is at the same level as your ankle on the stance leg (figure 7.4a).

Movement

Perform a low-amplitude single-leg lateral hop from the lowered position but not to full extension. At the same time, your non-weight-bearing leg moves from an extended to a flexed hip position (figure 7.4b). The hop and the landing are performed on the same leg. Reset to the initial starting position on the same leg to perform the next repetition. Perform this exercise on both legs.

Figure 7.4   Side skate jumps: (a) starting position and (b) hop.

Resisted Explosive Lateral Stride

Difficulty

Intermediate to advanced

Equipment

Heavy band, partner to provide resistance to the band

Purpose

While applying the same mechanics as the low skater lateral stride and side skate jumps, the resisted explosive lateral stride adds more rapid force production than the previous two exercises.

Starting Position

Assume the same starting position as the low skater lateral stride. Secure the band around your waist. Your partner holds the other end of the band and provides resistance. Lean away from and move your inside foot closer to the point of attachment to achieve approximately 45 degrees of body lean. To finish the setup, brace your core, squat down on the inside leg, and lower your torso (figure 7.5a).

Movement

The movement is the same as the low skater lateral stride; however, push off as rapidly as possible, performing a lateral bound (figure 7.5b).

Figure 7.5　Resisted explosive lateral stride: *(a)* starting position and *(b)* lateral bound.

Common Errors

The most common error in this movement is not starting from a low position. Most athletes assume the path of least resistance and start from a high stance; however, the goal is to maximize impulse. Therefore, assume the lowest starting stance that you can safely attain.

Progressions and Variations

Continuous Resisted Explosive Lateral Stride

Rather than resetting after each repetition, perform this pattern continuously with a rapid transition between repetitions.

Half-Kneeling Lateral Acceleration

Difficulty

Intermediate to advanced

Equipment

None

Purpose

This exercise integrates both the lateral stride and linear acceleration. The main focus is on force application throughout the lateral push-off start.

Starting Position

Assume a half-kneeling position. If you are moving to your right, your right knee is on the ground and vice versa. Brace your core, and shift your body weight forward and slightly in the direction of travel to load your front foot (figure 7.6a).

Movement

Extend your outside leg as rapidly as possible while lifting your knee off the ground. At the same time, open your hips and body in the direction of travel. At ground contact of your lead leg, be sure to have a positive shin angle to apply force efficiently in the direction you are moving (figure 7.6b). Accelerate linearly for approximately 33 feet (10 m).

Common Errors

One of the most common faults with this exercise is the upper body lagging at takeoff. Be sure to maintain core stability so your body moves in sequence.

Figure 7.6 Half-kneeling lateral acceleration: *(a)* starting position and *(b)* lateral move.

Stationary Skater Crossover

Difficulty

Beginner to intermediate

Equipment

Long strap or heavy band, stable structure to which to attach the strap

Purpose

The stationary skater crossover trains crossover stride mechanics, emphasizing the full hip, knee, and ankle extension of the crossunder leg while applying force throughout the entire motion.

Starting Position

Attach the strap to a stable structure such as a squat rack at approximately waist height. Place the strap around your waist, and make sure the strap is taut. Grip the strap with the free hand closest to the point of attachment. Lean away from the attachment and move your outside foot closer to the point of attachment to achieve approximately 45 degrees of body lean. To finish the setup, brace your core, squat down on the outside leg, and lower your torso (figure 7.7*a*).

Movement

Fully extend your stance leg in a slow and controlled manner from this lowered position, applying force in the medial direction (toward the point of attachment) throughout the movement. At the same time, your non-weight-bearing leg moves from an extended to a flexed hip position (figure 7.7b). To alter this exercise's difficulty, move your weight-bearing foot closer to the point of attachment to increase the intensity or away from the point of attachment to decrease the intensity.

Figure 7.7   Stationary skater crossover: *(a)* starting position and *(b)* movement.

Common Errors

The most common tendency is rushing this movement. Focus on getting as low as possible in the stride and performing the pattern with control.

Low Skater Crossover

Difficulty

Beginner to intermediate

Equipment

Long strap or heavy band, partner to provide resistance to the strap or band

Purpose

The purpose of the low skater crossover is the same as the stationary skater crossover; however, the addition of movement increases the demands on stability and coordination.

Starting Position

Use the same initial setup as the stationary skater crossover, only with a partner to provide resistance. Secure the strap around your waist, and make sure the strap is taut. Your partner holds the other end of the strap and provides resistance. Grip the strap with the free hand closest to your partner. Lean away from your partner, and move your outside foot closer to your partner to achieve approximately 45 degrees of body lean. To finish the setup, brace your core, squat down on the outside leg, and lower your torso (figure 7.8a).

Movement

Fully extend your stance leg in a slow and controlled manner from the lowered position, applying force in the medial direction (toward your partner) throughout the movement. At the same time, your non-weight-bearing leg moves from an extended to a flexed hip position, crosses over the stance leg, and finally, touches down on the ground, at which point weight is transferred to the lead leg (figure 7.8b). Reset to the initial starting position to perform the next repetition. To change the difficulty of this exercise, modify your range of motion. The partner has a lot of responsibility to move with the working athlete to maintain appropriate resistance. This technique might take some practice.

Figure 7.8   Low skater crossover: *(a)* starting position and *(b)* crossover.

Common Errors

The most common tendency is rushing this movement, which can create slack in the strap, causing it to be unstable. Focus on getting as low as possible in the stride and performing the pattern with control.

Resisted Explosive Crossover

Difficulty

Intermediate to advanced

Equipment

Heavy band, partner to provide resistance to the band

Purpose

While applying the same mechanics as the stationary skater crossover and low skater crossover, the resisted explosive crossover adds more rapid force production.

Starting Position

Assume the same starting position as the low skater crossover. Secure the strap around your waist, and make sure the strap is taut. Your partner holds the other end of the strap and provides resistance. Grip the strap with the free hand closest to your partner. Lean away from your partner, and move your outside foot closer to your part-

Figure 7.9 Resisted explosive crossover: *(a)* starting position and *(b)* crossover bound.

ner to achieve approximately 45 degrees of body lean. To finish the setup, brace your core, squat down on the outside leg, and lower your torso (figure 7.9a).

Movement

The movement is the same as the low skater crossover; however, push off as rapidly as possible, performing a crossover bound (figure 7.9b).

Common Errors

The most common error in this movement is not starting from a low position. Most athletes assume the path of least resistance and start from a high stance; however, the goal is to maximize impulse. Therefore, assume the lowest starting stance that you can safely attain.

Progressions and Variations

Continuous Resisted Explosive Crossover

Rather than resetting after each repetition, perform this pattern continuously with a rapid transition between repetitions.

Crossover to Base

Difficulty

Beginner, intermediate, advanced

Equipment

None

Purpose

The primary purpose of the crossover to base is to train crossover stride mechanics with an emphasis on full hip, knee, and ankle extension of the crossunder leg while applying force throughout the entire motion. The secondary purpose of this exercise is to begin to develop the capacity to change directions from the base position.

Starting Position

Set up in an athletic stance with your feet approximately shoulder-width apart.

Movement

Simultaneously bring your outside knee up and over the inside leg while the inside leg extends (figure 7.10a). For example, if you intend to move to your left, punch your right knee over the left leg while the left leg extends to create a powerful push. Immediately following the crossover push, assume the initial athletic position as quickly as possible (figure 7.10b).

Figure 7.10   Crossover to base: *(a)* crossover and *(b)* base athletic position.

Progressions and Variations

Crossover to Base and Return

Perform the same movement as the crossover to base; however, as soon as you reach the base position, immediately reverse the motion and return to the initial position as quickly as possible. Be sure that your shin and body angles are pointing in the direction you intend to travel during the transition between directions.

Corner Skate Jump

Difficulty

Intermediate to advanced

Equipment

None

Purpose

The purpose of the corner skate jump is to train crossunder mechanics and power development.

Starting Position

Begin in a low athletic position, and extend your right leg laterally as far as possible (figure 7.11*a*). Your left leg should bear most of your weight.

Movement

From the extended position, drive into the ground with your left leg, and simultaneously bring your right knee toward the middle and up into a flexed hip position. Drive into the ground with enough force to perform a low-level jump (figure 7.11*b*).

Figure 7.11   Corner skate jump: *(a)* starting position and *(b)* jump.

Upon landing, immediately return to the starting position. Perform this movement for the prescribed number of repetitions on both legs.

Half-Kneeling Crossover Acceleration

Difficulty

Intermediate to advanced

Equipment

None

Purpose

This exercise integrates both the crossover and linear acceleration. The main focus is on force application throughout the push of the crossunder leg.

Starting Position

Assume a half-kneeling position. If you are moving to your right, your left knee is on the ground and vice versa. Brace your core and shift your body weight forward and slightly in the direction of travel to load your front foot (figure 7.12*a*).

Figure 7.12 Half-kneeling crossover acceleration: *(a)* starting position and *(b)* crossover.

Movement

Extend your inside leg as rapidly as possible while lifting your knee off the ground. Swing your outside leg over your push leg, and rotate your hips and torso in the direction of travel (figure 7.12*b*). At ground contact of your crossover leg, be sure to have a positive shin angle to efficiently apply force in the direction you are moving. Then accelerate linearly for approximately 33 feet (10 m).

Common Errors

One of the most common faults with this exercise is the upper body lagging at takeoff. Be sure to maintain core stability so your body moves in sequence.

Linear Wall Drill, Single Exchange

Difficulty

Beginner

Equipment

A wall or stable structure to support your body weight, miniband

Purpose

During linear acceleration, leg action in front of the body is of primary importance. The athlete must drive their knee up in front of their body, and ground contacts typically occur behind the body because there is significant forward lean. This exercise helps the athlete maintain lumbo-pelvic control while leaning forward on one leg.

Starting Position

Stand with your feet shoulder-width apart, approximately 3 to 5 feet (1.0-1.5 m) away from the wall, depending on your height. Hold your arms directly in front of your body at shoulder height. While maintaining a straight line from your heels to shoulders, lean forward until your hands contact the wall. At this point, your body should form a 45-degree angle to the wall, and your heels should be slightly elevated off the ground. Engage your glute and core musculature, raise one knee so your hip flexes at approximately 90 degrees, and pull your toes toward your shin. The shin of your front leg should be parallel to your body.

Movement

While maintaining a stable torso and upper body, exchange your legs, bringing the stance leg up and front leg down and back as quickly as possible (figure 7.13). Contact the ground with the ball of your foot. The goal of this exercise is to maintain posture while rapidly exchanging your legs.

Common Errors

One common error with this exercise is bouncing off the back foot before the exchange. Focus on not moving your upper body and head during this exercise.

Figure 7.13   Linear wall drill, single exchange.

Progressions and Variations

Deliberate Wall Drill

If you cannot perform the linear wall drills while maintaining posture, regress it to simply hold the wall position with one knee up for approximately 5 seconds, then slowly switch legs and hold the opposite side. Continue this drill for the prescribed number of repetitions.

Double-Exchange Wall Drill

Once you have mastered the single exchange, perform a double exchange. This action is done by completing two rapid exchanges in succession so that you end on the same starting leg.

Continuous Wall Drill

Continuously perform this exercise for a prescribed number of repetitions or amount of time.

Figure 7.14   Linear wall drill, single exchange with miniband.

Linear Wall Drill, Single Exchange With Miniband

This exercise is performed the same way as the linear wall drills, single exchange; however, resistance is applied by placing a miniband around the balls of your feet (figure 7.14).

Low Skater Walk

Difficulty

Beginner to intermediate

Equipment

None

Purpose

The low skater walk builds a tolerance to moving and maintaining a low body position while tired, which is vital for skating because a low position (deep hip and knee flexion) is beneficial for skating efficiency.

Starting Position

Begin in a low athletic position.

Movement

Figure 7.15   Low skater walk.

Start the movement by stepping forward (figure 7.15), slightly tapping your back knee to the ground. Your body should remain low for the duration of the exercise, never rising to a standing position. Continuously repeat this movement.

Walking Acceleration Lunge

Difficulty

Beginner

Equipment

None

Purpose

The walking acceleration lunge trains the simultaneous action of hip extension and flexion with optimal body positioning. The secondary purpose of this exercise is to build lower-body strength.

Starting Position

Stand with feet shoulder-width apart.

Movement

Step forward with your right leg into a lunge position (figure 7.16a), with your right shin assuming a positive angle. Drive your right foot into the ground, stand up by fully extending your right hip, and simultaneously swing your leg through into full hip flexion (figure 7.16b). Hold this position for 1 second before stepping forward with your left leg. Perform this alternating pattern for the prescribed distance or number of repetitions.

Figure 7.16 Walking acceleration lunge: (a) lunge position with right leg and (b) swing left leg through.

Resisted March

Difficulty

Beginner to intermediate

Equipment

Thick band, partner to hold the band

Purpose

The resisted march is a progression from the wall drills and increases the coordination and stability demands. The resistance serves two purposes: it allows the athlete to achieve the forward lean posture without high-velocity movement, and the resistance provides the opportunity to apply more force throughout the entire range of motion.

Starting Position

Stand with your feet approximately shoulder-width apart, and place the band around your waist. Your partner holds the opposite end of the band and makes it taut. Brace your core, and begin to lean in the forward direction at approximately a 45-degree angle with your partner holding your weight.

Movement

March in the forward direction. This movement is a piston action; drive the knee up and back down slightly behind your hips with coordinated arm movement (figure 7.17). Contact the ground on the ball of your foot. Maintain a neutral (straight) spine throughout the movement.

Figure 7.17   Resisted march.

Resisted High-Knee Run

Difficulty

Intermediate to advanced

Equipment

Thick band, partner to hold the band

Purpose

The resisted high-knee run is a progression to the resisted march and increases the coordination demands by adding velocity to the movement.

Starting Position

Assume the same starting position as the resisted march. Stand with your feet approximately shoulder-width apart, and place the band around your waist. Your partner holds the opposite end of the band and makes it taut. Brace your core, and begin to lean in the forward direction at approximately a 45-degree angle with your partner holding your weight.

Movement

The movement pattern is the same as the resisted march; however, the leg exchanges and movement in the forward direction are much more rapid (figure 7.18). The legs should move in a piston-like action, up and down, during the acceleration phase, with foot contacts slightly behind your hips and with a positive shin angle. Avoid the tendency to turn this movement into a top-end speed run where you are in a more upright

Figure 7.18 Resisted high-knee run.

position and making ground contact with a vertical shin. Be sure to maximize your push and, as a result, maximize the impulse generated.

Falling Acceleration

Difficulty

Beginner, intermediate, advanced

Equipment

None

Purpose

The angle of the body relative to the ground is an important consideration when training acceleration. Falling accelerations help train and reinforce optimal body angle during the run.

Starting Position

Stand tall with your feet approximately shoulder-width apart (figure 7.19a).

Movement

While maintaining a straight line from your shoulders to heels, begin to lean forward, essentially falling to the ground (figure 7.19b). When you feel as though you cannot fall any farther, begin to accelerate as fast as possible forward (figure 7.19c).

Figure 7.19 Falling acceleration: (a) starting position, (b) lean forward, and (c) accelerate forward.

Progressions and Variations

Figure 7.20 Base position.

Falling Acceleration to Base

This drill is identical to the falling acceleration; however, when you reach the prescribed distance, decelerate as quickly as possible and stop in a half-squat base position (figure 7.20).

Get-Up Acceleration

Difficulty

Intermediate to advanced

Equipment

None

Purpose

The get-up acceleration is an excellent exercise where you start from a low position that emphasizes proper body and shin angles due to the starting position.

Starting Position

Assume the push-up position on the ground (figure 7.21a).

Movement

At the onset of the exercise, push up and drive one knee forward while pushing off the ground with the opposite foot (figure 7.21b). Your body should assume an angle of approximately 45 degrees from the ground. While driving one knee forward, simultaneously swing your opposite arm, with 90 degrees of elbow flexion, in the same direction and the other arm backward (figure 7.21c). Once your lead hip and knee both reach 90 degrees of flexion, immediately reverse their motion, and drive them back and down toward the ground. At ground contact, perform the same action on the opposite side. Keep your core engaged and chin tucked so your head is facing the ground. Accelerate 16 to 33 feet (5-10 m), maintaining your forward body lean.

Common Errors

The most common error observed in hockey players while performing this exercise is not attaining a full range of motion on the front side,

Figure 7.21 Get-up acceleration: *(a)* starting position, *(b)* drive knee forward, and *(c)* swing arms.

meaning that 90 degrees of hip and knee flexion are not achieved. Focus on driving the knee up and forward. The goal is to maintain a forward lean throughout the exercise. Avoid prematurely assuming an upright position.

On-Ice Acceleration Exercises

Although this book's focus is off-ice training for hockey, many performance qualities must also be trained on the ice. However, this is not a power skating book, and technical elements regarding the skating stride and edge work cannot be covered here in detail. Having said that, here are several on-ice acceleration exercises following the same pattern of progression as the off-ice acceleration exercises.

Linear Board Stride

Difficulty

Beginner

Equipment

None

Purpose

The linear board stride trains basic acceleration mechanics in a stationary and controlled environment.

Starting Position

Facing the boards, assume the low hockey stance position with your hands on the boards. Your feet should be approximately 1 to 2 feet (0.3-0.6 m) away from the boards.

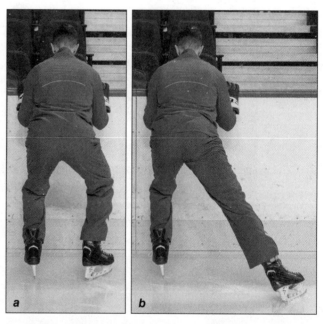

Figure 7.22   Linear board stride: *(a)* push for acceleration and *(b)* shave the ice.

Movement

If you are striding with your right leg, load your left leg with the toes pointing forward. Turn your right foot on a 45-degree angle because this is the angle of the push for acceleration (figure 7.22*a*). Then extend your right leg back at a 45-degree angle, shaving the ice (figure 7.22*b*). Be sure to extend your hip and knee fully while maintaining the load on your left leg and avoiding weight transfer to the right. As competency improves, increase the intensity and velocity of the push. During full-speed acceleration, as the velocity of movement increases, so does the angle of push.

Gliding Stride Mechanics With Heel Drag

Difficulty

Beginner

Equipment

None

Purpose

This exercise transitions from the stationary linear board stride to moving. This transition is done by performing a similar action moving in the forward direction. The heel drag is unorthodox but increases glute and quad activation and teaches the feeling of pushing maximally through these muscle groups.

Starting Position

Assume the low hockey stance position (figure 7.23a).

Movement

If you are striding with your right leg, load your left leg with the toes pointing forward. Turn your right foot on a 45-degree angle because this is the angle of the push for acceleration (figure 7.23b). Then extend your right leg back at a 45-degree angle to begin gliding on your left leg (figure 7.23c). Extend your hip and knee fully while maintaining the load on your left leg and avoiding weight transfer to the right. At this point, lift your right toe and lightly drag the heel for glute and quad activation (figure 7.23d). Focus on staying low, and alternate legs slowly as you glide down the ice.

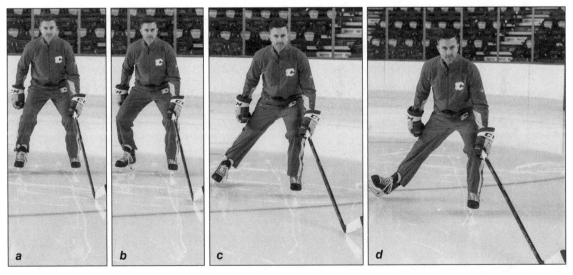

Figure 7.23 Gliding stride mechanics with heel drag: (a) starting position in low hockey stance, (b) right foot turns to a 45-degree angle, (c) right leg extends back at a 45-degree angle and glide begins, and (d) lift right toe and light heel drag.

Progressions and Variations

Gliding Stride Mechanics With Toe Drag

This exercise can be progressed to a toe drag instead of heel drag to mimic the actual full acceleration stride.

Gliding Stride Mechanics With Heel Drag at Full Speed

Increase the velocity of this pattern as competency improves until you are performing a full-speed acceleration.

V-Start Net Push

Difficulty

Intermediate

Equipment

Net

Purpose

The purpose of the V-start net push is to train acceleration with an external load to increase impulse.

Starting Position

Stand in front of the net with your hands on the crossbar. Assume a low hockey stance position as you lean forward into the net. Place both feet at 45-degree angles with your heels off the ice (figure 7.24a).

Movement

Explode forward. Focus on rapid stride turnover for the first three or four strides, pushing off the inside edge on the ball of your foot (figure 7.24b). Do not sacrifice your stride length at the expense of the stride rate. Focus on front side mechanics as well, bringing your knees up high to maximize drive and power (figure 7.24c). As your velocity increases, more of your skate blade will contact the ice and stride will lengthen.

Figure 7.24　V-start net push: *(a)* starting position, *(b)* push off, and *(c)* front side mechanics.

Flying Acceleration

Difficulty

Intermediate

Equipment

None

Purpose

During a game, you will rarely accelerate from a stationary position. This exercise trains accelerating while your body is already in motion.

Starting Position

Assume the low hockey stance position (figure 7.25a).

Movement

Commence movement by taking two or three strides, following the principles of the gliding stride mechanics exercise (with toe-off). Once your body is in motion, explode forward, focusing on rapid stride turnover for the first three or four strides, pushing off the inside edge on the ball of your foot (figure 7.25b).

Figure 7.25   Flying acceleration: (a) starting position and (b) push off inside edge.

Crossover Acceleration

Difficulty

Intermediate

Equipment

None

Purpose

During a change of direction in hockey, the most common start technique is a crossover start. This exercise trains acceleration from a crossover start.

Figure 7.26   Crossover acceleration: *(a)* lead skate on outside edge, rear skate on inside edge; and *(b)* crossover.

Starting Position

Assume the low hockey stance position, and point your stick in the direction of travel. Begin to lean in the direction in which you intend to travel. Your lead skate is on the outside edge while the rear skate is on the inside edge (figure 7.26*a*).

Movement

Begin the movement by punching your rear knee over top of the lead leg while simultaneously driving off the skate's outside edge in contact with the ice. Rotate your hips and body in the direction of travel (figure 7.26*b*). Once your body is in motion, focus on rapid stride turnover for the first three or four strides, pushing off the inside edge on the ball of your foot.

Backward Crossover Start

Difficulty

Intermediate

Equipment

None

Purpose

The backward crossover is the most effective technique for accelerating backward. Defense positions in particular should practice this starting technique.

Starting Position

Assume the low hockey stance position with your feet and body pointed toward the boards (figure 7.27a).

Movement

If you intend to travel to the left, perform a powerful C-cut on the inside edge of your skate with your right leg, finishing on the ball of your foot (figure 7.27b). At this point, the right leg crosses over the left (figure 7.27c). The left leg then performs a powerful outside edge kick (figure 7.27d). You will then be in a backward stride position from which you can continue to perform crossovers or C-cuts to build speed.

Figure 7.27 Backward crossover start: (a) starting position, (b) C-cut with right leg, (c) right leg crosses over left, and (d) left leg performs a powerful outside edge kick.

SUMMARY

In hockey, top-end speed or maximum velocity is rarely achieved due to the stop-and-start nature of the game. Accelerations, such as racing to a loose puck or breaking away from an opponent, typically occur over short distances. This chapter outlined many factors that influence the athlete's ability to accelerate, including the ability to produce force rapidly and the mechanics of movement. For youth and beginning hockey players, simply increasing force production improves acceleration. As with most training concepts, mechanics should be taught stepwise, starting from slow and controlled and progressing to fast and complex. Remember, slow is smooth, and smooth is fast.

Chapter 8

Change of Direction and Reactivity

The previous chapter focused on the ability to accelerate. It is important to keep in mind that in an invasion sport such as hockey, acceleration paints only a portion of the picture. The ability to change directions builds on the concept of acceleration. Change-of-direction speed is the ability to decelerate, followed by altering or changing direction and accelerating once again. When reactivity components are added, that is, when the athlete must react to a stimulus, the complexity of the change-of-direction equation increases. This reactivity component combined with a change of direction is referred to as *agility*. In hockey, change-of-direction speed and agility are essential in all areas of the game. Regardless of position, several qualities affect the change of direction and agility that all players must perform with proficiency.

QUALITIES AFFECTING CHANGE-OF-DIRECTION SPEED AND AGILITY

Several factors influence change-of-direction speed and agility. These factors include physical, biomechanical, and perceptual and cognitive qualities.

Physical Qualities

The purpose of change-of-direction (COD) or agility exercises is to quickly change the body's momentum to a new direction. Paul, Gabbett, and Nassis (2016) suggested that physical qualities represent the most significant determining factors of total time to complete an agility test. Although the ability to react to a stimulus, such as an opposing player, is essential, if the athlete does not possess the appropriate physical capabilities to perform the task, the cognitive abilities can never be realized.

Many scientific studies have highlighted the relationship between muscular strength and the ability to change direction. One such study demonstrated strong correlations between maximal dynamic strength; eccentric, concentric, and isometric strength; and COD performance (Spiteri et al. 2014). However, this same study noted that these factors did not influence agility performance when a cognitive or reactive component was present.

Since changing directions involves all three phases of muscle action (eccentric, isometric, and concentric), it has been demonstrated that improving these qualities alone will have a significant impact on the ability to redirect the momentum of the body in an organized manner. Spiteri et al. (2014) also highlighted the importance of braking capacity (eccentric strength) and suggested that eccentric strength is the main predictor of performance for COD tasks when the intensity and the total number of direction changes increases. Chapter 5 outlines in detail various strength training techniques that directly affect the COD ability.

On the other hand, training to improve power has also been shown to enhance COD performance. For example, Váczi et al. (2013) demonstrated slight but significant COD ability improvements resulting from a six-week plyometric training program. There is conflicting evidence regarding power training and COD performance, however. Tricoli et al. (2005) demonstrated that power training protocols such as weightlifting and vertical jump training improved vertical jump and sprinting performance but not COD performance. These authors suggested that power transfer to more complex agility tasks is difficult and could be influenced to a greater degree by motor control factors such as technique.

Biomechanical Qualities

Like all dynamic sporting movements, COD and agility performance are governed by the athlete's technical skills. The strength and power developed in the gym must be transferred effectively and efficiently to complex sporting movements to optimize the performance of these tasks. The gym setting is typically a more controlled environment with clearly defined actions; therefore, it is also imperative to train the sporting task's technical skills. These technical skills must first be identified then progressively trained by increasing speed, complexity, and reactivity.

Coaches and practitioners should not begin training at the endpoint. Far too often, reactive agility training is the starting point when athletes do not possess the ability to perform simple tasks such as decelerating from a linear acceleration. These skills need to be broken down, beginning with slow and simple and progressing appropriately to fast and reactive. The end goal is fluid and efficient movement in the face of external stimuli.

Perceptual and Cognitive Qualities

Perceptual and cognitive qualities come into question when reactivity and decision-making are added to a task or during a game or practice. The majority of the scientific literature on strength and power training and its effects on COD and agility focuses primarily on predetermined skills. The literature that does examine agility often demonstrates that strength and power training have negligible performance benefits. This fact is due to the perceptual, cognitive, and decision-making skills necessary to react to a specific stimulus and optimize agility. Coaches often attempt to train reaction time; however, real-time agility during a game is far more complex. Data suggest that the most agile athletes in a game or competition exhibit more accurate and faster responses due to their capacity to anticipate what will happen (Roca et al. 2011). This anticipation comes by recognizing the opponent's postural orientation, recognizing structure and patterns in game situations, and correctly predicting what the opponent is going to do. Roca et al. (2011) also studied the visual patterns between skilled and less skilled soccer players and found that the skilled players' visual searching during play was more abundant and shorter. The skilled soccer players also alternated their visual fixation more frequently between the player in possession of the ball, the ball itself, and other game play areas. These data highlight the importance of information gathering and processing on agility performance.

CLOSED VERSUS OPEN SKILLS

When examining various sports and training exercises, the constraints and environment must be considered. McMorris (2014) outlines two categories of skill classification: closed and open skills. Closed skills are completed in the same or similar environment using the same technique every time, such as hitting a golf ball. In contrast, open skills require greater information processing, are completed in constantly changing environments, and are rarely repeated. Based on these definitions, hockey is an open-skill sport in which the environment is ever-changing and the information-processing demands on the player are significantly increased.

When viewed through the lens of the two categories listed above, closed-skill training includes predetermined drills in a set environment and attempts to improve the athlete's COD speed. On the other hand, open-skill training includes drills that are unpredictable with environmental changes that the athlete must read and respond to appropriately. Rather than jumping straight into open-skill training drills with our athletes, we must progress from mastering closed skills, focusing on technique and mechanics, before advancing to open skills, such as agility training, using the continuum in figure 8.1.

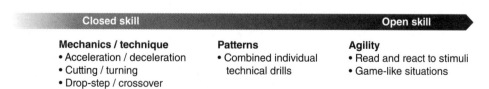

Closed skill		Open skill
Mechanics / technique • Acceleration / deceleration • Cutting / turning • Drop-step / crossover	**Patterns** • Combined individual technical drills	**Agility** • Read and react to stimuli • Game-like situations

Figure 8.1 Change of direction and agility continuum.

CHANGE-OF-DIRECTION AND AGILITY TRAINING FOR YOUTH

Training COD and agility in youth hockey players follows similar trends to that of strength and acceleration training. Early improvements in COD speed before puberty mainly result from central nervous system development and improved motor control. Progress during and after puberty is likely facilitated by hormonal influences on force production and muscle morphology (Lloyd et al. 2013). Lloyd et al. (2013) outlined three agility training elements: fundamental movement skills (emphasizing core and lower-limb joint stability), COD speed (closed skills), and reactive agility training (open skills). The percentage of time spent on these elements in each stage of development is outlined in table 8.1.

Table 8.1 Percentage of Time Allocated to the Three Agility Training Elements of Fundamental Movement Skills, Change of Direction Speed, and Reactive Agility Training

Stage of development	Movement skills	Change of direction (closed skills)	Reactive agility (open skills)
Before puberty	60%	25%	15%
During puberty	30%	40%	30%
After puberty	20%	20%	60%

CLOSED-SKILL CHANGE-OF-DIRECTION SPEED EXERCISES

COD speed exercises are performed in a closed (nonchanging) environment where the task is predetermined from start to finish. The perceptual–cognitive demand during these drills is negligible, and the athlete's primary focus is performing the drill as quickly and efficiently as possible. COD speed exercises are typically implemented linearly and gradually progressed to various COD patterns both off and on the ice. Mastery of these exercises is vital in the overall development of agility in a game scenario.

Acceleration to Base

Difficulty

Beginner

Equipment

Cones

Purpose

The ability to decelerate with postural control and organization is an essential characteristic of COD speed. Hockey players must be able to decelerate before they can master COD.

Starting Position

Set two cones 33 to 49 feet (10-15 m) apart on the floor. Assume a staggered-stance athletic position at the first cone.

Movement

Begin by linearly accelerating as rapidly as possible to the second cone 33 to 49 feet (10-15 m) away. As you approach the cone, begin to decelerate, stopping in an athletic half-squat or athletic position at the cone with your feet parallel and your hips back.

Progressions and Variations

Acceleration to Staggered Base

As you progress in skill, begin to decelerate and stop in a staggered athletic stance with your hips down and back.

Acceleration to Base and Return

Perform the exercise in the same manner as the acceleration to base; however, instead of stopping at the cone, immediately reverse your movement and backpedal to the first cone.

Continuous Acceleration to Base and Return

Continuously perform the second progression, acceleration to base and return. Upon return to the initial cone, immediately reverse your motion and accelerate back to the second cone. Repeat for the prescribed number of repetitions.

On-Ice Acceleration to Base

These drills can also be performed on the ice. The only difference in the base position is a two-foot stop in either direction. Alternate between stopping directions.

Acceleration and Deceleration 90 Runs

Difficulty

Beginner to intermediate

Equipment

Cones

Purpose

The acceleration and deceleration 90 runs exercise incorporates acceleration and deceleration techniques while adding a 90-degree crossover transition. The COD is controlled to focus on technique.

Starting Position

Set four cones up in a square on the floor with 33 feet (10 m) between them. Assume a staggered-stance athletic position at one of the cones.

Movement

Begin by linearly accelerating as rapidly as possible to the first cone. As you approach the cone, begin to decelerate, stopping in an athletic half-squat position at the cone with your feet parallel and your hips back. Immediately cross over, transitioning your body 90 degrees, and accelerate to the next cone. Complete this pattern until you reach all four cones. As your competency improves, increase the velocity of your crossover transition.

Progressions and Variations

On-Ice Acceleration and Deceleration 90 Runs

This exercise can also be performed on the ice. The only difference is that the base position is a two-foot stop facing the direction in which you intend to travel (figure 8.2), removing the requirement of a crossover acceleration to the next cone.

Figure 8.2 On-ice acceleration and deceleration 90 runs two-foot stop.

Acceleration to 45-Degree Cut

Difficulty

Intermediate

Equipment

Cones

Purpose

Performing controlled cutting exercises trains high-velocity COD movements that are important in hockey to evade or defend against the opposition.

Starting Position

Set four cones on the floor in a Y shape with 33 to 49 feet (10-15 m) between them. Assume a staggered-stance athletic position at the cone at the bottom of the Y.

Movement

Begin by linearly accelerating as rapidly as possible to the first cone Y. At the cone, cut and change directions, and accelerate to the cone on the left or right. To initiate the cut, place your cutting foot (right foot if cutting to the left and vice versa) outside the center of body mass. Your shin and body angles are pointing in the direction of travel. Drive off the cutting leg, and accelerate to the final cone. Perform this exercise with postural control, with your torso and hips moving together.

Progressions and Variations

On-Ice Acceleration to 45-Degree Cut

This exercise can also be performed on the ice.

Lateral Shuffle to Linear Acceleration

Difficulty

Intermediate

Equipment

Cones

Purpose

The lateral shuffle to linear acceleration exercise trains the transition from lateral to linear movement.

Starting Position

Place three cones on the floor in an L shape with 33 feet (10 m) between them. Stand in an athletic half-squat position facing the direction of the linear movement.

Movement

In a rapid but controlled manner, shuffle laterally to the second cone. At the cone, change directions by transitioning from the lateral shuffle to linear acceleration. To initiate the direction change, place your lead foot slightly outside the center of body mass. Your shin and body angle transition to the forward acceleration techniques described in chapter 7. As you approach the final cone, begin to decelerate, stopping in an athletic half-squat position at the cone with your feet parallel and your hips back.

Progressions and Variations

Lateral Shuffle to Linear Acceleration to Drop-Step

On reaching the final cone, drop-step (open) to the inside, rotating your body 180 degrees. Then accelerate back to the second cone, transitioning to the lateral shuffle to the first cone.

Goalie Butterfly to Lateral Shuffle

Difficulty

Intermediate

Equipment

Cones

Purpose

This goalie-specific exercise focuses on the transition from the butterfly kneeling position to a lateral shuffle.

Starting Position

Place two cones on the floor approximately 16 feet (5 m) apart. Assume the butterfly kneeling position at the first cone (figure 8.3a).

Movement

Begin the exercise by quickly assuming your standing position from the floor (figure 8.3b). In a rapid but controlled manner, shuffle laterally to the second cone (figure 8.3c). At the second cone, assume the butterfly position once again, and repeat the exercise in the opposite direction.

Figure 8.3 Goalie butterfly to lateral shuffle: *(a)* starting position, *(b)* standing position, and *(c)* shuffle.

Progressions and Variations

Goalie Butterfly to Lateral Shuffle and Return

Perform the exercise in the same fashion; however, immediately reverse your shuffle back to the first cone once you reach the second. When you reach the cone, assume the butterfly position on the ground.

Repetitive Goalie Butterfly to Standing With Lateral Shuffle

In this progression, go from the butterfly position to standing position one to three times before performing the lateral shuffle.

On-Ice Goalie Butterfly to Lateral Shuffle

These exercises can also be performed on the ice.

OPEN-SKILL AGILITY EXERCISES

During closed-skill exercises, all aspects are predetermined from start to finish, making the perceptual–cognitive demand negligible. In contrast, open-skill agility exercises are performed in a random or unpredictable environment, introducing significant perceptual–cognitive challenges. These challenges act to reinforce a game-like reaction to an unexpected stimulus.

Read and React 45-Degree Cut

Difficulty

Intermediate

Equipment

Cones, partner for visual or verbal cues

Purpose

Performing cutting exercises in which the direction of cut is unknown at the onset of the exercise trains high-velocity COD movements where the athlete must react to a stimulus. This type of exercise is vital in hockey to evade or defend against an unpredictable opposing player.

Starting Position

Set four cones on the floor in a Y shape with 33 to 49 feet (10-15 m) space between them. Assume a staggered-stance athletic position at the cone at the bottom of the Y. Your partner stands at the second cone, facing you.

Movement

Begin by linearly accelerating as rapidly as possible to the second cone. As you approach the second cone, your partner points to the right or left or says the words "right" or "left." React to this stimulus by cutting in the cue's direction, and accelerate to that cone. The cutting procedure is the same as acceleration to 45-degree cut. Perform this exercise with postural control, with your torso and hips moving together.

Common Errors

Due to the uncertainty of direction change, athletes often lose focus on the technique of the movement. It is imperative to maintain body posture and technique during these exercises.

Progressions and Variations

On-Ice Read and React 45-Degree Cut

This exercise can also be performed on the ice.

Four-Cone Drill With Visual Cues

Difficulty

Intermediate to advanced

Equipment

Cones, partner for visual cues

Purpose

The four-cone drill with visual cues trains agility in multiple directions under the guidance of external stimuli to mimic game-like scenarios.

Starting Position

Set four cones on the floor in a square with 16 to 33 feet (5-10 m) between them. Stand directly in the middle of all four cones in an athletic half-squat position, facing your partner.

Movement

Your partner points to one cone, at which point you will immediately accelerate to that cone, touch it, and rapidly move back to the center of the square. When you return to the center, your partner points to another cone, and the process is continued. Perform this drill for the prescribed number of repetitions or amount of time.

Progressions and Variations

Four-Cone Partner Mirror Drill

This exercise can be progressed to mirroring another athlete. Simply create a second square by adding two more cones. Both athletes stand in the center of their respective squares. The leading athlete moves as rapidly as possible to a cone of their choice, with the reacting athlete attempting to mirror them with as little gap as possible.

On-Ice Four-Cone Drill With Visual Cues

These exercises can also be performed on the ice.

Partner Mirroring

Difficulty

Intermediate to advanced

Equipment

Partner to mirror

Purpose

Partner mirroring trains agility in multiple directions under the guidance of external stimuli to mimic game-like scenarios. This exercise can be performed either by lateral shuffling or linear movement (forward and backward).

Starting Position

For the lateral shuffle partner mirror, stand on the floor facing each other in an athletic half-squat position. For the linear partner mirror, stand side by side with your partner, facing the same direction.

Movement

One partner leads, and the other attempts to mirror them step by step. The lead partner decides which direction to travel and when to change directions. The leading athlete moves as rapidly as possible in their direction of choice, with the reacting athlete attempting to mirror them with as little gap as possible.

Progressions and Variations

On-Ice Partner Mirroring

This exercise can also be performed on the ice.

Goalie Butterfly to Lateral Shuffle With Ball Toss

Difficulty

Intermediate to advanced

Equipment

Cones, tennis ball, partner

Purpose

This goalie-specific exercise focuses on the transition from the butterfly kneeling position to a lateral shuffle with a ball toss. The goalie must react and catch the ball while performing the exercise.

Starting Position

The starting position is the same as the goalie butterfly to lateral shuffle. Place two cones on the floor approximately 16 feet (5 m) apart. Assume the butterfly kneeling position at the first cone (figure 8.4a).

Movement

This exercise is performed in the same fashion as the goalie butterfly to lateral shuffle. Begin the exercise by quickly assuming a standing position from the floor (figure 8.4*b*). In a rapid but controlled manner, shuffle laterally to the second cone (figure 8.4*c*). At any point throughout the drill, your partner randomly tosses a tennis ball to you. Catch the ball (figure 8.4*d*). At the second cone,

Figure 8.4 Goalie butterfly to lateral shuffle with ball toss: *(a)* starting position, *(b)* standing position, *(c)* lateral shuffle, and *(d)* ball catch.

assume the butterfly position once again and repeat the exercise in the opposite direction.

Progressions

Goalie Butterfly to Lateral Shuffle and Return With Ball Toss

Perform the exercise in the same fashion; however, immediately reverse your shuffle back to the first cone once you reach the second. Your partner randomly tosses the ball to you at any point during the drill. Catch the ball. When you reach the cone, assume the butterfly position on the ground.

Repetitive Goalie Butterfly to Standing With Lateral Shuffle and Ball Toss

In this progression, go from the butterfly position to standing position one to three times before performing the lateral shuffle. Your partner randomly tosses the ball to you during the drill. Catch the ball.

On-Ice Goalie Butterfly to Lateral Shuffle With Shot

These exercises can also be performed on the ice, but instead of a tennis ball, a puck can be used. Catch the puck with your glove and drop it when you reach the cone.

Goalie Read and React

Difficulty

Intermediate to advanced

Equipment

Tennis ball, wall against which to throw the ball, partner to throw the ball

Purpose

This exercise challenges the athlete's ability to read where the ball is coming from and react to that stimulus by moving laterally to catch it. This is a challenging exercise because the athlete does not know the ball's direction until it hits the wall.

Starting Position

Stand approximately 10 feet (3 m) away from a wall, facing the wall in an athletic half-squat position. Your partner sets up behind you with the tennis ball (figure 8.5*a*).

Movement

Your partner tosses the tennis ball off the wall in various directions. React to the trajectory of the ball and shuffle laterally to catch it (figure 8.5*b*).

Figure 8.5 Goalie read and react: *(a)* starting position and *(b)* shuffle laterally to catch the ball.

Small-Sided Games

Small-sided games involve fewer players than a regulation game playing on a smaller surface, often with modified rules. Young et al. (2013) outlined three characteristics of small-sided games that increase the agility demand and number of maneuvers players perform per game:

1. Increasing density or having more players in a given space

2. Reducing the total number of players in a game

3. Rule changes (e.g., reducing the number of passes allowed before shooting)

Small-sided games can be creatively crafted, and the possibilities are endless. However, rule changes must be thoughtful because not all rule changes result in an increased agility demand. Coaches must evaluate and potentially reimagine small-sided games depending on the outcomes.

PERCEPTUAL–COGNITIVE TRAINING

Once the physical foundation has been laid, evidence suggests that perceptual and cognitive factors separate the high- and low-skilled agility performers (Paul, Gabbett, and Nassis 2016). Certain training methods can be used to train perceptual and cognitive aspects of anticipation and tracking. Visual occlusion is one such method. It typically involves a video of an action, such as a slap shot, in which the video is edited into segments from which portions of the visual information are removed (Causer, Smeeton, and Williams 2017). This removal of visual information alters the availability of cues that influence the athlete's perception and judgments. This type of training has been shown to have some benefits in team sport athletes. For example, Nimmerichter et al. (2015) administered temporal occlusion training twice a week for six weeks and demonstrated improvements in decision-making time and reactive agility sprint time. An example for a hockey goalie is a video of an approaching player in the process of shooting the puck. At the point of or immediately before the release of the puck the video is blacked out. The blacking out of the video at puck release requires the goalie to make judgments about the trajectory of the puck based on visual cues from the shooting player prior to and during the shot. Performing this type of training regularly, approximately two to three times per week, might elicit improvements in visual information processing and anticipation skills. Position players can also benefit from this type of training.

SUMMARY

Invasion sports such as hockey rely almost entirely on agility rather than predictable COD speed due to the game's unpredictability. That said, athletes must possess the COD foundational elements such as motor control, muscular strength, movement mechanics, and technique to excel in agility tasks. As with training any aspect of performance, certain COD and agility skills must be mastered before progressing to more advanced techniques.

Chapter 9

Recovery and Reducing Injury Risk

Being a hockey player is a physically and mentally demanding task year-round. During the off-season, hockey players typically train 5 or 6 days per week, often with multiple sessions per day. Those demands are compounded during the season with the addition of games, travel, and other psychological stressors. As a result, fatigue is inevitable. This fatigue, however, is often critical to the physiological adaptations to training. Many adaptations occur in response to training but are accompanied by fatigue. The physiological adaptations are often not realized until a recovery period, where performance variables typically exceed the baseline measurements, known as supercompensation.

There is a fine line between fatigue and recovery, and this must be monitored and acted on using different strategies throughout the calendar year. These strategies vary depending on the goals of training. For example, the amount of acceptable fatigue present during the off-season is likely different from during the season. The primary concern during the season is being physically and mentally ready to perform in games and competition. According to Calder (2003), there are four types of training and competition fatigue:

1. Metabolic fatigue, which is characterized by depletion of energy stores and buildup of metabolites
2. Neural fatigue, which affects both the peripheral nervous system (localized force production) and central nervous system (drive and motivation)
3. Psychological fatigue, which is characterized by emotional and social stress factors
4. Environmental fatigue, which is characterized by climate and travel

It is essential to understand the types of fatigue and stress experienced by the athlete to reduce their negative impacts. This chapter discusses how to monitor fatigue levels, the role fatigue plays in injury risk, and recovery strategies to mitigate fatigue throughout the calendar year.

MONITORING FATIGUE

The type and nature of fatigue must be identified and monitored to prescribe the appropriate recovery modalities and protocols. Monitoring fatigue levels also provides insight into how the defined recovery strategies are influencing fatigue. Chapter 2 highlighted several monitoring strategies, including daily wellness and sleep questionnaires, heart rate variability, and performance monitoring. Following are two additional monitoring techniques that can be used to assess fatigue status.

Heart Rate Recovery

Heart rate recovery is the rate at which heart rate decreases after exercise. This measurement is usually taken about 1 minute after an activity is stopped. Like heart rate variability, heart rate recovery can provide insights into how the nervous system responds to exercise and training load. For example, Lamberts et al. (2010) demonstrated that a decrease in heart rate recovery is associated with attenuated improvement in endurance performance. This impaired improvement suggests that heart rate recovery can be used to predict an individual's ability to deal with the training load and associated fatigue. These same authors suggested measuring heart rate recovery after a standardized warm-up to optimize the training program that follows. Individual heart rate recovery values will vary; therefore, it is essential to regularly monitor how each individual responds to the training.

Joint Range of Motion

Regular assessment of joint range of motion can provide insight into fatigue and training status. Thorpe et al. (2017) highlighted that joint range of motion typically decreases for approximately 24 to 48 hours after a game. Chapter 3 discussed how a decreased joint range of motion might be a predictor of injury risk; therefore, regularly assessing joint range of motion provides feedback on the joints and muscles' structural status and how they are affected by fatigue. The techniques outlined in chapter 2 can help identify joint range of motion and mobility restrictions. The results can guide the recovery protocols and treatments in the period after activity.

FATIGUE AND INJURY

Preventing injury is a significant concern of all strength and conditioning practitioners. Therefore, one of the primary questions that needs to be analyzed is, Does fatigue increase the risk of injury? The body of research within hockey is limited; however, inferences can be drawn from the research available on other sports. Verschueren et al. (2020) conducted an extensive review of the scientific literature and found that acute fatigue does affect lower-extremity injury risk. They suggested that injury risk increases due to several factors, including decreases in muscular strength and alterations to proprioception and postural control. Verschueren et al. (2020) also highlighted that various forms of fatigue do not affect all individuals in the same way, and the fatigue mitigation approach must be individualized. The effects of fatigue on the individual cannot be overlooked, and there is no one-size-fits-all approach to recovery. The hockey players that I have worked with exist on a spectrum of fatigue tolerance. For example, some players seem to be less affected by the presence of fatigue than others, evident in the daily and weekly monitoring of performance, kinematic, and psychological variables. Ultimately, we might never know if our interventions have prevented an injury, but by examining the current body of evidence, it is safe to assume that minimizing fatigue through various recovery strategies will affect the injury risk profile of the athlete.

RECOVERY MODALITIES

A vast number of recovery modalities can be used to minimize fatigue. This section focuses primarily on modalities that are simple and accessible to all athletes. For any modality to be effective, the athlete must be able to perform the task with ease.

Sleep

Sleep is one of the most critical recovery strategies, because it plays a significant role in the muscle regeneration process. However, sleep is a recovery strategy that is often overlooked. Due to high-level hockey's competitive demands (e.g., late-night games and travel), sleep is often difficult to accomplish for many athletes. For example, a late-night hockey game might increase arousal and promote wakefulness in the hours after the match. Travel complicates the sleep equation further by decreasing mood, inducing acute fatigue, and causing difficulty sleeping at the arrival destination (Fullagar et al. 2015). It is known that sleep deprivation is linked to cognitive impairment and negatively affects metabolic and immune systems as well as restorative physiologic processes (Samuels 2009).

Three aspects that determine the beneficial impact of sleep include (Samuels 2009) the following:

1. *Total sleep time:* A dose-response relationship exists between sleep duration and cognitive function. Typically, between 7 and 10 hours is desirable.

2. *Sleep quality:* Even if an athlete achieves adequate total sleep time, sleep quality might not be optimal to be completely restorative. These athletes typically have higher arousal periods during sleep, causing sleep fragmentation (i.e., periods of light sleep and recurrent periods of wakefulness).

3. *Timing of sleep:* Every athlete has a different circadian rhythm, and this rhythm guides their appropriate sleep schedule. Typically, athletes are

either night owls or morning birds. The night owls prefer to go to bed and wake up later, and the morning birds prefer to go to bed and wake up earlier. Issues can arise when night owls wake up early for training, missing critical periods of restorative sleep.

Sleep hygiene is characterized by behavioral and environmental recommendations that are aimed to promote healthy and restful sleep. Irish et al. (2015) have outlined several sleep hygiene recommendations:

- Avoid consumption of stimulants such as caffeine and nicotine in the hours leading up to bedtime, because they increase arousal.
- Avoid alcohol consumption before bedtime due to its effects on one's ability to fall asleep and its predisposition to increase arousal during the second half of the night.
- Exercise regularly but not close to bedtime.
- Minimize stress before bedtime by engaging in relaxing activities, such as mindfulness meditation (described later in this chapter).
- Minimize the amount of noise in your sleeping environment.
- Attempt to go to bed within the same time frame every night. The ability to accomplish this might be diminished during the season with late game times.

In addition to these items, it has been demonstrated that mobile phone and tablet use in the hours leading to bedtime can disrupt sleep (Cabré-Riera et al. 2019). One of the primary concerns of screen time before bed is the effects of exposure to blue light emitted by the screen. Blue light exposure has been shown to alter sleep patterns because it suppresses melatonin, a hormone produced by the brain that helps promote healthy sleep. Not using a phone or tablet in the evening might be difficult, particularly with young players. Therefore, an acceptable workaround to eliminating screen time is to invest in blue light–blocking glasses. Burkhart and Phelps (2009) showed that using blue light–blocking glasses for three hours before sleep significantly improved sleep quality. Quality sleep of appropriate duration is one of the best tools in the recovery arsenal.

Nutrition and Hydration

Nutrition and hydration play a vital role in the recovery process. A well-balanced diet consisting of mainly whole, high-quality foods is essential to optimizing recovery and performance. Adequate nutrition increases the available nutrients required during competition and provides the nutrients to rebuild and remodel tissues that might have been affected by training and competition. The saying, "You cannot out-train a bad diet" means that training outcomes and adaptations rely on proper nutritional choices to be optimized. Outlined in this section are specific dietary factors and strategies to maximize recovery between training sessions and competitions.

Protein Consumption

Protein plays a vital role in many human physiological processes, and its consumption is essential around the training and competition window. Protein intake during this time has been shown to influence both performance and recovery positively. For example, Cintineo et al. (2018) highlighted that protein consumption immediately after resistance exercise aided in the recovery of muscle function, likely due to muscle protein remodeling and increases in muscle protein synthesis rates. It has been suggested that the timing of protein consumption is less critical than consuming adequate daily calories and protein (0.12 oz/lb/day [1.6 g/kg/day]) (Jäger et al. 2017). However, it is advisable to consume protein (approximately 0.07-.1 oz [20-40 g]) immediately before and after exercise or competition to aid in recovery. Athletes and active individuals should strive to consume about 0.1 ounces per pound per day (1.4-1.6 g/kg/day) of protein.

Carbohydrate Consumption

Replenishment of carbohydrates after exercise or competition is another crucial nutritional strategy that must be considered for hockey players. Carbohydrate is a primary fuel source for hockey players during moderate- to high-intensity games and practices because it is an easily accessible and rapid fuel source. Carbohydrate uptake into muscles and glycogen (the carbohydrate storage molecule) resynthesis is accelerated in the postexercise period (Williams 2004). This author also outlined that the amount of carbohydrate consumed immediately after exercise should be in the range of 0.08 to 0.12 ounces per pound (1.0-1.5 g/kg) of body weight. This amount should be consumed at 2-hour intervals following intense exercise or competition. Not all carbohydrates are created equally, though. The type of carbohydrate also influences the recovery process. Consuming high-glycemic-index foods, such as simple sugars, rice, or potatoes, might speed muscle glycogen resynthesis (Murray and Rosenbloom 2018).

Combined Protein and Carbohydrate Consumption

Due to the multifactorial nature of hockey training and competition, it is advised to consume a mixture of both protein and carbohydrates following intense activity. The addition of protein to carbohydrates will also aid in the rapid replenishment of muscle glycogen stores because of its effects on blood insulin levels; insulin is a hormone that affects carbohydrate uptake into the muscle (Murray and Rosenbloom 2018). Combining these ingredients into an easy-to-consume shake might be the most straightforward avenue to allow these nutrients to do their magic and aid in the recovery process.

Hydration and Electrolytes

Although hockey is a winter sport, many of the playing conditions result in significant sweat loss. Often, arenas filled with fans are warm, and the addition of protective equipment can simulate a hot and humid environment for the player. In these cases, when sweat loss is high, replenishment of fluid and electrolytes (salt) is an essential aspect of recovery, because dehydration can affect performance both physically and mentally. Maughan and Shirreffs (1997) suggested that ingesting a carbohydrate–electrolyte drink resulted in greater rehydration than drinking water alone, which does not address the salt lost in the sweat. Because rehydration is highly individual based on the amount of sweat lost, the simplest way to assess the amount of fluid and electrolyte to consume after activity is to measure body weight before and after training or competition and calculate the difference between the two body weights. The athlete should then consume approximately 120 percent of the volume equivalent of weight lost in an electrolyte drink; 1 pound (0.5 kg) of water weight lost is equivalent to 0.45 liters. For example, if one loses 2 pounds (the equivalent of 0.9 liters) of weight during practice, one should consume 1.1 liters (0.2 gal) of electrolyte fluid to rehydrate.

Active Recovery

The two general types of recovery are passive and active. Passive recovery or rest is usually in the form of inactivity or sleep. Active recovery is typically characterized by performing light aerobic activities such as jogging, walking, swimming, or other light recreational activities. Active recovery can be performed during and after training sessions and games as well as on off days. There is some conflicting evidence to using active recovery during high-intensity intermittent exercise. For example, Dorado, Sanchis-Moysi, and Calbet (2004) found that active recovery (cycling at 20% of $\dot{V}O_2$max) enhanced work capacity during high-intensity intermittent exercise. These authors suggested this was due to improved energy contribution from the aerobic system. In contrast, Ohya, Aramaki, and Kitagawa (2013) found that passive recovery (25 and 50 seconds of recovery) after 5-second maximal sprints was better than active recovery for subsequent power production. However, once the recovery duration reached 100 seconds, no difference was recorded between passive and active recovery. Therefore, when examining within-session recovery, the work-to-rest ratios and intensity of exercise must be considered to prescribe the appropriate recovery mode.

After training or games, active recovery might provide more benefit than passive recovery in removing metabolites within the muscle. Bastos et al. (2012) found that active recovery after high-intensity exercise was better at eliminating lactate than passive recovery. The greater removal of metabolites out of the muscle is due to increased blood flow to the active muscle, accelerating metabolite movement across the muscle fiber membrane (Bastos et al. 2012). Therefore, the addition of approximately 10 minutes of light aerobic activity (e.g., cycling, walking, or jogging) after on- and off-ice training and games provides additional recovery benefit as opposed to passive recovery alone. This light aerobic activity should be performed at the following heart rate: max heart rate – (50-65 beats).

Sport Massage and Self-Myofascial Release

Sport massage and self-myofascial release (SMR) are forms of mechanical manipulation of human tissue using rhythmical pressure with the goal of health promotion and recovery (Best et al. 2008). These authors conducted a review of several randomized controlled trials regarding the effects of massage on recovery. They found that massage could restore strength and power after fatigue, decrease the decline in cycling work output, increase mobility and flexibility, lessen delayed-onset muscle soreness, and reduce levels of markers of muscle damage (i.e., creatine kinase) (Best et al. 2008). Another review of the scientific literature highlighted that SMR helped restore range of motion and positively affected muscle soreness and fatigue (Schroeder and Best 2015). Chapter 3 outlined many SMR variations that can also be used for recovery purposes; refer to the section on inhibition of tight tissues.

Cold-Water Immersion and Cryotherapy

Cold-water immersion (CWI) and cryotherapy are common methods used by hockey players to enhance or accelerate recovery. CWI is typically characterized by water temperatures ranging from 5 to 20 degrees Celsius (41-68 degrees Fahrenheit) and immersion times ranging from 5 to 20 minutes in a single immersion or immersion intervals of 1 to 5 minutes with periods out of the water of 1 to 2.5 minutes (Versey, Halson, and Dawson 2013). Pournot et al. (2011) found that immersion in cold water of 10 degrees Celsius (50 degrees Fahrenheit) for 15 minutes decreased the amount of metabolites in the blood from muscle damage, which they suggested might increase the force production during subsequent exercise. Table 9.1 outlines various water immersion protocols for recovery.

Whole-body cryotherapy (WBC) is becoming a popular recovery technique in the world of sports. It is characterized by exposure to temperatures between -110 and -190 degrees Celsius (-166 to -310 degrees Fahrenheit) for 2 to 5 minutes. Rose et al. (2017) highlighted that WBC positively influenced muscle and athletic performance, muscle pain, and inflammation. That said, CWI is more accessible for most athletes than WBC, and the benefits appear to be similar.

Contrast Water Therapy

Contrast water therapy (CWT) is another common form of water immersion therapy used by athletes to enhance recovery. It is accomplished by alternating between cold-water (<20 degrees Celsius [<68 degrees Fahrenheit]) and hot-water (>36 degrees Celsius [>97 degrees Fahrenheit]) immersion. Various CWT protocols are outlined in table 9.1. After reviewing the scientific literature, Versey, Halson, and Dawson (2013) noted some debate as to how CWT affects recovery and performance. However, many of the studies reviewed outlined positive performance recovery benefits as a result of CWT, including the recovery of jump performance, muscle strength, and running performance.

Table 9.1 Various Cold-Water Immersion and Contrast Water Therapies for Recovery

Protocol	Duration	Repetitions
Cold (CWI)	5-20 min	1
Cold/hot/cold (CWT)	5 min/2 min/5 min	1
Hot/cold (CWT)	3 min/1 min	3-6
Hot/cold (CWT)	5 min/5 min	1-3

Compression

Compression in multiple forms offers a promising avenue to enhance recovery in athletes. Wearing compression garments, such as socks and lower-body tights, after exercise and competition has been shown to increase muscle strength and power recovery, decrease the severity of delayed-onset muscle soreness, and reduce the amount of muscle damage markers in the blood (Hill et al. 2014). Dynamic compression using a pneumatic (air) compression device has also been shown to enhance recovery. These devices apply compression in a sequential order (moving toward the body) via different compartments in the garment sleeve. For example, the compartment around the foot inflates, then after some time (typically 1 minute), the next compartment around the shin and calf inflates, and so forth. Dynamic compression in this manner has been shown to further reduce recovery time from muscle soreness relative to constant pressure in the form of a classic compression garment (Winke and Williamson 2018). This increased recovery might be due to higher pressure inducing greater arterial blood flow, which, in turn, might promote an increased removal of muscle damage metabolites and fluid in the affected limb.

Diaphragmatic Breathing

Diaphragmatic breathing, or abdominal breathing, is performed by pulling the diaphragm down and expanding the abdomen instead of flaring the rib cage up and out. Martarelli et al. (2011) studied the effects of diaphragmatic breathing on athletes after exhaustive exercise. They found that the relaxation induced by this type of breathing reduced the oxidative stress as evidenced by decreases in cortisol (stress hormone) and reactive oxygen metabolites and increases in melatonin, a potent antioxidant. Various forms of diaphragmatic breathing are outlined below.

Diaphragmatic Breathing Technique

Purpose

The purpose of this breathing technique is to induce relaxation and promote recovery.

Setup and Starting Position

Lie comfortably on your back, relax your shoulders, and place a pillow under your knees. Place one hand on your chest and the other on your abdomen.

Procedure

Breathe through your nose for a 2 to 4-second count. Expand your abdomen as you bring air into your lungs, keeping your chest as still as possible. Press gently on your abdomen, and exhale gently out of your mouth through pursed lips for another 2 to 4 seconds. Repeat this procedure for approximately 5 to 10 minutes. As you become comfortable with the process, gradually increase the duration over time.

Diaphragmatic Rib Cage Breathing

Purpose

Diaphragmatic rib cage breathing is another breath control technique that focuses on expanding the rib cage rather than the abdomen during the breathing process. This technique is another practice to gain control over conscious breathing.

Setup and Starting Position

Lie comfortably on your back, relax your shoulders, and place a pillow under your knees. Place one hand on your chest and the other on your abdomen.

Procedure

In contrast to the diaphragmatic breathing technique, gently contract your abdominal muscles during the initial inhalation of air. This abdominal contraction limits the diaphragm's movement, forcing the rib cage to expand and lift, increasing the thoracic cavity's size. Gently breathe through your nose for 2 to 4 seconds, followed by a 2- to 4-second exhalation through pursed lips.

4-7-8 Breathing

Purpose

The 4-7-8 breathing technique is another method of diaphragmatic breathing designed to promote relaxation and reduce anxiety and stress.

Setup and Starting Position

Assume a comfortable sitting position with a straight spine in a chair or on a couch, and place the tip of your tongue on the tissue right behind your upper front teeth.

Procedure

Start by completely exhaling all the air from your lungs. Breathe in gently through your nose for 4 seconds, expanding your abdomen. Once your lungs are full, hold your breath for 7 seconds. Then, through pursed lips, exhale forcefully out of your mouth (around your tongue) for 8 seconds. Repeat this process four times.

Mindfulness Meditation

Psychological stress has been shown to affect many physiological variables negatively. Mohammed, Pappous, and Sharma (2018) examined the effects of stress on injured athletes. They suggested that the worry and tension that result from the stress can decrease an athlete's ability to achieve their optimal performance and potentially impede the rehabilitation process. These authors suggested that mindfulness meditation practices can reduce the severity of pain athletes experience. Along with pain modification, these injured athletes could regulate their emotions more effectively, potentially reducing negative attitudes and improving thinking patterns. Another study demonstrated that an eight-week mindfulness meditation training program positively influenced the immune system (Davidson et al. 2003). Studies like these highlight the brain's power over physiological variables that can affect recovery in hockey players.

Mindfulness meditation techniques often use variations of the breathing techniques outlined in the previous section. The breathing exercises alone can be a form of mindfulness, prompting the athlete to focus on the breath and be present in the moment. In addition to the breathing exercises listed previously, following are some other examples of mindfulness meditation.

A critical element of this type of meditation is that if one notices one's attention and thoughts drifting away from the present, one should note this experience and return the focus to the present moment's sensations. The more one practices these types of meditation, the better one will get at being mindful in the moment.

Body Scan Meditation

Purpose

Be mindful of the present moment, and focus on the sensations within each part of your body to promote relaxation and reduce stress.

Setup and Starting Position

With your eyes closed, lie on your back with your arms at your sides and palms turned up.

Procedure

Breathe slowly in through your nose and out of your mouth, using the diaphragmatic breathing technique described earlier. While breathing slowly, focus your attention on each body part (typically from head to toe or vice versa). Notice sensations of touch, pressure, and so on during this exercise. Your mind and thoughts might wander, and that is perfectly normal. When you notice your mind wandering, simply redirect these thoughts back to the sensations your body is experiencing. Perform this exercise for up to 30 minutes, starting with shorter durations and gradually building to longer durations.

Walking Meditation

Purpose

Be mindful of the present, and focus on the sensations while walking intentionally to reduce anxiety and stress.

Setup and Starting Position

Find a location that will allow you to take approximately 10 to 20 steps. This location should be peaceful, and being outdoors in nature, although not necessary, is preferred.

Procedure

Slowly walk 10 to 20 steps, then pause and breathe for a few moments. Turn back and walk in the other direction for another 10 to 20 steps, and repeat the process. Walking is typically an automatic activity; however, you should deliberately think about each step and the sensations that your feet and body experience during this exercise. Like with other forms of meditation, your mind and thoughts may wander. When you notice your mind wandering, simply redirect these thoughts back to the sensations your body is experiencing.

SUMMARY

This chapter detailed the importance of recovery, particularly during high training and competition stress, and many methods that promote recovery. It should be noted that sleep, nutrition, and hydration are an athlete's top recovery priorities. These factors are often overlooked because they are simple and seemingly mundane, but they pack a big punch. When sleep, nutrition, and hydration are optimized and combined with other recovery modalities, athletes provide their bodies with the best tools to recover and, therefore, the best chance for success down the road.

Chapter 10

Technological Advances

In 2011, my first year as a head strength and conditioning coach in the NHL, daily use of performance or monitoring technology was not an ordinary endeavor around the league. A few teams utilized heart rate technology for on-ice monitoring, and even fewer teams employed off-ice performance and monitoring technologies such as force plates and heart rate variability (HRV) devices. Within 10 years, the landscape in the NHL (and other leagues around the world) had changed drastically. These days, most organizations use various technologies to measure and monitor their athletes and teams and are building entire sport science departments within their organizations. These changes are, in part, due to rapid advances in the development and availability of technology and in the education of the strength and conditioning and sport science teams.

As an organization, a fundamental issue to think about is whether the use of technology is essential. The answer depends on many factors. As alluded to previously in this book, it is challenging to influence performance, readiness, and wellness variables in a meaningful way if these variables are not measured and evaluated. However, advanced technologies are not always necessary to measure these factors. Therefore, if an individual or organization does not possess the resources to acquire specific technologies, many low-tech options, outlined previously in this book, can garner meaningful and actionable information. If the choice is made to use technology, the collected data must be valid and reliable to guide modification to daily training programs and recovery strategies if necessary. Do not use technology for its own sake. The collected information must be put to work to advance and fine-tune the athlete's physical and health status.

This chapter highlights common technologies currently used at the highest levels of the game. However, this is not an exhaustive list, because technology is advancing at a rapid rate. We will explore both on-ice and off-ice technologies used in performance and in monitoring rehabilitation, training, workload, and readiness.

OFF-ICE TECHNOLOGY

The off-ice technologies highlighted in this chapter are presented in figure 10.1. They typically fall under two categories:

1. Performance or rehab monitoring and training, which includes monitoring of performance metrics and of return-to-play metrics, as well as training devices
2. Workload and readiness monitoring, which includes monitoring of workload data (e.g., external and internal load) and of readiness data (e.g., HRV, sleep, and fatigue).

Many off-ice technologies are also used on the ice to monitor the same metrics in a more specific environment.

Force Plates

Scientists and researchers have used force plate technology for decades; however, its prevalence in high-performance sport has increased significantly in the past ten years, primarily due to increased accessibility. Force plates can measure ground reaction forces in multiple planes (i.e., vertical, horizontal, and lateral) during human movement.

The most common movements measured at the elite levels of hockey are vertical jump variations. However, many other actions such as lower-body strength exercises and other athletic endeavors (e.g., cutting) can also be measured to evaluate athletes. Many variables can be derived from the measurement of ground reaction force. Table 10.1 outlines several important diagnostic variables when considering the use of force plates.

Why Use It?

As with all technology, objective data collected from the force plates is used to guide evidence-based training decisions and objectives. Data from the force plates allow the sport science and strength and conditioning teams to ask a whole new set of questions about performance and readiness and to monitor fatigue. For example, force plates can be used to obtain an individual's force–velocity profile. This force–velocity profile (see chapter 5) can then be used to guide individualized training prescriptions. An athlete who presents with low force at low velocities but high force at higher velocities might benefit from additional maximum strength training. With regard to readiness, weekly force plate monitoring might be beneficial. If an athlete's power or velocity decreases over time, it might signify fatigue or detraining, prompting the use of various recovery modalities or additional recovery sessions or days.

When to Use It

During the off-season, force plate monitoring should be performed every week. This monitoring should be conducted on the first training day of each week when the athlete has recovered from the previous week's training.

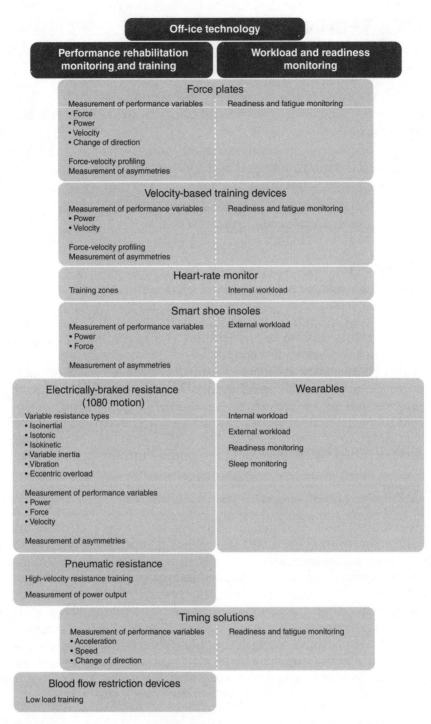

Figure 10.1 Summary of off-ice technology used in hockey. Each technology can be classified as performance or rehab monitoring and training or workload and readiness monitoring. Many of the technologies listed fall under both categories.

Table 10.1 Diagnostic Variables Commonly Measured in Hockey Using Force Plate Technology

Variable	Definition
Ground reaction force	Force exerted by the ground on the body
Power	Combination of force and velocity
Takeoff velocity	Vertical velocity of the center of mass at takeoff
Rate of force development	Explosive strength, how rapidly force can be produced
Impulse	Amount of force in a given time
Modified reactive strength index	Ability to change from eccentric to concentric phases of the jump; represents ability to use the stretch-shortening cycle
Kinetic asymmetries (eccentric CMJ)	Difference in force production between right and left leg during the eccentric phase of CMJ
Kinetic asymmetries (concentric CMJ)	Difference in force production between right and left leg during the concentric phase of CMJ
Kinetic asymmetries (early phase of concentric SJ)	Difference in force production between right and left leg during the early phase (hip dominant) of SJ
Kinetic asymmetries (late phase of concentric SJ)	Difference in force production between right and left leg during the late phase (knee dominant) of SJ

CMJ = countermovement jump; SJ = squat jump

In-season use of force plate monitoring is often governed by the game and travel schedules of the team. The goal during the season is to perform force plate monitoring one or two times per month.

Velocity-Based Training Devices

Currently, velocity-based training (VBT) devices such as GymAware are some of the most accessible and valuable technologies on the market. These devices measure the speed and distance traveled of the barbell, weight, or body in motion via linear position transducers. Other devices use accelerometer and laser optic technology to measure velocity. Several other variables (table 10.2) can be calculated from the velocity and distance traveled.

Why Use It?

The data obtained from VBT devices can be used for both performance and readiness or fatigue monitoring. From a performance standpoint, these devices allow for the development of an individual's force–velocity profile. The importance of this profile was outlined in the previous section on force plate technology. During the power and high-velocity phases of the training program, measuring velocity is an important monitoring tool. Knowing the movement's velocity allows for acute adjustments to the loading parameters, rest periods, set volume, and coach's cues during the training session. For

Table 10.2 Variables Measured or Calculated Via a VBT Training Device

Variable	Definition
Distance traveled	How far the bar, weight, or body moved
Mean power	Average power during the concentric phase of the lift
Peak power	Highest power observed
Mean velocity	Average velocity during the concentric phase of the lift
Peak velocity	Highest velocity observed
Barbell path	The trajectory of the bar during the lift; indication of lifting technique

example, during a velocity phase, an athlete might perform as many repetitions as possible until the velocity drops to a certain percentage of the peak velocity with each set. Additionally, when an athlete is aware of the velocity of movement, that could drive internal motivation and the movement's intent as they continually attempt to achieve a higher velocity on subsequent repetitions.

When viewing VBT through the lens of readiness and fatigue monitoring, these devices can be valuable. Typically, when an athlete is tired, their velocity of movement decreases. Therefore, collecting velocity data might be helpful in identifying when an athlete might require microadjustments in rest and recovery within their program. For example, consistently using a VBT device during specific warm-up lifts or movements allows the coach to identify the presence of neuromuscular fatigue if the velocity of motion is slower than usual. The coach can make acute decisions on training variables such as intensity, volume, rest, and recovery within the training session from this data.

When to Use It

VBT devices should be used year-round to monitor continuously the readiness status of the athletes. During the off-season's power and velocity phases, these devices become even more critical for monitoring the quality of training and generating motivation and intent within the athlete. Velocity should be measured on any key lifts or movements during this period.

Heart Rate Monitor

A heart rate monitor is a device that measures how many times per minute the heart is beating. A traditional heart rate monitoring chest strap measures the electrical impulses that make the heart beat. Wearable devices (e.g., watches and wristbands) measure heart rate through the skin. These devices typically rely on the emission of LED light through the surface of the skin. When the light enters the skin, it is either transmitted or reflected back to the device's sensor. The changes in how the light reacts to blood flow changes in the vessels can be used to calculate heart rate. Many heart rate monitors also measure HRV and internal workload (training impulse, or TRIMP), discussed in chapter 2.

Why Use It?

Measuring heart rate is helpful for both performance training and workload or readiness monitoring. For energy systems training (chapter 4), many training prescriptions rely on heart rate feedback to ensure the athlete works in the appropriate training zone. These heart rate values can also be used to calculate a training efficiency index. For example, if an athlete's heart rate at a specific workload decreases over time, it could indicate an improvement in fitness. Training allows the athlete to express greater output for a given heart rate.

Measuring HRV also provides insight into the nervous system's readiness status, outlined in chapter 2. When HRV is high, the parasympathetic and sympathetic nervous systems are in balance. When HRV is low, these systems are out of balance, typically seen with sympathetic dominance. HRV provides insights into chronic fatigue and training readiness that can be used daily to individualize training plans to avoid overtraining or chronic fatigue.

A third area where heart rate monitoring is beneficial is in measuring the internal workload of exercise. The internal workload is usually characterized by the TRIMP score, which provides insight into how the individual's physiology reacts to the applied training stimulus both off and on the ice. These can also be used to calculate a training efficiency index, provided that external workload is monitored in conjunction.

When to Use It

Heart rate monitoring can be used daily year-round to monitor performance, training, and readiness variables.

Smart Shoe Insoles

The past several years have seen an increase in product development regarding the smart shoe insole market. Companies such as Plantiga use an inertial measurement unit embedded in the shoe insole that measures acceleration, position, and orientation. These variables and artificial intelligence provide feedback on performance characteristics and how the athlete is moving. The insoles can give valuable data similar to the force plate data (table 10.1); however, the actions are not limited to the laboratory setting.

Why Use It?

The most valuable reason to use smart shoe insole technology is to bridge the gap between laboratory testing and field testing. Many of these devices provide information similar to that obtained via force plates; however, measurements can now be made on the field or on-ice environments. These insoles allow for data collection of performance and training variables as well as external workload monitoring. This data can then be used to influence acute training modifications.

When to Use It

Smart insoles can be used daily to monitor performance, training, and workload variables both off and on the ice.

Wearable Devices

Wearable devices are a fast-growing sector of health and wellness technology. These devices are typically worn on the skin (e.g., watch or bracelet), where they collect biological and health information. Data collected often include heart rate, temperature, blood oxygen levels, respiration rate, movement, or steps, to name a few. From the measured data, calories burned, physical workload, physical readiness, and sleep metrics can be calculated.

Why Use It?

These devices are readily accessible to all athletes and can provide valuable health and wellness information that can be used to monitor the individual's training and health status. For example, suppose the device demonstrates that the daily readiness of the athlete is not optimal. In that case, the strength and conditioning coach can make recovery, training, and potentially lifestyle adjustments to the daily plan.

When to Use It

Wearables can be used daily to monitor performance, training, workload, and readiness variables. The more consistently the device is worn, the more valuable the data is because trends can be observed in response to many training or health interventions.

Motorized Resistance

Motorized resistance machines, such as the 1080 Motion devices, are a potent tool in the performance training toolbox. This device offers many forms of resistance (table 10.3) and collects real-time power, force, and velocity data within the training session. These different forms of resistance can be customized to different velocities and resistance independently in the eccentric and concentric phases of movement. These tools can be used at different periods within the training program to enhance the desired training effects' outcomes.

Why Use It?

Compared to traditional free weights, a system with motorized resistance, such as the 1080 Motion, is highly adaptable within a specific exercise. Whereas free weights rely on the laws of gravity, electrically braked resistance depends on a motor to control the variables of the load on the individual. These added elements of control allow for specific manipulation of resistance variables that can be used to modify the athlete's force–velocity profile with a high degree of precision.

Table 10.3 Types of Resistance Offered by Motorized Resistance Machines

Type of resistance	Definition
Isoinertial	Simulates normal weight stack resistance
Isotonic	Constant resistance throughout the range of motion
Isokinetic	Limiting the speed of the movement will maximize concentric force output
Variable inertia	Inertia only present during acceleration, no inertia during deceleration of weight, eases load on joints and tendons
Vibration	Can be added to the resistance for neuromuscular benefits
Eccentric overload	Can add greater eccentric load relative to concentric safely and effectively

The real-time data collection of force, velocity, power, and acceleration variables allows for close monitoring of each exercise set. As with VBT devices, real-time monitoring of these variables allows for acute adjustments to the loading parameters, rest periods, set volume, and coach's cues used during the training session. This data can also be used to monitor readiness and fatigue because it can be cross-referenced with previous data collected on the device. For example, if an exercise with the same load is significantly slower than previous trials or days, this could indicate fatigue accumulation and might require adjustments to the training session and specific recovery and lifestyle interventions, such as nutrition modifications, the addition of recovery modalities, and sleep interventions.

When to Use It

Due to its adaptability of the resistance and monitoring capabilities, this technology can be used year-round for many different training objectives. For example, the eccentric overload resistance option can be used early in the off-season to elicit more significant muscle morphology changes than traditional free weights alone. In contrast, concentric-only resistance can be used during the season to minimize muscle soreness.

Pneumatic Resistance

Pneumatic resistance machines, such as Keiser equipment, use air compression rather than free weights for resistance. Because air compression resistance does not rely on gravity, these machines provide isotonic or constant resistance throughout the entire range of motion. In contrast, with free weights, momentum can be generated, changing the input required for keeping the load in motion. Along with the benefit of isotonic resistance, this type of equipment also provides power output information.

Why Use It?

Pneumatic resistance differs from traditional free weights in that it relies on air compression rather than gravity to achieve specific loads. The air compression allows for constant loading throughout the entire range of motion. The fact that the load remains constant lets the athlete perform high-velocity movements with control and eliminates the risk of the kickback seen with traditional free weight stacks.

Close monitoring of the real-time power data within each exercise set permits acute adjustments to the loading parameters, rest periods, set volume, and coach's cues used during the training session. Additionally, when an athlete is aware of their power output, that can improve internal motivation and the intent of the movement as they continually attempt to achieve a higher power on subsequent repetitions.

When to Use It

Pneumatic resistance can be used year-round, but it might have greater specificity during high-velocity and power phases of the training program due to the isotonic loading qualities.

Timing Solutions

Many different timing solutions are on the market. They typically fall into two categories: conventional timing gates and continuous laser timing. Traditional timing gates use a beam of light that the athlete passes through, triggering the timing system. Continuous laser timing uses a laser beam pointed at the athlete, sampling instantaneously for the duration of the activity. Continuous laser timing might involve increased variability in the measurements, making it difficult to determine if a meaningful change has occurred (Bond, Willaert, and Noonan 2017). Both types of timing technology can provide valuable information on acceleration, velocity, and change-of-direction (COD) capabilities of the athlete.

Why Use It?

The main reason to use a timing system is to monitor performance changes in specific acceleration and speed tests. This technology also can be used for on-ice acceleration and speed testing. Consistently measuring these variables can aid in coaching decisions surrounding program adjustments (if needed) and the fatigue or readiness status of the athlete.

Like other technologies, the instant feedback from the timing system can improve internal motivation and the movement's intent as athletes continually attempt to achieve better scores on subsequent repetitions.

When to Use It

From a logistical perspective, it is best to use these timing solutions during the off-season. Athletes should test 98-foot (30 m) sprint times with 33- and

66-foot (10 and 20 m) splits weekly in conjunction with force plate testing. Like force plate testing, testing of speed and acceleration is to be performed on the first training day of each week to ensure the athlete is recovered from the previous week of training. Sprint testing is not advised during the season because the athletes are not running regularly, which increases the risk of injury. That said, if time and logistics permit, on-ice speed testing can be a valuable tool to monitor athlete status throughout the season. Please refer to chapter 2 for various off- and on-ice speed and COD tests.

Blood Flow Restriction Devices

Blood flow restriction (BFR) or occlusion training devices use a tourniquet to minimize blood flow to various parts of the body. This restricted blood flow creates a low-oxygen environment in the working muscle, which in turn causes high metabolic stress. This stress is vital for muscle hypertrophy and even strength improvements and can be accomplished using significantly reduced loads (e.g., 30% 1-repetition max).

Why Use It?

BFR can be a useful training tool during the season, when physical demands are high. Muscle hypertrophy and strength improvements can be attained while minimizing the muscle's mechanical loading, reducing the amount of delayed-onset muscle soreness experienced by the athlete. Because injuries are common due to hockey's full-contact nature, BFR can be a valuable rehabilitation tool. For example, if an athlete presents with a knee or ankle injury, BFR training can be used to maintain or improve muscle strength and hypertrophy in the affected limb with very light loads, minimizing the stress on the injured body part. Note that BFR training should be done only with specific BFR devices that monitor the amount of pressure on the limb.

When to Use It

BFR training can be used year-round for low-load finishing sets at the end of workouts in healthy individuals or during the season to accumulate training load without inducing excessive mechanical stress on the muscles and joints. This training can be performed one to four times per week, depending on the specific situation. Injured athletes might also benefit from BFR training two to four times per week until they can progressively increase the load on the injured body part.

ON-ICE TECHNOLOGIES

The on-ice technologies highlighted in this chapter are presented in figure 10.2. Like the off-ice technologies, they typically fall under the same two categories:

1. Performance or rehab monitoring and training
2. Workload and readiness monitoring

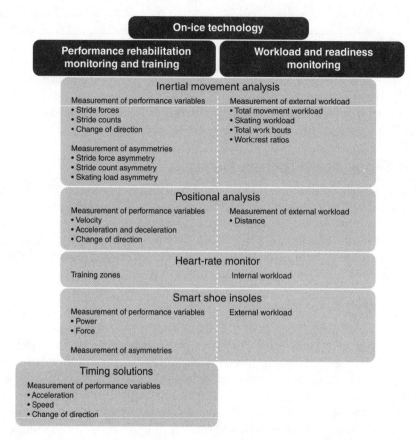

Figure 10.2   Summary of on-ice technology used in hockey. Each technology can be classified as performance or rehab monitoring and training or workload and readiness monitoring. Many of the technologies listed fall under both categories.

This is not an exhaustive list of on-ice technologies but rather a highlight of standard technologies used at the highest levels of hockey.

Inertial Movement Analysis

Inertial movement analysis (IMA) devices, such as the Catapult system, use both accelerometer and gyroscope technology. The accelerometer measures accelerations and decelerations in three dimensions, whereas the gyroscope measures rotation. The data points from the accelerometer and gyroscope measure the magnitude of every movement an athlete makes on the ice. Based on specific algorithms, these devices can detect acceleration, deceleration, and COD.

Why Use It?

IMA devices collect both performance and workload information. From a performance and rehabilitation perspective, information on stride forces and counts, COD, and right and left asymmetries can be measured. This data can then guide specific training requirements or return-to-play protocols for injured athletes. For example, if an athlete's stride forces decrease over time, off-ice strength training interventions can be implemented. Conversely, if an athlete is returning from an injury, the on-ice asymmetry data can be cross-referenced to information collected before the injury to assess the rehabilitation protocol's effectiveness and provide insight into when the athlete can return to play.

Historically, coaches often programmed practices based on gut feelings rather than objective workload information. Utilizing the IMA technology, external workload information for each practice, drill, and game can be collected. This objective information creates an environment where on-ice practices can be planned precisely according to the team's or individual's specific workload needs. This data can also be used to determine positional differences within practices and games. For example, suppose the team's defense core consistently performs more work than the forwards during practices. In that case, this might require an adjustment to the drill selection to ensure the defense is not overworked or the forwards underworked.

When to Use It

IMA technology should be used at all times on the ice, provided there are no restrictions (e.g., NHL players currently cannot wear these devices during games).

Positional Analysis

Positional analysis or global positioning system (GPS) units measure the athlete's locomotion on the ice. These devices work by communicating with satellite receivers installed within the hockey arena (figure 10.3). These satellites and GPS units work together to determine the location of the athlete on the ice. This positional data is used to determine velocity, acceleration, deceleration, COD, and distance traveled.

Why Use It?

Positional analysis devices provide valuable information on performance metrics as well as workload information. Athlete skating velocities and acceleration

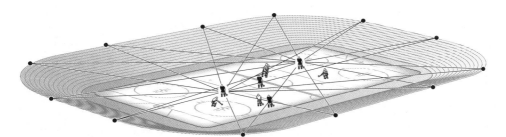

Figure 10.3 How a positional analysis system works to determine the precise location of the athlete on the ice.

and deceleration capabilities can be monitored during practices and games. Monitoring these variables provides insight into off- or on-ice programming adjustments that might be necessary in response to changes observed over time. For example, if an athlete's average velocity decreases throughout the season, this could indicate detraining or fatigue accumulation. In the case of detraining, additional speed or power work might be required to augment the decline in performance. If it is determined that fatigue is a factor, specific recovery protocols might be implemented, or a decrease in workload might be required.

Total distance traveled during practices and games can also be a measure of workload. However, using distance alone might be an incomplete metric for workload because many other variables (e.g., shooting, collisions, and velocity of movement) play significant roles in determining the athlete's total workload. Therefore, it is advised to use positional analysis information and IMA data to obtain a complete picture of what the athlete experiences on the ice.

When to Use It

Positional analysis technology should be used at all times on the ice, provided there are no restrictions (e.g., NHL players currently cannot wear these devices during games).

SUMMARY

Performance and readiness variables must be measured and monitored regularly to influence training in a meaningful and directed way. These variables can be monitored using the technologies outlined in this chapter. Since sport technology is advancing rapidly, this is not an exhaustive list but shows relatively common technologies used in hockey today. It is understood that advanced technologies are not always necessary to monitor athletes. Therefore, if an individual or organization does not possess the resources to acquire specific technologies, many low-tech options can be used as monitoring tools, which have been outlined previously in this book. If the choice is made to use technology as part of your daily coaching or training routine, opt for technology with a proven track record of validity and reliability to ensure that meaningful changes can be made.

Chapter 11

Yearly Training Plan and Program Development

The famous French aviator Antoine de Saint-Exupéry eloquently said, "A goal without a plan is just a wish." This statement could not be more accurate concerning training program design for hockey players. Without weekly, monthly, and yearly plans, it is difficult to assess the effectiveness of the training variables and interventions on specific performance characteristics we are attempting to modify.

One of the most critical considerations is the design of training programs and how they fit within the calendar year to optimize performance potential for future dates and minimize the risk of excessive fatigue leading up to those dates (Smith 2003). This chapter outlines the principles of training responsible for directing the training process and the use of periodization, the method of manipulating training variables to meet specific goals, considering the focus of yearly, monthly, weekly, and daily training.

PRINCIPLES OF TRAINING

The theory and methodology of athletic development are guided by the principles of training, which are based on physiological, psychological, and educational science (Bompa and Haff 2009). These principles are responsible for directing the process of athlete training on a global level and include the following:

• *Multilateral development:* As outlined in the long-term player development model in chapter 1, early athletic development should prioritize multilateral development (early diversification) instead of early specialization. Multilateral development focuses on the athlete's overall physical progress and sets the foundation to specialize in the later training stages (Bompa and Haff 2009).

- *Progressive overload:* Physical adaptations occur in response to the training loads imposed on the body. If the load on the body is not progressed over time in a structured and sequential manner, specific adaptations either slow or stop completely as the body eventually reaches equilibrium. Once the planned transformation has occurred, the training load must be systematically increased to progress physically. Training load can be increased by modifying intensity and volume, which are discussed later in this chapter.

- *Specificity:* This principle suggests that physical adaptation is specific to the cells and structures that are experiencing the training load. Training adaptations are specific to the individual, type of movement, speed, intensity, and duration of the activity. Therefore, when designing training plans, it is critical to train under similar conditions to those experienced during a game.

- *Nonlinear relationship:* A nonlinear relationship exists between the training load and physical adaptation. In younger or inexperienced athletes, adaptations and performance improvements appear more quickly than in athletes of a higher training age. The need for systematic planning of training loads increases as athletes mature, to continually push the boundaries of the physical and technical capacities.

- *Reversibility:* We have all heard the phrase, "Use it or lose it." If the training load is not consistent, is decreased, or is removed, the specific adaptation will diminish over time. This process might be acceptable for certain qualities at particular times, but in general, the training plan should be designed to minimize this detraining effect.

- *Retrogression:* Decreases in performance often occur before improvements, whether due to fatigue or other factors. Retrogression might need to be explained to athletes, especially because more training load in these cases might not be the path forward. Adding training load in this state could worsen the problem and potentially lead to overtraining.

- *Recovery:* Recovery is a crucial factor in the training plan; the greater the volume and intensity of training, the greater the need for a recovery period. As with any training variable, recovery must be systematically planned to ensure continued progress.

- *Individualization:* Like specificity, training affects individuals differently based on genetics, training age, gender, and general health. Individualization is often difficult in team settings, but it must be done. This is where individual monitoring comes into play. The tracking of a particular athlete's adaptations to training allows for scientific reflection on the training process. These assessments can be used to evaluate the training model and adjust it based on the individual's specific needs.

- *Variation:* Novel tasks typically increase the rate of technical skill and performance adaptations, but this rate will slow when athletes perform the same tasks repetitively (Bompa and Haff 2009). This training monotony can lead to decreases in performance. Adjustments in training volume, intensity, frequency, and exercise selection can provide variety. On the other hand, if the variation is too frequent, complete adaptation to the training stimulus might not be acquired. The variation must be structured into the training plan carefully to achieve the desired outcomes.

• *Awareness:* This principle is particularly important for mature and advanced athletes. Mature athletes must be aware of the training philosophy and plan to become active participants in their development.

PERIODIZATION

Periodization is defined as a systematic method of manipulating training variables to optimize and achieve specific performance goals (Stone et al. 1999). In essence, periodization is the training plan that encompasses all the training variables required to reach a particular level of performance and allows for the breakdown of the entire training plan into manageable blocks or periods, enabling peak performance at precise times. As with any blueprint, it should serve as a guideline with checks and periods of reflection along the way.

Intensity and volume are two training variables manipulated during periodization. Intensity and volume must be carefully planned to ensure continued progress and minimize the effects of fatigue on the athlete.

Intensity

Training intensity is often classified as a function of the work performed in a given amount of time; however, this definition can also be applied to sessional density. According to Bompa and Haff (2009), intensity can also be classified as a function of neuromuscular activation. This activation pattern is influenced by the external load, speed, fatigue, and type of activity. When prescribing intensity in training, the variable is specific to the action performed. During a hockey practice, intensity can be prescribed using heart rate parameters or skating velocities. During strength training, intensity can be prescribed using the percentage of weight lifted relative to the 1-repetition maximum or maximum power output.

Volume

Volume is the total quantity of training performed and can be broken down by week, month, year, or any other predetermined amount of time scheduled in the training plan (Smith 2003). As athletes progress over time, more volume might be necessary to elicit the specific physical adaptations required to improve performance. Volume is a factor of training duration and density. Training duration is the amount of time it takes to complete a training session, and density is the number of training sessions within a specific time frame (e.g., day or week). Like intensity, assessment of volume is specific to the activity performed. In strength training, volume can be quantified by multiplying the number of sets, repetitions, and weight lifted: volume = sets × repetitions × weight lifted. When considering energy systems development, volume can be quantified by distance traveled or the number of sets multiplied by distance or time.

TRAINING LOAD

The term *training load* refers to the interaction between the intensity and volume of training. In general, intensity and volume are inversely related, meaning that as intensity increases, volume decreases, and vice versa. However, there might be periods when both intensity and volume are high. Smith (2003) describes various types of training load:

- *Excessive load:* A training load above the individual's functional capacity, which might result in overtraining
- *Trainable load:* The load required for a specific training adaptation
- *Maintenance load:* The load required to minimize or eliminate detraining
- *Recovery load:* A training load that promotes recovery and typically follows an excessive or trainable load
- *Useless load:* A training load less than what is required to achieve adaptation

---

YEARLY TRAINING PLAN

The yearly training plan is typically cyclical, containing three types of cycles: macrocycle, mesocycle, and microcycle. In hockey, a microcycle is usually one training week (seven days). A mesocycle is composed of several microcycles (on average three to six microcycles). The macrocycle is the combination of all the mesocycles and is usually distinguished as the annual training cycle.

For sports with one competitive phase, like hockey, the yearly training plan usually has one macrocycle. However, hockey players' training cycle does not necessarily contain one specific peak in performance. Periodization is not restricted to the yearly plan structure. It includes periodization and planning of the various physiological components (i.e., speed, power, strength, agility, and energy systems) within the yearly training cycle. For example, in hockey, peaks for physical abilities such as power and strength usually occur around the competition phase's commencement, and peaks for technical and tactical aspects of the game and potentially specific speed, agility, and reaction time generally happen later in the competition cycle.

Macrocycle

For sports with one competitive phase, like hockey, the macrocycle is usually composed of three main phases: preparatory, stabilization (competition), and transition (recovery). The macrocycle breakdown for each player or team will likely vary depending on the athlete's previous season and training experience or age. For example, if an NHL team does not make the playoffs, the transition phase might begin in April, whereas for the team that wins the championship, the transition phase likely starts in June. Additionally, training experience and age directly affect the physiological starting point for the athlete. Although younger athletes with less experience typically follow the same macrocycle structure, the degree of complexity is often lower, the duration phases can vary, and rates of progression are usually slower.

Preparatory Phase

The preparatory phase forms the foundation of physical qualities that allow an athlete to excel during the competition phase. For hockey players, this phase is generally four or five months long. According to Bompa and Haff (2009), this preparatory phase is potentially the most important of the annual plan. Bompa and Haff (2009) also outlined several goals of the preparatory phase, which include but are not limited to the following:

- Improve general physical tolerance and training capacity.
- Improve specific physiological characteristics required for hockey.
- Develop technical skills.

The preparatory phase can be divided further into a general preparation phase and a specific preparation phase.

General Preparatory Phase The general preparatory phase's primary purpose is to increase the athlete's work capacity, usually in the first two months of the off-season. The increase in work capacity is mainly accomplished by increasing training volume, where training intensity is secondary to volume and should account for approximately 40 percent of the training load in this phase (Bompa and Haff 2009). During the general preparatory phase, the primary physiological variables programmed include structural tolerance of tissue, movement capacity, aerobic capacity, aerobic power, work capacity, and general and maximal strength.

Specific Preparatory Phase The primary purpose of the specific preparatory phase, like that of the general preparatory phase, is to increase the athlete's work capacity. However, a greater focus is placed on endeavors closer to what the athlete will experience during a game. This phase typically occurs in months three and four of the off-season. While volume remains high for the first part of this phase, it usually tapers down in the later parts leading into training camp, when the training intensity increases. During the specific preparatory phase, the significant physiological variables programmed include movement capacity (transitioning to more dynamic agility movements), anaerobic power and capacity (including speed, lactate production, and lactate capacity), aerobic power, power development, and strength and power endurance. A greater emphasis is placed on performing many movement capacity, acceleration, change-of-direction, and energy systems program variables on the ice in full equipment during this phase.

Stabilization (or Competition) Phase

The stabilization phase in hockey includes precompetition (preseason) and main competition (in-season) components. During this phase, the physical capacities developed during the preparatory phase are maintained, and the focus shifts primarily to optimizing the technical and tactical skills on the ice. The off-ice training volume is significantly reduced, and an emphasis is placed on maintaining strength, power, and mobility and on optimizing recovery.

Transition (or Recovery) Phase

The transition phase, also known as the recovery phase, is usually two to six weeks long, immediately follows the stabilization phase, and is designed to promote psychological and physiological regeneration. A common misconception is that the transition phase is for complete rest. On the contrary, during this phase, the athlete participates in low-level general activity to minimize the detraining effect on the physical qualities built during the macrocycle's other phases.

Hockey-Specific Macrocycle

A sample hockey-specific macrocycle is outlined in table 11.1. This schematic helps a hockey player visualize the calendar year. This outline is highly adaptable to any individual situation. For instance, if the team plays until mid-May, the preparatory phase might not begin until the beginning of June and would be shorter in duration.

Mesocycle

The mesocycle is a combination of several microcycles. Each mesocycle has specific training objectives and goals. These training objectives guide the construction of the training plan and the microcycles that make up the mesocycle. If the main training objective for the mesocycle is maximum strength development, that does not mean that the program cannot include aspects of muscular power and endurance development; it means that the primary focus of the mesocycle is maximum strength. Each mesocycle is approximately three to six weeks long. Mesocycles can be further subdivided, if required, to focus on specific aspects of the primary focus. For example, a mesocycle designed to develop maximal strength can be divided into smaller blocks focusing on eccentric, isometric, or concentric strength. Tables 11.2 and 11.3 outline examples of mesocycles within the macrocycle for various strength and energy systems development variables.

The training load is the combination of volume and intensity. The number of microcycles in a mesocycle generally dictates the training load pattern within the mesocycle. For example, in a four-week mesocycle with four microcycles,

Table 11.1 Sample Hockey-Specific Macrocycle

Month	May	June	July	August	September	October	November	December	January	February	March	April
Phase	Preparatory				Stabilization							Transition
Subphase	General preparation	Specific preparation			Precom- petition	Competition						
Physiological focus	Movement capacity	Movement capacity			Technical and tactical							Aerobic base
	Structural tolerance	Anaerobic power, capacity			Strength maintenance							Movement capacity
	Aerobic capacity	Aerobic power			Power maintenance							Low-level general strength
	Aerobic power	Power develop- ment			Mobility and recovery							
	Work capacity	Strength and power endurance										
	Strength											

Table 11.2 Mesocycle Structure for Strength Variables Within a Macrocycle

Month	May	June	July	August	September	October to March
Phase	Preparatory				Stabilization	
Subphase	General		Specific		Precompetition	Competition
Mesocycle	Reintegration, morphological adaptation	Max strength	Power and speed development		Maintenance	
Number of microcycles	3-4	4-6	6		>26	

the typical loading pattern is 3:1, meaning that the training load is increased over the first three microcycles. The fourth microcycle is a recovery or deload microcycle. Several types of loading patterns (figures 11.1 through 11.3) can be used during a mesocycle.

Table 11.3 Mesocycle Structure for Energy Systems Development Variables Within a Macrocycle

Month	May	June	July	August	September	October to March
Phase	Preparatory				Stabilization	
Subphase	General		Specific		Precompetition	Competition
Mesocycle	Aerobic capacity and power	Aerobic capacity and power, work capacity	Anaerobic and aerobic power	Anaerobic power and capacity	Maintenance	
Number of microcycles	3	3	4	4	≥26	

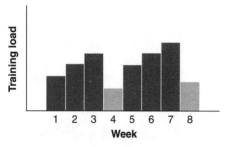

Figure 11.1 Ascending step loading pattern over eight weeks. Ascending step loading is characterized by progressive overload followed by recovery or deload. In this example, weeks 4 and 8 represent a deloading period.

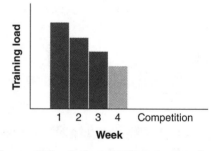

Figure 11.2 A descending step loading pattern leading into competition. Descending step loading typically is used leading into training camp and is characterized by a decrease in weekly load. Descending step loading is often classified as a taper period to optimize readiness.

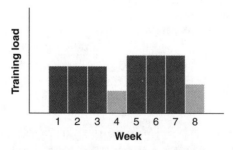

Figure 11.3 A flat loading pattern over eight weeks. In flat loading, training load remains constant throughout the mesocycle. This type of loading typically is used by more advanced athletes later in the macrocycle preparatory phase. In this example, weeks 4 and 8 represent a deloading period.

Microcycle

The microcycle is one week within the training cycle and contains the precise details used to accomplish the specific training goals. According to most experts, the microcycle is the most critical programming tool in the coaching toolbox (Bompa and Haff 2009). The microcycle helps guide and mold the meso- and macrocycles. It has been established that the meso- and macrocycles are general plans that can be adapted based on the physical changes observed during the microcycles. By monitoring athletes daily and weekly, coaches can quantify the adaptations that are occurring. If the expected outcomes are not observed within the microcycles, the meso- and macrocycles might need to be adapted.

Within the microcycle, many factors must be considered. Issurin (2008) and Bompa and Haff (2009) highlighted the following considerations:

- Training modalities and methods and main training objectives
- Training frequency, volume, and intensity
- Placement of the most critical training days. These are the days that determine the microcycle's primary outcomes and typically do not immediately follow a recovery or off-day.
- Placement and assignment of supportive training days. The training load from these days affects primary outcomes and recovery.
- Placement of recovery days and workouts
- Monitoring techniques to ensure the microcycle has the desired effects
- Competition schedule

Types of Microcycles

Many types of microcycles can be used to achieve specific training goals. The terminology used to describe the types of microcycles varies between sources; however, the contents and purpose are what matters. Issurin (2008) outlined several kinds of microcycles:

- *Adjustment:* Initial load adaptations with a gradual increase in workload
- *Loading:* For strength and conditioning development that uses high workloads
- *Impact or shock:* For strength and conditioning development that uses very high or extreme workloads
- *Precompetition:* Fine-tuning for upcoming competition using medium workloads
- *Restoration or deload:* Active recovery using low workloads

Figures 11.4 through 11.6 show examples of microcycle placement within a mesocycle for different scenarios.

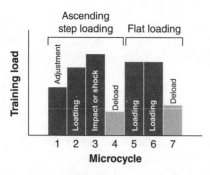

Figure 11.4 Microcycle breakdown for two preparatory-phase mesocycles for an intermediate- or advanced-level hockey player.

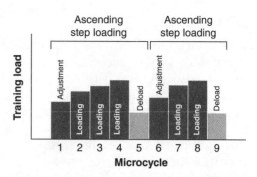

Figure 11.5 Microcycle breakdown for two preparatory-phase mesocycles for a beginner- or intermediate-level hockey player.

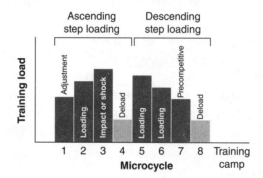

Figure 11.6 Microcycle breakdown for two preparatory-phase mesocycles for an intermediate- or advanced-level hockey player leading into training camp.

Designing the Microcycle

When designing a microcycle, many factors must be considered. The number of training days within the microcycle typically ranges from three to five during the preparatory phases, and each microcycle might have one or two high-demand days. Figures 11.7 through 11.10 illustrate examples of off-season and in-season microcycle breakdowns.

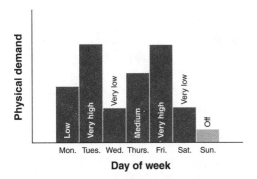

Figure 11.7 Daily physical demand breakdown of a four-day preparatory-phase microcycle with two very high-demand days. The very low days include unstructured light aerobic, mobility, and recovery modalities. This structure can be used at any level.

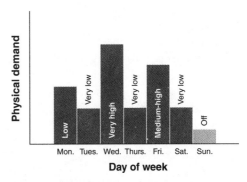

Figure 11.8 Daily physical demand breakdown of a three-day preparatory-phase microcycle with one very high-demand day. The very low days include unstructured light aerobic, mobility, and recovery modalities. This structure can be used at any level.

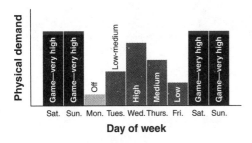

Figure 11.9 Daily physical demand breakdown of a competition or stabilization phase microcycle when games are played on weekends (e.g., college hockey).

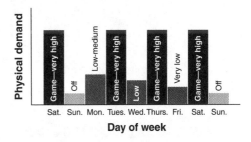

Figure 11.10 Daily physical demand breakdown of a competition or stabilization phase microcycle with three games played and a fourth game on the eighth day (e.g., professional hockey).

MODELS OF PERIODIZATION

Several styles and models of periodization can be used to plan training for hockey players. Each model has merits and can be used with success, but the periodization model's selection must be made after considering the individual, team, and game and training schedules. These are often unchangeable variables; therefore, the periodization model used must make sense in the given scenario.

The periodization models highlighted in this chapter include linear periodization, nonlinear periodization, and concurrent periodization.

Linear Periodization

Linear periodization is the most common form of periodization. It is characterized by increasing intensity and decreasing volume throughout the macrocycle's preparatory phases. This is the form of periodization best suited for youth and beginner athletes who do not have an extensive training foundation. Figure 11.11 outlines a typical sequence of mesocycle focus and corresponding volumes and intensities.

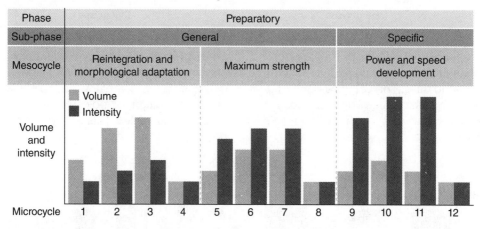

Phase	Preparatory											
Sub-phase	General								Specific			
Mesocycle	Reintegration and morphological adaptation				Maximum strength				Power and speed development			
	▨ Volume ■ Intensity											
Volume and intensity												
Microcycle	1	2	3	4	5	6	7	8	9	10	11	12

Figure 11.11 Linear periodization of volume and intensity in a 12-week off-season training program.

Nonlinear Periodization

Nonlinear periodization is characterized by weekly variations in volume and intensity within a mesocycle. With this style of periodization, many different physiological qualities can be trained simultaneously. Nonlinear periodization is ideal for advanced athletes who have a high training age and training foundation. Figure 11.12 outlines a typical sequence of mesocycle focus and corresponding volumes and intensities. Although volume and intensity undulate from week to week, the emphasis is placed on the primary focus of each mesocycle (e.g., maximum strength or power development), and within each session, only the primary movements are periodized in this fashion.

Concurrent Periodization

In concurrent periodization, multiple physiological qualities are trained within each session and across numerous mesocycles; it is like nonlinear periodization. Speed, power, strength, and energy systems are all trained daily within this model, but volumes and intensity are adjusted accordingly to account for the mesocycle's primary focus. Concurrent periodization in a nonlinear fashion is often the model of choice for hockey players due to the typical off-season's short duration; however, the selected model must be appropriate for the individual athlete.

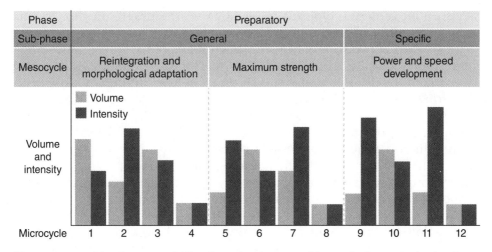

Figure 11.12 Nonlinear periodization of volume and intensity in a 12-week off-season training program.

DAILY TRAINING PARAMETERS

The training variables modified within each training session are known as the daily training parameters. These are the nuts and bolts of the program and are ultimately responsible for determining the physiological adaptations. The training program's primary goals should guide the exercise selection, order, and balance of movements. The desired training outcomes should also dictate the volume and intensity of training and rest periods between exercises or blocks of exercises.

Exercise Selection

The exercise selection is one of the most crucial daily training variables. Many things must be considered, including multijoint versus single-joint exercises, the plane of movement, complexity of movement, and load type, to name a few. Multijoint exercises, outlined in chapter 5, focus on specific movement patterns and involve multiple joints and muscle groups, as the name suggests. These exercises should make up the bulk of the training program. Single-joint exercises focus on specific muscles and are primarily used for accessory work (e.g., rotator cuff or isolated hamstring exercises).

The plane of movement (i.e., sagittal, frontal, and transverse) is another important consideration because hockey is a multiplanar sport. Exercises that move through different planes or a combination of planes are used to target specific performance requirements or balance overused planes. For example, off-ice lower-body training during the season should use the sagittal plane more frequently to balance the frontal plane skating load experienced on the ice. Another consideration for planes of movement is the position of the individual. For example, goalies might require additional frontal plane movements in the preparatory phases of the off-season. The complexity of the exercise or movement is typically guided by the athlete's training experience. Young or beginner athletes must master exercises with low complexity before progressing. In contrast, athletes who have high training experience might require more complex exercises to elicit specific physiological adaptations. Exercise complexity should also transition from low complexity early in the off-season's general preparatory phase to higher complexity and specificity in the specific preparatory phase.

The last consideration for exercise selection is the type of load. Typically, free weights and cables are preferred over machine loading due to the greater degree of freedom, increasing the neurological load. Free weights and cables require more coordination than machine loading; this coordination is essential for hockey performance. However, machine loading can be useful in specific instances. For example, injured athletes might benefit from the decreased coordination demand required by machine loading before they progress to free weights. These instances should be carefully evaluated on an individual basis.

Exercise Order and Balance

The order in which exercises are performed within a training session is critical to ensure the appropriate adaptations occur. In general, the primary exercises should follow these ordering rules:

- Fast to slow (perform speed and power exercises before slower strength exercises)
- High-intensity or -complexity to low-intensity or -complexity (exercises with the most neurological demand before exercises with low neurological demand)
- Multijoint to single-joint

These ordering rules are not always hard and fast. Coaches can deviate from these rules, but these deviations need to be thoughtfully planned to induce the specific adaptations. For example, with advanced hockey players, power and speed movements can be placed at the end of the training session while the player is under significant fatigue. This technique might have benefits for power endurance and should only be used in the advanced training stages.

The movement patterns must also be balanced throughout the microcycle, meaning that each pattern is equally used throughout the microcycle. An appropriate balance between squat, hinge, upper-body push and pull, and core patterns is crucial when designing training sessions. An example of this movement pattern balance within a microcycle is outlined in figure 11.13. Again, a coach can deviate from this balanced approach in special cases, such as rehabbing an injury that might require more attention.

	Day 1	Day 2	Day 3	Day 4
Block 1	**Power movement**	**Power complex**	**Power movement**	**Power complex**
	Core: anti-extension	Hip mobility	Core: whole body integration	Hip mobility
	Hip mobility		Hip mobility	
Block 2	Squat pattern (bilateral)	**Horizontal push**	Hinge pattern (bilateral)	**Vertical push**
	Vertical pull	Core: anti-extension	Horizontal pull	Core: anti-extension
	Core: anti-lateral flexion	Shoulder and T-spine mobility	Core: anti-lateral flexion	Shoulder and T-spine mobility
Block 3	Squat pattern (unilateral)	**Vertical push**	Hinge pattern (unilateral)	**Horizontal push**
	Horizontal pull	Core: hip flexor and lower ab	Vertical pull	Core: hip flexor and lower ab
	Hip mobility	Hip and adductor accessory	Hip and adductor mobility	Hip and adductor accessory
Block 4	Rotator cuff	Rotator cuff	Rotator cuff	Rotator cuff
	Core: anti-rotation	Core: anti-rotation	Core: anti-rotation	Core: anti-rotation

Figure 11.13 Movement balance within a four-training-day preparatory phase microcycle.

Volume, Intensity, and Rest

The final training parameters that must be considered include volume, intensity, and rest within the training session. These are known as the *loading parameters* and are the main variables for determining the physiological adaptations to the exercises performed. The microcycle's primary exercises are prioritized in terms of periodization and are where the main loading parameters are applied. Dr. Matthew Jordan from the Canadian Sport Institute–Calgary outlined these training parameters and targeted physiological adaptations in figure 11.14. During the competitive season, the volume is usually dictated by the game schedule. At the NHL level, teams play games every other night, on average. In this scenario, microdoses of specific training at various intensities must be applied. Microdosing implies frequent doses of very low volumes of intensities deemed appropriate for the given scenario. This technique allows for the accumulation of training stimulus while minimizing fatigue throughout the competitive season.

TUT(s)	Strength zone	Strength method	Target strength ability	Rep	Intensity	Sets	Tempo	Interset rest	
< 10	Zone 1	Reactive strength	Stretch-shortening cycle ability	6-10	Body mass	3-6	Short-long	1-2	Neural adaptations
		Heavy power	Maximal muscle power	3-6	60-80%	4-6	Fast	1.5-3	
		Heavy RFD	Late rate of force development	3-6	60-80%	4-6	Fast	1.5-3	
		Light power	Maximal muscle power	5-8	20-60%	5-8	Fast	1-2.5	
		Light RFD	Initial rate of force development	5-8	20-60%	5-8	Fast	1-2.5	
5-20		Eccentric deceleration and braking	Eccentric rate of force development	3-5	Body mass to 60%	3-5	X:1-3:1	1-2.5	
	Zone 3	Maximal strength	Maximal muscle strength	1-5	90-100% (very heavy)	3-5	2-4:1-3:X	2.5-5	
		Maximal eccentric strength	Maximal eccentric muscle strength	3-5	90-110% (very heavy)	3-5	2-10:0:A	2.5-5	Muscle morphology adaptation
20-40	Zone 2	Max rep exhaustive	Muscle hypertrophy	5-12	70-85% (heavy)	3-4	2-4:1-3:1-3	2-3	
		Max set exhaustive	Muscle hypertrophy	5-12	50-70% (moderate)	5-10	1-3:1-2:1-3	1-2	
		Assistant strength	Structural balance	8-15	60-80% (moderate)	2-4	1-3:1-3:1-3	1-2	
40-60		Slow tempo exhaustive	Muscle hypertrophy	5-8	60-80% (moderate)	3-5	4-6:1-3:4-6	1-3	
		Low load exhaustive	Muscle hypertrophy and strength endurance	15-30	30-60% (light)	2-4	1-2:0:1	2-3	
		Technical development	Movement competency and motor control	2-8	Light	3-10	NA	1-2	

Figure 11.14 Various loading parameters to target specific strength abilities.

Used with permission of Matthew Jordan.

SUMMARY

This chapter outlined the principles of training and how to develop an annual training plan for hockey players. Specific physiological responses and adaptations (e.g., strength, power, and speed) must be prioritized at various times within the calendar year. Understanding how to develop an annual plan will set the stage to allow athletes to reach their full physical potential. The overall training plan generally dictates the efficacy of the physiological responses to the training stimulus, but the annual plan must be adaptable based on daily and weekly monitoring of the physiological and psychological responses to the training. This chapter also outlined the importance of the daily training parameters and the importance of balance within the microcycle. This chapter's ultimate goal is to provide a blueprint for developing a training plan from the macro to micro levels.

Chapter 12

Postseason Training

The competitive hockey season is physically and mentally demanding. The sheer number of games played, combined with practices, off-ice training, and travel, significantly stresses the individual. If an athlete does not undertake a period of recovery and regeneration, they will be at risk of burnout. The macrocycle's transition phase is a critical period to reset. As stated in chapter 11, this phase follows the competitive in-season and links two annual training cycles. This transition contains a short period of complete rest, an active recovery block, and the postseason training phase. These elements are designed to enable mental and physical recovery and restoration before the yearly training plan's preparatory phase.

PASSIVE REST AND RECOVERY

Immediately following the competitive season, a short period of passive rest and recovery is advised. The duration of passive rest and recovery should not exceed seven days. Bompa and Haff (2009) highlight that a complete interruption of training could lead to detraining syndrome within two to three weeks. Although rare in hockey players, this syndrome is often characterized by insomnia, anxiety, depression, and appetite loss (Bompa and Haff 2009). Additionally, specific motor abilities, such as aerobic endurance, maximum strength, anaerobic endurance, strength endurance, and speed, decline at different rates after cessation of training. Issurin (2008) outlined these rates of decline in his book *Block Periodization*. He suggested the following duration (in days) that these motor abilities can be retained after training cessation:

- Aerobic endurance: 30±5 days
- Maximum strength: 30±5 days
- Anaerobic endurance: 18±4 days

- Strength endurance: 15±5 days
- Speed: 5±3 days

Therefore, to avoid detraining these variables, passive rest and recovery should be of short duration.

ACTIVE RECOVERY

Immediately following the short period of passive rest and recovery, an active recovery period of approximately one to two weeks should commence. During this period, the focus is on unstructured, enjoyable, and mainly aerobic activities. These activities can include playing other recreational sports, swimming, cycling, hiking, and so on. This active recovery period should not involve any hockey-specific technical or tactical training. It is designed to promote psychological and physical recovery, and any structured practice is discouraged during this time. The transition phase should include participation in various sports and activities for youth hockey players, outlined in the long-term player development model in chapter 1.

POSTSEASON TRAINING

Following the two to three weeks of passive and active recovery, postseason training commences to further prepare the athlete for the upcoming preparatory phase of the annual training cycle. This postseason training phase is generally two to three weeks in duration and includes movement capacity, general resistance training, and aerobic training. The aerobic activity in this portion of the transition phase should continue to be unstructured and enjoyable, as in the active recovery period. Two levels of programming (beginner to intermediate and advanced) are outlined in the following sections.

WHAT IS TEMPO?

The tempo of the exercise is the velocity or time in which the movement is performed. Tempo is broken down into four phases: eccentric phase, the transition between eccentric and concentric phases, concentric phase, and the transition between concentric and eccentric phases. For example, a tempo of 3-0-1-0 means 3 seconds of lowering the weight in the eccentric phase, no pause between eccentric and concentric phases, a 1-second concentric phase, and no pause between the concentric and eccentric phases. An X in the tempo represents an explosive movement.

Beginner to Intermediate Postseason Training

The beginner to intermediate postseason training block is intended for younger athletes and athletes without extensive off-ice training experience. This programming level consists of two movement capacity sessions (table 12.1), two general strength sessions (table 12.2), and three or four days of unstructured aerobic training. During this phase, the training emphasis is placed on movement mechanics and acclimatizing the individual to off-ice training before the preparatory phase. The main challenge with a two-day general strength program is in the design and structural balance. The goal is to build a balanced program that checks all the movement pattern boxes, including the squat, hinge, upper-body push, upper-body pull, and core patterns.

Table 12.1 Sample Two-Day Beginner to Intermediate Postseason Movement Capacity Program

Day 1					
		Week 1		**Week 2**	
Category	**Exercise**	**Sets**	**Reps, distance, or time**	**Sets**	**Reps, distance, or time**	**Page**
Inhibition of tight tissue	Hip flexors SMR	1	30 sec each side	1	30 sec each side	43
	Tensor fasciae latae (TFL) SMR	1	30 sec each side	1	30 sec each side	44
	Iliotibial (IT) band SMR	1	30 sec each side	1	30 sec each side	44
	Quadriceps SMR	1	30 sec each side	1	30 sec each side	44
	Adductors SMR	1	30 sec each side	1	30 sec each side	44
	Hamstrings SMR	1	30 sec each side	1	30 sec each side	44
	Calf muscles SMR	1	30 sec each side	1	30 sec each side	44
	Pectoralis minor SMR	1	30 sec each side	1	30 sec each side	45
	Latissimus dorsi SMR	1	30 sec each side	1	30 sec each side	45
	Prone quadriceps static stretch	1	30 sec each side	1	45 sec each side	48

(continued)

Table 12.1 *(continued)*

		Week 1		Week 2		
Category	Exercise	Sets	Reps, distance, or time	Sets	Reps, distance, or time	Page
Inhibition of tight tissue	Quadruped adductor static stretch	1	30 sec	1	45 sec	50
	Supine hamstring static stretch	1	30 sec each side	1	45 sec each side	51
	Corner pec static stretch	1	30 sec	1	45 sec	52
	Banded over-head static stretch	1	30 sec each side	1	45 sec each side	53
Joint mobilization	Ankle distraction	1	30 sec each side	1	30 sec each side	55
	Ankle glide	1	15	1	15	56
	Hip distraction	1	30 sec each side	1	30 sec each side	57
	Hip rotations	1	3 each side	1	4 each side	58
	T-spine distrac-tion	1	10 sec each level	1	10 sec each level	59
	Shoulder distrac-tion	1	30 sec each side	1	30 sec each side	60
Muscle activation	Glute bridge	1	10	1	10	97
	Groin squeeze	1	10 × 2 second hold	1	10 × 2 second hold	107
	Shoulder com-plex: Ys, Ts, Ls	1	10 each exercise	1	10 each exercise	63
Movement integration	Stationary knee hug	1	5 each side	1	5 each side	65
	Stationary quad pull	1	5 each side	1	5 each side	65
	Linear march	1	49 ft (15 m)	1	49 ft (15 m)	65
	Straight-leg march	1	49 ft (15 m)	1	49 ft (15 m)	66

Day 1 *(continued)*

		Week 1		Week 2		
Category	Exercise	Sets	Reps, distance, or time	Sets	Reps, distance, or time	Page
Inhibition of tight tissue	Hip flexors SMR	1	30 sec each side	1	30 sec each side	43
	Tensor fasciae latae (TFL) SMR	1	30 sec each side	1	30 sec each side	44
	Iliotibial (IT) band SMR	1	30 sec each side	1	30 sec each side	44
	Quadriceps SMR	1	30 sec each side	1	30 sec each side	44
	Adductors SMR	1	30 sec each side	1	30 sec each side	44
	Hamstrings SMR	1	30 sec each side	1	30 sec each side	44
	Calf muscles SMR	1	30 sec each side	1	30 sec each side	44
	Pectoralis minor SMR	1	30 sec each side	1	30 sec each side	45
	Latissimus dorsi SMR	1	30 sec each side	1	30 sec each side	45
Muscle length	Half-kneeling hip flexor AIS	1	10 each side	1	10 each side	48
	Prone quadriceps AIS	1	10 each side	1	10 each side	49
	Quadruped adductor rock back	1	10	1	10	50
	Supine hamstring AIS	1	10 each side	1	10 each side	52
	Corner pec AIS	1	10	1	10	53
	Banded over-head AIS	1	10 each side	1	10 each side	54
Joint mobilization	Ankle glide	1	15 each side	1	15 each side	56
	Hip distrac-tion and glide (medial–lateral)	1	10 each side	1	10 each side	57
	T-spine glide (flex-ion–extension)	1	10	1	10	59

(continued)

Table 12.1　*(continued)*

		\multicolumn{2}{c}{Week 1}	\multicolumn{2}{c}{Week 2}	
			Reps,		Reps,	
			distance,		distance,	
Category	Exercise	Sets	or time	Sets	or time	Page
Muscle activation	Front plank	1	30 sec	1	30 sec	94
	Side plank	1	30 sec each side	1	30 sec each side	99
	Glute bridge	1	10	1	10	97
	Shoulder complex: Ys, Ts, Ls	1	10 each exercise	1	10 each exercise	64
Movement integration	Stationary knee hug	1	5 each side	1	5 each side	65
	Stationary quad pull	1	5 each side	1	5 each side	65
	Lateral lunge	1	5 each side	1	5 each side	66
	Drop lunge	1	5 each side	1	5 each side	66
	Drop step squat	1	5 each side	1	5 each side	67

Heading above the table: **Day 2 *(continued)***

Table 12.2　Sample Two-Day Beginner to Intermediate Postseason General Resistance Training Program

Day 1	Tempo	Rest	Week 1	Week 2	Page
A1. Bodyweight squat	3-0-1-0		2 × 15	2 × 12	116
A2. Push-up	3-0-1-0		2 × 10	2 × 12	131
A3. Romanian deadlift (RDL) with dowel	3-0-1-0		2 × 10	2 × 10	123
A4. Rings row	3-0-1-0		2 × 8	2 × 10	135
A5. Front plank	N/A	60 sec	2 × 30 sec	2 × 35 sec	94
Day 2	**Tempo**	**Rest**	**Week 1**	**Week 2**	**Page**
A1. Split squat (body weight)	3-0-1-0		2 × 10 each side	2 × 10 each side	119
A2. Kneeling cable pull-down	3-0-1-0		2 × 12	2 × 12	138
A3. Stability ball leg curl	3-0-1-0		2 × 8	2 × 8	129
A4. Push-up (feet on bench)	3-0-1-0		2 × 6-8	2 × 8-10	131
A5. Side plank	N/A	60 sec	2 × 20 sec each side	2 × 25 sec each side	99

Advanced Postseason Training

The advanced postseason training block is intended for athletes who have extensive off-ice training experience. This programming level consists of three movement capacity sessions (table 12.3), three general strength sessions (table 12.4), and three or four days of unstructured aerobic training. Like the beginner to intermediate program, the training emphasis is placed on movement mechanics and acclimatizing the individual to off-ice training before the commencement of the preparatory phase that follows. The program should balance movement patterns, including the squat, hinge, upper-body push, upper-body pull, and core patterns.

Table 12.3 Sample Three-Day Advanced Postseason Movement Capacity Program

		Day 1						
			Week 1		Week 2		Week 3	
Category	Exercise	Sets	Reps, distance, or time	Sets	Reps, distance, or time	Sets	Reps, distance, or time	Page
Inhibition of tight tissue	Hip flexors SMR	1	30 sec each side	1	30 sec each side	1	30 sec each side	43
	Tensor fasciae latae (TFL) SMR	1	30 sec each side	1	30 sec each side	1	30 sec each side	44
	Iliotibial (IT) band SMR	1	30 sec each side	1	30 sec each side	1	30 sec each side	44
	Quadriceps SMR	1	30 sec each side	1	30 sec each side	1	30 sec each side	44
	Adductors SMR	1	30 sec each side	1	30 sec each side	1	30 sec each side	44
	Hamstrings SMR	1	30 sec each side	1	30 sec each side	1	30 sec each side	44
	Calf muscles SMR	1	30 sec each side	1	30 sec each side	1	30 sec each side	44
	Pectoralis minor SMR	1	30 sec each side	1	30 sec each side	1	30 sec each side	45
	Latissimus dorsi SMR	1	30 sec each side	1	30 sec each side	1	30 sec each side	45
Muscle length	Half-kneeling hip flexor static stretch	1	30 sec each side	1	45 sec each side	1	60 sec each side	47

(continued)

Table 12.3 *(continued)*

		Day 1 *(continued)*						
			Week 1		Week 2		Week 3	
Category	Exercise	Sets	Reps, distance, or time	Sets	Reps, distance, or time	Sets	Reps, distance, or time	Page
Muscle length	Quadruped adductor static stretch	1	30 sec	1	45 sec	1	60 sec each side	50
	Supine hamstring static stretch	1	30 sec each side	1	45 sec each side	1	60 sec each side	51
	Corner pec static stretch	1	30 sec	1	45 sec	1	60 sec each side	52
	Banded overhead static stretch	1	30 sec each side	1	45 sec each side	1	60 sec each side	53
Joint mobilization	Ankle distraction	1	30 sec each side	1	30 sec each side	1	30 sec each side	55
	Hip distraction	1	30 sec each side	1	30 sec each side	1	30 sec each side	57
	Hip rotations	1	3 each side	1	4 each side	1	4 each side	58
	T-spine distraction	1	10 sec each level	1	10 sec each level	1	10 sec each level	59
	Shoulder distraction	1	30 sec each side	1	30 sec each side	1	30 sec each side	60
Muscle activation	Glute bridge	1	10	1	10	1	10	97
	Groin squeeze	1	10 × 2 sec hold	1	10 × 2 sec hold	1	10 × 2 sec hold	107
	Shoulder complex: Ys, Ts, Ls	1	10 each exercise	1	10 each exercise	1	10 each exercise	63
Movement integration	Stationary knee hug	1	5 each side	1	5 each side	1	5 each side	65
	Stationary quad pull	1	5 each side	1	5 each side	1	5 each side	65
	Elbow to instep	1	5 each side	1	5 each side	1	5 each side	65
	Linear march	1	49 ft (15 m)	1	49 ft (15 m)	1	49 ft (15 m)	65
	Straight-leg march	1	49 ft (15 m)	1	49 ft (15 m)	1	49 ft (15 m)	66

		Day 2						
		Week 1		Week 2		Week 3		
Category	Exercise	Sets	Reps, distance, or time	Sets	Reps, distance, or time	Sets	Reps, distance, or time	Page
Inhibition of tight tissue	Hip flexors SMR	1	30 sec each side	1	30 sec each side	1	30 sec each side	43
	Tensor fasciae latae (TFL) SMR	1	30 sec each side	1	30 sec each side	1	30 sec each side	44
	Iliotibial (IT) band SMR	1	30 sec each side	1	30 sec each side	1	30 sec each side	44
	Quadriceps SMR	1	30 sec each side	1	30 sec each side	1	30 sec each side	44
	Adductors SMR	1	30 sec each side	1	30 sec each side	1	30 sec each side	44
	Hamstrings SMR	1	30 sec each side	1	30 sec each side	1	30 sec each side	44
	Calf muscles SMR	1	30 sec each side	1	30 sec each side	1	30 sec each side	44
	Pectoralis minor SMR	1	30 sec each side	1	30 sec each side	1	30 sec each side	45
	Latissimus dorsi SMR	1	30 sec each side	1	30 sec each side	1	30 sec each side	45
Muscle length	Supine assisted PNF hip flexor stretch	1	3 each side	1	4 each side	1	4 each side	47
	Prone quad-riceps PNF stretch	1	3 each side	1	4 each side	1	4 each side	48
	Butterfly adductor PNF stretch	1	3	1	4	1	4	50
	Supine ham-string PNF stretch	1	3 each side	1	4 each side	1	4 each side	52
	Corner pec PNF stretch	1	3	1	4	1	4	53
	Banded over-head PNF stretch	1	3 each side	1	4 each side	1	4 each side	54

(continued)

Table 12.3 *(continued)*

			Day 2 *(continued)*					
			Week 1		**Week 2**		**Week 3**	
Category	**Exercise**	**Sets**	**Reps, distance, or time**	**Sets**	**Reps, distance, or time**	**Sets**	**Reps, distance, or time**	**Page**
Muscle length	Hip distraction and glide (medial–lateral)	1	10 each side	1	10 each side	1	10 each side	57
	T-spine distraction and glide	1	5 each level	1	5 each level	1	5 each level	59
	Shoulder distraction and glide	1	10 each side	1	10 each side	1	10 each side	61
Muscle activation	Front plank	1	30 sec	1	45 sec	1	45 sec	94
	Side plank	1	30 sec each side	1	30 sec each side	1	30 sec each side	99
	Linear miniband walk	1	33 ft (10 m) (forward and backward)	1	33 ft (10 m) (forward and backward)	1	33 ft (10 m) (forward and backward)	63
	Shoulder complex	1	10 each exercise	1	10 each exercise	1	10 each exercise	63
Movement integration	Stationary knee hug	1	5 each side	1	5 each side	1	5 each side	65
	Stationary quad pull	1	5 each side	1	5 each side	1	5 each side	65
	Lateral lunge	1	5 each side	1	5 each side	1	5 each side	66
	Drop lunge	1	5 each side	1	5 each side	1	5 each side	66
	Drop step squat	1	5 each side	1	5 each side	1	5 each side	67
			Day 3					
			Week 1		**Week 2**		**Week 3**	
Category	**Exercise**	**Sets**	**Reps, distance, or time**	**Sets**	**Reps, distance, or time**	**Sets**	**Reps, distance, or time**	**Page**
Inhibition of tight tissue	Hip flexors SMR	1	30 sec each side	1	30 sec each side	1	30 sec each side	43

Day 3 *(continued)*								
		Week 1		Week 2		Week 3		
Category	Exercise	Sets	Reps, distance, or time	Sets	Reps, distance, or time	Sets	Reps, distance, or time	Page
Inhibition of tight tissue	Iliotibial (IT) band SMR	1	30 sec each side	1	30 sec each side	1	30 sec each side	44
	Quadriceps SMR	1	30 sec each side	1	30 sec each side	1	30 sec each side	44
	Adductors SMR	1	30 sec each side	1	30 sec each side	1	30 sec each side	44
	Hamstrings SMR	1	30 sec each side	1	30 sec each side	1	30 sec each side	44
	Calf muscles SMR	1	30 sec each side	1	30 sec each side	1	30 sec each side	44
	Pectoralis minor SMR	1	30 sec each side	1	30 sec each side	1	30 sec each side	45
	Latissimus dorsi SMR	1	30 sec each side	1	30 sec each side	1	30 sec each side	45
Muscle length	Half-kneeling hip flexor AIS	1	10 each side	1	10 each side	1	10 each side	48
	Prone quadriceps AIS	1	10 each side	1	10 each side	1	10 each side	49
	Quadruped adductor rock back	1	10	1	10	1	10	50
	Supine hamstring AIS	1	10 each side	1	10 each side	1	10 each side	52
	Corner pec AIS	1	10	1	10	1	10	53
	Banded overhead AIS	1	10 each side	1	10 each side	1	10 each side	54
Joint mobilization	Ankle glide	1	15 each side	1	15 each side	1	15 each side	56
	Hip distraction and glide (anterior–posterior)	1	10 each side	1	10 each side	1	10 each side	57
	Hip rotations	1	5 each side	1	5 each side	1	5 each side	58
	T-spine glide (flexion–extension)	1	10	1	10	1	10	59

(continued)

Table 12.3 *(continued)*

			Week 1		Week 2		Week 3		
Category	Exercise	Sets	Reps, distance, or time	Sets	Reps, distance, or time	Sets	Reps, distance, or time	Page
Joint mobilization	Shoulder external rotation	1	5 each side	1	5 each side	1	5 each side	61
Muscle activation	Front plank	1	30 sec	1	45 sec	1	45 sec	94
	Glute bridge	1	10	1	10	1	10	97
	Lateral mini-band walk	1	33 ft (10 m) each way	1	33 ft (10 m) each way	1	33 ft (10 m) each way	64
	Shoulder complex	1	10 each exercise	1	10 each exercise	1	10 each exercise	63
Movement integration	Stationary knee hug	1	5 each side	1	5 each side	1	5 each side	65
	Stationary quad pull	1	5 each side	1	5 each side	1	5 each side	65
	Elbow to instep	1	5 each side	1	5 each side	1	5 each side	65
	Drop lunge	1	5 each side	1	5 each side	1	5 each side	66
	Drop unders	1	5 each side	1	5 each side	1	5 each side	67
	Straight-leg march	1	49 ft (15 m)	1	49 ft (15 m)	1	49 ft (15 m)	66

Day 3 (continued)

Table 12.4 Sample Advanced Postseason General Resistance Training

Day 1	Tempo	Rest	Week 1	Week 2	Week 3	Page
A1. Goblet squat	3-0-1-0		2 × 15	3 × 12	3 × 10	117
A2. Push-up	3-0-1-0		2 × 15	3 × 20	3 × 25	131
A3. Front plank	N/A		2 × 30 sec	3 × 45 sec	3 × 60 sec	94
A4. Four-way cable hip series	1-0-1-0	60 sec	2 × 5 each pattern	2 × 5 each pattern	2 × 5 each pattern	108
B1. Romanian deadlift (RDL)	3-0-1-0		2 × 10	3 × 10	3 × 10	123
B2. Rings row	3-0-1-0		2 × 10	3 × 10-12	3 × 12	135

Day 1	Tempo	Rest	Week 1	Week 2	Week 3	Page
B3. Side plank	N/A		2 × 30 sec each side	3 × 30 sec each side	3 × 45 sec each side	99
B4. Shoulder external rotation	2-0-2-0	60 sec	2 × 12 each side	2 × 12 each side	2 × 12 each side	104
Day 2	**Tempo**	**Rest**	**Week 1**	**Week 2**	**Week 3**	**Page**
A1. Split squat	3-0-1-0		2 × 12 each side	3 × 10 each side	3 × 8 each side	119
A2. Kneeling cable pull-down	3-0-1-0		2 × 12	3 × 12	3 × 10	138
A3. Upward cable X to extension	2-0-2-0	60 sec	2 × 10	2 × 10	2 × 10	105
B1. Stability ball leg curl	3-0-1-0		2 × 8	3 × 10	3 × 10	129
B2. Half-kneeling landmine press	3-0-1-0		2 × 12 each side	3 × 10 each side	3 × 8 each side	133
B3. Half-kneeling Pallof press	1-2-1-0	60 sec	2 × 10 each side	2 × 10 each side	2 × 10 each side	101
Day 3	**Tempo**	**Rest**	**Week 1**	**Week 2**	**Week 3**	**Page**
A1. Trap bar dead-lift	3-0-1-0		2 × 12	3 × 10	3 × 8	125
A2. Push-up, hands on BOSU ball	3-0-1-0		2 × 10-12	3 × 10-12	3 × 12-15	131
A3. Glute bridge	2-1-1-0		2 × 10	3 × 12	3 × 12	97
A4. Downward cable X to extension	2-0-2-0	60 sec	2 × 10	2 × 10	2 × 10	106
B1. Reverse lunge to hip lock	3-0-1-0		2 × 10 each side	3 × 10 each side	3 × 10 each side	120
B2. Staggered stance single-arm dumbbell row	3-0-1-0		2 × 12 each side	3 × 10 each side	3 × 8 each side	137
B3. Half-kneeling stability lift	2-0-1-0		2 × 10 each side	3 × 10 each side	3 × 12 each side	102
B4. Glute bridge groin squeeze (hold)	N/A	60 sec	2 × 10 sec	2 × 10 sec	2 × 10 sec	108

SUMMARY

The postseason is a time in which recovery and regeneration are emphasized. This period allows the athlete to recover physically and mentally from the previous season without detraining. Most of the activities during the postseason should be fun and enjoyable while at the same time preparing the athletes for the upcoming demands of the preparatory phase. Hockey-specific activities such as on-ice tactical sessions are to be avoided during the postseason or transition phase. That said, unstructured on-ice shinny and fun games are acceptable if the athlete wishes, but off-ice activities should be emphasized.

Chapter 13

Off-Season Training

The off-season is the most critical period for developing the physiological performance characteristics that support a hockey player's on-ice playing abilities. These performance characteristics include movement capacity, strength, power development, acceleration, speed, and ability to change directions. A needs analysis for each athlete should be performed before a training program is designed for the athlete. This needs analysis includes many of the physical assessments outlined in chapter 2 and helps the coach develop a specific set of goals to accomplish in the off-season. By following the planning and programming guidelines in chapter 11, the individualized training plan is developed based on the needs analysis and goal setting. As the athlete progresses through the training program, daily and weekly monitoring of physiological and psychological variables must be conducted to fine-tune the training program from week to week. As mentioned in chapter 11, the overall plan is highly adaptable and must be guided by the acute adaptations to training on the micro level. This test/retest cycle must be ongoing to ensure the athlete reaches their predetermined goals.

OFF-SEASON PROGRAM

Regardless of age or experience, the general daily training breakdown should abide by the following order of operations:

1. Movement capacity
2. Movement skill and strength, acceleration, and change of direction
3. Power and strength training
4. Energy systems development

This order of operations is an adaptable guideline based on the requirements of the training plan. For example, an athlete performing a two-day power and strength program might perform only movement capacity, movement skill and strength, and energy systems development on specific days. However, the order of operations remains the same in most cases.

In general, movement capacity training should be performed every training day and potentially on off-days as well. Chapter 3 outlined the specific movement capacity sequence as follows:

1. Inhibition of tight tissue
2. Muscle lengthening
3. Joint mobilization
4. Muscle activation
5. Movement integration
6. Structural and neural priming

This sequence is crucial to prepare the joints and tissues for the training session to follow and cannot be overlooked.

BEGINNER AND INTERMEDIATE OFF-SEASON PROGRAM

The beginner and intermediate off-season program is a three-day program consisting of movement strength and skill, power and strength, and energy systems development. These sessions typically follow linear progressions; however, in some cases, the power and strength sessions can be accomplished through nonlinear concurrent progressions throughout the off-season phases.

Beginner and Intermediate Movement Strength and Skill

Movement strength and skill training for the beginner and intermediate player is designed to develop linear, lateral, and multidirectional movement skills. Young and inexperienced athletes must learn to walk before they can run. The movement skills and patterns that young athletes acquire early in their development set the stage for their long-term development as athletes. Therefore, it is imperative not to skip steps along the way, and progressions should be based on the athlete's competencies. Tables 13.1 through 13.3 outline sample movement skill and strength training programs for the macrocycle's preparatory phase.

Table 13.1 Sample Phase 1: Three-Day Beginner and Intermediate Off-Season (Preparatory Phase) Movement Strength and Skill Training Program

	Day 1 linear				
	Week 1	Week 2	Week 3	Week 4	Page
Rudimentary hop series: linear, double-leg forward	1 × 6	1 × 7	1 × 8	1 × 10	69
Rudimentary hop series: linear, double-leg backward	1 × 6	1 × 7	1 × 8	1 × 10	69
Drop squat	2 × 3	2 × 3	1 × 4	N/A	159
Drop squat, eyes closed	N/A	N/A	1 × 4	2 × 5	159
Noncountermovement jump (land on box)	2 × 5	2 × 5	1 × 5	N/A	173
Countermovement jump to box	N/A	N/A	1 × 5	2 × 5	161
Medicine ball chest toss	1 × 5	1 × 5	1 × 5	1 × 5	185
Medicine ball slam	1 × 5	1 × 5	1 × 5	1 × 5	186
Deliberate wall drill	1 × 5 sec each side	1 × 5 sec each side	1 × 5 sec each side	N/A	206
Linear wall drill, single exchange	N/A	1 × 3 each side	1 × 4 each side	1 × 5 each side	205
Resisted march	1 × 49 ft (15 m)	2 × 49 ft (15 m)	3 × 49 ft (15 m)	2 × 49 ft (15 m)	209
Falling acceleration	N/A	N/A	4 × 33 ft (10 m)	4 × 33 ft (10 m)	211
	Day 2 lateral				
	Week 1	Week 2	Week 3	Week 4	Page
Rudimentary hop series: lateral, double-leg	1 × 6 each way	1 × 7 each way	1 × 8 each way	1 × 10 each way	69
Drop squat	2 × 3	2 × 3	1 × 4	N/A	159
Drop squat, eyes closed	N/A	N/A	1 × 4	2 × 5	159
Lateral noncountermovement jump (land on box)	2 × 5 each way	2 × 5 each way	1 × 5 each way	N/A	149

(continued)

Table 13.1 *(continued)*

	Day 2 lateral *(continued)*				
	Week 1	**Week 2**	**Week 3**	**Week 4**	**Page**
Countermovement jump to box: lateral, double-leg	N/A	N/A	1 × 5 each way	2 × 5 each way	161
Medicine ball perpendicular toss	2 × 3 each side	2 × 4 each side	2 × 5 each side	2 × 3 each side	180
Stationary skater stride	1 × 5 each side	1 × 6 each side	1 × 7 each side	1 × 5 each side	191
Low skater lateral stride	N/A	N/A	1 × 33-49 ft (10-15 m) each way	1 × 33-49 ft (15 m) each way	193
	Day 3 crossover				
	Week 1	**Week 2**	**Week 3**	**Week 4**	**Page**
Rudimentary hop series: linear, single-leg	1 × 5 each way	1 × 5 each way	1 × 5 each way	1 × 5 each way	69
Rudimentary hop series: lateral, single-leg	1 × 5 each way	1 × 5 each way	1 × 5 each way	1 × 5 each way	69
Noncountermovement jump (land on box)	1 × 3 each side	1 × 4 each side	1 × 5 each side	1 × 5 each side	147
Noncountermovement jump to box, lateral, inside foot	1 × 3 each side	1 × 4 each side	1 × 5 each side	1 × 5 each side	147
Medicine ball slam	1 × 3	1 × 4	1 × 5	1 × 3	186
Medicine ball chest toss	1 × 3	1 × 4	1 × 5	1 × 3	185
Stationary skater crossover	1 × 5 each side	1 × 6 each side	1 × 7 each side	1 × 5 each side	198
Low skater crossover	N/A	N/A	1 × 33-49 ft (10-15 m) each way	1 × 49 ft (15 m) each way	199

Table 13.2 Sample Phase 2: Three-Day Beginner and Intermediate Off-Season (Preparatory Phase) Movement Strength and Skill Training Program

	Day 1 linear				
	Week 1	**Week 2**	**Week 3**	**Week 4**	**Page**
Rudimentary hop series: linear, double-leg forward	1 × 10	1 × 10	1 × 10	1 × 10	69
Rudimentary hop series: linear, double-leg backward	1 × 10	1 × 10	1 × 10	1 × 10	69
Drop squat, eyes closed	2 × 5	N/A	N/A	N/A	159
Drop squat, single-leg	1 × 3 each side	2 × 3 each side	1 × 4 each side	1 × 4 each side	159
Drop squat, single-leg, eyes closed	N/A	1 × 3 each side	2 × 4 each side	2 × 4 each side	159
Countermovement jump, over 6-in. (15 cm) hurdles	2 × 6	1 × 6	N/A	N/A	30
Double-contact jump, over 6-in. (15 cm) hurdles	N/A	1 × 6	2 × 6	2 × 6	167
Medicine ball chest toss	1 × 5	1 × 5	1 × 5	1 × 5	185
Medicine ball slam	1 × 5	1 × 5	1 × 5	1 × 5	186
Linear wall drill, single exchange	1 × 5 each side	N/A	N/A	N/A	205
Double-exchange wall drill	1 × 3 each side	2 × 3 each side	N/A	N/A	206
Resisted march	3 × 49 ft (15 m)	4 × 49 ft (15 m)	4 × 49 ft (15 m)	2 × 49 ft (15 m)	209
Resisted high-knee run	N/A	2 × 49 ft (15 m)	3 × 49 ft (15 m)	4 × 49 ft (15 m)	210
Falling acceleration	2 × 33 ft (10 m)	2 × 33 ft (10 m)	3 × 33 ft (10 m)	3 × 33 ft (10 m)	211
Falling acceleration to base	2 × 33 ft (10 m)	3 × 33 ft (10 m)	4 × 33 ft (10 m)	4 × 33 ft (10 m)	212

(continued)

Table 13.2 *(continued)*

	Day 2 lateral				
	Week 1	**Week 2**	**Week 3**	**Week 4**	**Page**
Rudimentary hop series: lateral, double-leg	1 × 10 each way	1 × 10 each way	1 × 10each way	1 × 10 each way	69
Lateral countermovement jump, over 6-in. (15 cm) hurdles	2 × 6 each way	1 × 6 each way	N/A	N/A	163
Lateral double-contact jump, over 6-in. (15 cm) hurdles	N/A	1 × 6 each way	2 × 6 each way	2 × 6 each way	167
Low skater lateral stride	3 × 49 ft (15 m) each way	1 × 49 ft (15 m) each way	1 × 49 ft (15 m) each way	N/A	193
Resisted explosive lateral stride	N/A	2 × 49 ft (15 m) each way	2 × 49 ft (15 m) each way	3 × 49 ft (15 m) each way	196
Noncountermovement lateral bound	2 × 5 each side	1 × 5 each side	N/A	N/A	155
Countermovement lateral bound	N/A	1 × 5 each side	2 × 5 each side	1 × 5 each side	164
Double-contact lateral bound	N/A	N/A	N/A	1 × 3 each side	167
Half-kneeling lateral acceleration	2 × 33 ft (10 m) each way	3 × 33 ft (10 m) each way	3 × 33 ft (10 m) each way	2 × 33 ft (10 m) each way	197
	Day 3 crossover				
	Week 1	**Week 2**	**Week 3**	**Week 4**	**Page**
Rudimentary hop series: linear, single-leg, forward and backward	1 × 5 each way	1 × 5 each way	1 × 5 each way	1 × 5 each way	69
Rudimentary hop series: lateral, single-leg	1 × 5 each way	1 × 5 each way	1 × 5 each way	1 × 5 each way	69
Countermovement jump, over 6-in. (15 cm) hurdles	1 × 6 each side	1 × 6 each side	N/A	N/A	30
Double-contact jump: linear, single-leg over 6-in. (15 cm) hurdles	N/A	N/A	1 × 6 each side	1 × 6 each side	167

	Day 3 crossover *(continued)*				
	Week 1	**Week 2**	**Week 3**	**Week 4**	**Page**
Forward step medicine ball perpendicular toss	1 × 5 each side	1 × 5 each side	1 × 5 each side	1 × 5 each side	181
Low skater crossover	3 × 49 ft (15 m) each way	1 × 49 ft (15 m) each way	1 × 49 ft (15 m) each way	N/A	199
Resisted explosive crossover	N/A	2 x 15m each way	2 x 15m each way	3 x 15m each way	201
Crossover to base	N/A	2 × 3 each way	1 × 3 each way	N/A	202
Crossover to base and return	N/A	N/A	1 × 3 each way	2 × 3 each way	203
Half-kneeling crossover acceleration	2 × 33 ft (10 m) each way	3 × 33 ft (10 m) each way	3 × 33 ft (10 m) each way	2 × 33 ft (10 m) each way	204

Table 13.3 Sample Phase 3: Three-Day Beginner and Intermediate Off-Season (Preparatory Phase) Movement Strength and Skill Training Program

	Day 1 linear				
	Week 1	**Week 2**	**Week 3**	**Week 4**	**Page**
Rudimentary hop series: linear, double-leg forward	1 × 10	1 × 10	1 × 10	1 × 10	69
Rudimentary hop series: linear, double-leg backward	1 × 10	1 × 10	1 × 10	1 × 10	69
Double-contact jump, over 6-in. (15 cm) hurdles	1 × 6	N/A	N/A	N/A	167
Continuous jump: double-leg, over 6-in. (15 cm) hurdles	1 × 6	2 × 6	2 × 6	1 × 6	168
Medicine ball chest toss	1 × 5	1 × 5	1 × 5	1 × 5	185
Medicine ball slam	1 × 5	1 × 5	1 × 5	1 × 5	186
Resisted march to resisted high-knee run (transition)	4 × 33 ft (10 m) + 33 ft (10 m)	5 × 33 ft (10 m) + 33 ft (10 m)	3 × 33 ft (10 m) + 33 ft (10 m)	2 × 33 ft (10 m) + 33 ft (10 m)	209, 210

(continued)

Table 13.3 *(continued)*

	Day 1 linear *(continued)*				
	Week 1	**Week 2**	**Week 3**	**Week 4**	**Page**
Get-up acceleration	2 × 33 ft (10 m)	2 × 33 ft (10 m)	2 × 33 ft (10 m)	N/A	212
Acceleration to base and return	2 × 33 ft (10 m)	2 × 33 ft (10 m)	2 × 33 ft (10 m)	1 × 33 ft (10 m)	225
Partner mirroring, linear	N/A	2 × 49 ft (15 m)	2 × 49 ft (15 m)	3 × 49 ft (15 m)	232
	Day 2 lateral				
	Week 1	**Week 2**	**Week 3**	**Week 4**	**Page**
Rudimentary hop series: lateral, double-leg	1 × 10 each way	1 × 10 each way	1 × 10 each way	1 × 10 each way	69
Lateral double-contact jump, over 6-in. (15 cm) hurdles	1 × 6	N/A	N/A	N/A	167
Continuous jump: lateral, double-leg, over 6-in. (15 cm) hurdles	1 × 6	2 × 6	2 × 6	1 × 6	168
Resisted explosive lateral stride	3 × 49 ft (15 m) each way	3 × 49 ft (15 m) each way	2 × 49 ft (15 m) each way	1 × 49 ft (15 m) each way	196
Double-contact lateral bound	1 × 3 each side	N/A	N/A	N/A	167
Continuous lateral bound	1 × 3 each side	2 × 4 each side	2 × 3 each side	1 × 3 each side	169
Half-kneeling lateral acceleration	2 × 33 ft (10 m) each way	2 × 33 ft (10 m) each way	2 × 33 ft (10 m) each way	1 × 33 ft (10 m) each way	197
Lateral shuffle to linear acceleration	2 × 33 ft (10 m) each direction	3 × 33 ft (10 m) each direction	3 × 33 ft (10 m) each direction	1 × 33 ft (10 m) each direction	227
	Day 3 crossover				
	Week 1	**Week 2**	**Week 3**	**Week 4**	**Page**
Rudimentary hop series: linear, single-leg, forward and backward	1 × 5 each way	1 × 5 each way	1 × 5 each way	1 × 5 each way	69

	Day 3 crossover *(continued)*				
	Week 1	**Week 2**	**Week 3**	**Week 4**	**Page**
Rudimentary hop series: lateral, single-leg	1 × 5 each way	1 × 5 each way	1 × 5 each way	1 × 5 each way	69
Double-contact jump, over 6-in. (15 cm) hurdles	1 × 6 each side	N/A	N/A	N/A	167
Continuous jump: linear, over 6-in. (15 cm) hurdles	1 × 6 each side	2 × 6 each side	2 × 6 each side	1 × 6 each side	168
Forward step medicine ball perpendicular toss	1 × 5 each side	1 × 5 each side	1 × 5 each side	1 × 5 each side	181
Resisted explosive crossover	3 × 49 ft (15 m) each way	3 × 49 ft (15 m) each way	2 × 49 ft (15 m) each way	1 × 49 ft (15 m) each way	201
Crossover to base and return	2 × 3 each way	N/A	N/A	N/A	203
Half-kneeling crossover acceleration	2 × 33 ft (10 m) each way	2 × 33 ft (10 m) each way	2 × 33 ft (10 m) each way	1 × 33 ft (10 m) each way	204
Acceleration and deceleration 90 runs	1 × each way	2 × each way	2 × each way	1 × each way	206
Four-cone drill with visual cues	2 × 10 sec	3 × 10 sec	2 × 15 sec	1 × 15 sec	231

Beginner and Intermediate Power and Strength

Power and strength training for beginner and intermediate players is designed with movement pattern balance in mind. Each movement pattern outlined in chapter 5 is represented within the power and strength program. As a reminder, these include the squat, hinge, upper-body push and pull, core and shoulder variations, and other accessory exercises. Training for beginner and intermediate players must focus primarily on the fundamental movement patterns and lifts. The main goal is to excel at these patterns, because this will set the tone for future power and strength development. As the athlete matures, these basic movement patterns will be staples in the training program, often with modifications that might increase the training stimulus. Tables 13.4 through 13.6 outline sample beginner and intermediate power and strength training programs for the macrocycle's preparatory phase.

Table 13.4 Sample Phase 1: Three-Day Beginner and Intermediate Off-Season (Preparatory Phase) Power and Strength Training Program

			Day 1				
	Tempo	Rest	Week 1	Week 2	Week 3	Week 4	Page
A1. Goblet squat	3-0-1-0		2 × 15	3 × 12	3 × 10	3 × 10	117
A2. Push-up	3-0-1-0		2 × 10-12	3 × 10-12	3 × 12-15	3 × 12-15	131
A3. Front plank	N/A		2 × 30 sec	3 × 45 sec	3 × 60 sec	3 × 60 sec	94
A4. Half-kneeling hip flexor AIS	1-2-1-0	60 sec	2 × 10 each side	3 × 12 each side	3 × 15 each side	3 × 15 each side	48
B1. Romanian deadlift (RDL)	3-0-1-0		2 × 10	3 × 10	3 × 10	3 × 10	123
B2. Rings row	3-0-1-0		2 × 10	3 × 10-12	3 × 12	3 × 12	135
B3. Side plank	N/A		2 × 30 sec each side	3 × 30 sec each side	3 × 45 sec each side	3 × 45 sec each side	99
B4. Prone quadriceps AIS	1-2-1-0	60 sec	2 × 10 each side	2 × 12 each side	3 × 12 each side	3 × 12 each side	49
C1. Shoulder external rotation	2-0-2-0		2 × 12 each side	2 × 12 each side	2 × 12 each side	2 × 12 each side	104
C2. Four-way cable hip series	1-0-1-0	60 sec	2 × 5 each pattern	2 × 5 each pattern	2 × 5 each pattern	2 × 5 each pattern	108

			Day 2				
	Tempo	Rest	Week 1	Week 2	Week 3	Week 4	Page
A1. Split squat	3-0-1-0		2 × 12 each side	3 × 10 each side	3 × 8 each side	3 × 8 each side	119
A2. Kneeling cable pull-down	3-0-1-0		2 × 12	3 × 12	3 × 10	3 × 10	138
A3. Half-kneeling hip flexor static stretch	N/A	60 sec	2 × 30 sec each side	3 × 45 sec each side	3 × 60 sec each side	3 × 60 sec each side	47
B1. Stability ball leg curl	3-0-1-0		2 × 8	3 × 10	3 × 10	3 × 12	129
B2. Half-kneeling landmine press	3-0-1-0		2 × 12 each side	3 × 10 each side	3 × 8 each side	3 × 8 each side	133

			Day 2 *(continued)*				
	Tempo	**Rest**	**Week 1**	**Week 2**	**Week 3**	**Week 4**	**Page**
B3. Banded overhead AIS	1-2-1-0	60 sec	2 × 10 each side	3 × 10 each side	3 × 10 each side	3 × 10 each side	54
C1. Upward cable X to extension	2-0-2-0		2 × 10	2 × 10	2 × 10	2 × 10	105
C2. Half-kneeling Pallof press	1-2-1-0		2 × 10 each side	2 × 10 each side	2 × 10 each side	2 × 10 each side	101
C3. Groin squeeze	N/A	60 sec	2 × 10 sec	2 × 15 sec	2 × 20 sec	2 × 25 sec	107
			Day 3				
	Tempo	**Rest**	**Week 1**	**Week 2**	**Week 3**	**Week 4**	**Page**
A1. Trap bar deadlift	3-0-1-0		2 × 12	3 × 10	3 × 8	3 × 8	125
A2. Push-up, hands on BOSU ball	3-0-1-0		2 × 10-12	3 × 10-12	3 × 12-15	3 × 12-15	131
A3. Glute bridge	2-1-1-0		2 × 10	3 × 12	3 × 12	3 × 12	97
A4. Hip flexor and quadriceps combination	1-2-1-0	60 sec	2 × 10 each side	3 × 10 each side	3 × 10 each side	3 × 10 each side	49
B1. Cable resisted slide board lateral lunge	3-0-1-0		2 × 10 each side	3 × 10 each side	3 × 10 each side	3 × 10 each side	109
B2. Staggered stance single-arm dumbbell row	3-0-1-0		2 × 12 each side	3 × 10 each side	3 × 8 each side	3 × 8 each side	137
B3. Half-kneeling stability lift	2-0-1-0	60 sec	2 × 10 each side	3 × 10 each side	3 × 12 each side	3 × 12 each side	102
C1. Downward cable X to extension	2-0-2-0		2 × 10	2 × 10	2 × 10	2 × 10	106
C2. Stability ball rollout from knees	1-2-1-0		2 × 10	2 × 12	2 × 12	2 × 12	95
C3. Glute bridge groin squeeze (hold)	N/A	60 sec	2 × 10 sec	2 × 10 sec	2 × 10 sec	2 × 10 sec	108

Table 13.5 Sample Phase 2: Three-Day Beginner and Intermediate Off-Season (Preparatory Phase) Power and Strength Training Program

	Day 1						
	Tempo	Rest	Week 1	Week 2	Week 3	Week 4	Page
A1. Countermovement jump to box, linear	Explosive		3 × 5	3 × 5	3 × 5	2 × 5	161
A2. Dumbbell bench press	2-0-X-0		3 × 6	3 × 6	3 × 6	2 × 6	132
A3. Stability ball rollout	2-0-1-0		3 × 10	3 × 12	3 × 14	2 × 14	96
A4. Hip flexor and quadriceps combination AIS	1-2-1-0	60 sec	2 × 10 each side	3 × 10 each side	3 × 10 each side	3 × 10 each side	49
B1. Front squat	3-0-X-0		2 × 6, 1 × 10	3 × 6, 1 × 10	3 × 6, 1 × 10	1 × 6, 1 × 10	118
B2. Chin-up	2-0-X-0		3 × 6	4 × 5	4 × 4	2 × 4	139
B3. Side plank	N/A		3 × 30 sec each side	3 × 45 sec each side	3 × 60 sec each side	2 × 60 sec each side	99
C1. Single-leg RDL to hip lock	2-0-1-0		2 × 10 each side	3 × 10 each side	3 × 10 each side	2 × 10 each side	127
C2. Half-kneeling stability chop	2-0-1-0		2 × 10 each side	3 × 10 each side	3 × 10 each side	2 × 10 each side	101
C3. Shoulder external rotation	2-0-2-0	60 sec	2 × 12 each side	2 × 12 each side	2 × 12 each side	2 × 12 each side	104
D1. Slide board finisher, isometric hold		90 sec	2 sets	3 sets	3 sets	2 sets	142
	Day 2						
	Tempo	Rest	Week 1	Week 2	Week 3	Week 4	Page
A1. Noncountermovement trap bar jump	2-0-X-0		3 × 5	3 × 5	3 × 5	2 × 5	171
A2. Half-kneeling hip flexor static stretch	N/A	90-120 sec	2 × 30 sec each side	3 × 45 sec each side	3 × 60 sec each side	3 × 60 sec each side	47
B1. Rear foot–elevated split squat, bottom up	3-1-X-0		3 × 6 each side	3 × 6 each side	4 × 6 each side	2 × 6 each side	121
B2. Rings row	2-0-X-0		3 × 8	3 × 8	3 × 8	2 × 8	135

			Day 2 *(continued)*				
	Tempo	Rest	Week 1	Week 2	Week 3	Week 4	Page
B3. Stability ball rollout	2-0-1-0		3 × 10	3 × 12	3 × 14	2 × 14	96
B4. Corner pec AIS	1-2-1-0	60 sec	3 × 10	3 × 10	3 × 10	2 × 10	53
C1. Stability ball leg curl	2-0-1-0		3 × 10	3 × 10	3 × 12	2 × 12	129
C2. Dumbbell overhead press	2-0-1-0		3 × 8 each side	3 × 8 each side	3 × 8 each side	2 × 8 each side	135
C3. Half-kneeling stability lift	2-0-1-0		3 × 10 each side	3 × 10 each side	3 × 10 each side	2 × 10 each side	102
			Day 3				
	Tempo	Rest	Week 1	Week 2	Week 3	Week 4	Page
A1. Medicine ball perpendicular toss	Explo-sive		3 × 5	3 × 5	3 × 5	2 × 5	180
A2. Half-kneeling landmine press	2-0-1-0		3 × 8 each side	3 × 8 each side	3 × 8 each side	2 × 8 each side	133
A3. Dowel figure 8	Con-trolled		3 × 8 each side	3 × 10 each side	3 × 12 each side	2 × 12 each side	111
A4. Hip flexor and quadriceps combination AIS	1-2-1-0	60 sec	2 × 10 each side	3 × 10 each side	3 × 10 each side	3 × 10 each side	49
B1. Trap bar deadlift	3-0-X-0		3 × 8	3 × 6	4 × 6	2 × 6	125
B2. Staggered stance single-arm dumbbell row	3-0-X-0		3 × 6 each side	3 × 6 each side	4 × 5 each side	2 × 5 each side	137
B3. Single-arm farmer's carry	N/A		3 × 30 sec each side	3 × 35 sec each side	3 × 40 sec each side	2 × 40 sec each side	100
B4. Quadruped adductor rock back	Con-trolled	60 sec	3 × 10 each side	3 × 10 each side	3 × 10 each side	3 × 10 each side	50
C1. Nordic hamstring curl	3-0-1-0		3 × 6	3 × 8	3 × 8	2 × 8	130
C2. Upward cable X to extension	1-2-1-0		2 × 12	3 × 12	3 × 12	2 × 12	105
C3. Antirotation chop	2-0-1-0	60 sec	2 × 10 each side	3 × 10 each side	3 × 10 each side	2 × 10 each side	103
D1. Slide board finisher, isometric hold		90 sec	2 sets	3 sets	3 sets	2 sets	142

Table 13.6 Sample Phase 3: Three-Day Beginner and Intermediate Off-Season (Preparatory Phase) Power and Strength Training Program

	Day 1						
	Tempo	Rest	Week 1	Week 2	Week 3	Week 4	Page
A1. Single-arm dumbbell snatch	Explosive		3 × 3 each side	4 × 3 each side	4 × 3 each side	2 × 3 each side	179
A2. Wheel rollout	2-0-1-0		3 × 10	3 × 12	3 × 12	2 × 12	96
A3. Hip flexor and quadriceps combination AIS	1-2-1-0	90 sec	3 × 10 each side	3 × 10 each side	3 × 10 each side	2 × 10 each side	49
B1. T-spine distraction and glide	Controlled		3 × 12	3 × 12	3 × 12	2 × 12	59
B2. Trap bar deadlift	2-0-X-0		3 × 5	4 × 5	3 × 5	2 × 5	125
B3. Falling acceleration	N/A		3 × 33 ft (10 m)	4 × 33 ft (10 m)	3 × 33 ft (10 m)	2 × 33 ft (10 m)	211
B4. Pull-up	2-0-X-0		2 × 6, 1 × AMRAP	3 × 6, 1 × AMRAP	2 × 6, 1 × AMRAP	2 × 6	27
B5. Medicine ball slam	Explosive	90 sec	3 × 5	4 × 5	3 × 5	2 × 5	186
C1. Stability ball leg curl	2-0-X-0		3 × 8	3 × 8	3 × 8	2 × 8	129
C2. Dumbbell bench press, single-arm	2-0-X-0		3 × 6-8 each side	4 × 6-8 each side	3 × 6-8 each side	2 × 6-8 each side	132
C3. Split stance antirotation chop	2-0-1-0		2 × 12 each side	2 × 12 each side	2 × 12 each side	2 × 12 each side	103
C4. Four-way cable hip series	Controlled	90 sec	3 × 6 each way	3 × 6 each way	3 × 6 each way	2 × 6 each way	108
	Day 2						
	Tempo	Rest	Week 1	Week 2	Week 3	Week 4	Page
A1. Half-kneeling lateral bound	Explosive		3 × 5 each side	4 × 5 each side	4 × 5 each side	2 × 5 each side	153
A2. Quadruped adductor rock back	N/A	90 sec	3 × 10 each side	3 × 10 each side	3 × 10 each side	2 × 10 each side	50
B1. T-spine glide	Controlled		3 × 10	3 × 10	3 × 10	2 × 10	59
B2. Reverse lunge to hip lock	2-0-X-0		3 × 6 each side	4 × 6 each side	3 × 6 each side	2 × 6 each side	120
B3. Countermovement hop to box	Explosive		3 × 4 each side	4 × 4 each side	3 × 4 each side	2 × 4 each side	162
B4. Single-arm explosive cable row	2-0-X-0		3 × 6 each side	3 × 6 each side	3 × 6 each side	2 × 6 each side	187

			Day 2 *(continued)*				
	Tempo	Rest	Week 1	Week 2	Week 3	Week 4	Page
B5. Copenhagen side plank	N/A		3 × 15 sec each side	3 × 20 sec each side	3 × 25 sec each side	2 × 25 sec each side	100
C1. Rings push-up	2-0-X-0		3 × 10	3 × 10	3 × 8-10	2 × 8-10	133
C2. Countermovement medicine ball chest toss	Explosive		3 × 4	3 × 4	3 × 4	2 × 4	186
C3. Forward step medicine ball perpendicular toss	Explosive		3 × 5 each side	3 × 5 each side	3 × 5 each side	2 × 5 each side	181
			Day 3				
	Tempo	Rest	Week 1	Week 2	Week 3	Week 4	Page
A1. Countermovement jump squat	Explosive		3 × 5	3 × 5	3 × 4	2 × 4	174
A2. Dowel figure 8	Controlled		3 × 10 each side	3 × 10 each side	3 × 10 each side	2 × 10 each side	111
A3. Hip flexor and quadriceps combination AIS	1-2-1-0	90 sec	2 × 10 each side	3 × 10 each side	3 × 10 each side	3 × 10 each side	49
B1. Skater squat to hip lock	3-0-X-0		3 × 6 each side	4 × 6 each side	3 × 6 each side	2 × 6 each side	121
B2. Half-kneeling rotational bound	Explosive		3 × 3 each side	4 × 3 each side	3 × 3 each side	2 × 3 each side	155
B3. Half-kneeling landmine press	2-0-X-0		3 × 6 each side	4 × 6 each side	3 × 6 each side	2 × 6 each side	133
B4. Single-arm farmer's carry	N/A		3 × 45 sec each side	3 × 50 sec each side	3 × 60 sec each side	2 × 60 sec each side	100
B5. Supine hamstring AIS	Controlled	60 sec	3 × 10 each side	3 × 10 each side	3 × 10 each side	2 × 10 each side	52
C1. Single-leg hip thrust	2-0-X-0		3 × 6 each side	3 × 6 each side	3 × 6 each side	2 × 6 each side	126
C2. Staggered stance single-arm dumbbell row (no support)	2-0-X-0		3 × 6 each side	3 × 6 each side	3 × 6 each side	2 × 6 each side	137
C3. Countermovement medicine ball slam	Explosive		3 × 3	3 × 3	3 × 3	2 × 3	187
C4. Horizontal cable chop	1-0-X-0	90 sec	3 × 6 each side	3 × 8 each side	3 × 8 each side	2 × 6 each side	183

*AMRAP = as many reps as possible

ADVANCED OFF-SEASON PROGRAM

The advanced off-season program consists of four movement strength and skill sessions, power and strength sessions, and energy systems development sessions per week. The movement strength and skill sessions typically follow linear progressions, whereas the power and strength sessions typically follow nonlinear concurrent progressions throughout the off-season phases.

Advanced Movement Strength and Skill

Movement strength and skill training for the advanced athlete are designed to develop linear, lateral, and multidirectional movement skills. Much like the beginner and intermediate athlete, the advanced athlete must progress from simple to complex movement skills throughout the off-season. Movement progressions should be tailored to the individual's competencies, and special care should be taken not to skip steps of movement development along the way. Tables 13.7 through 13.9 outline sample advanced movement skill and strength training programs for the macrocycle's preparatory phase.

Table 13.7 Sample Phase 1: Four-Day Advanced Off-Season (Preparatory Phase) Movement Strength and Skill Training Program

	Day 1 linear				
	Week 1	Week 2	Week 3	Week 4	Page
Rudimentary hop series: linear, double-leg forward	1 × 6	1 × 7	1 × 8	1 × 10	69
Rudimentary hop series: linear, double-leg backward	1 × 6	1 × 7	1 × 8	1 × 10	69
Drop squat	2 × 3	N/A	N/A	N/A	159
Drop squat, eyes closed	2 × 3	1 × 3	1 × 3	N/A	159
Drop squat, single-leg	N/A	2 × 3 each side	2 × 3 each side	1 × 3 each side	159
Drop squat, single-leg, eyes closed	N/A	N/A	N/A	1 × 3 each side	159
Noncountermovement jump, over 6-in. (15 cm) hurdles	N/A	2 × 6	1 × 6	1× 6	147
Countermovement jump, over 6-in. (15 cm) hurdles	N/A	N/A	1 × 6	1 × 6	30

	Day 1 linear *(continued)*				
	Week 1	Week 2	Week 3	Week 4	Page
Double-contact jump, over 6-in. (15 cm) hurdles	N/A	N/A	N/A	1 × 6	167
Medicine ball chest toss	N/A	1 × 5	2 × 5	1 × 5	185
Medicine ball slam	1 × 5	1 × 5	2 × 5	1 × 5	186
Deliberate wall drill	2 × 5 sec each side	N/A	N/A	N/A	206
Linear wall drill, single exchange	2 × 5 each side	2 × 5 each side	N/A	N/A	205
Double-exchange wall drill	N/A	1 × 3 each side	2 × 3 each side	N/A	206
Low skater walk	1 × 15m	2 × 49 ft (15 m)	2 × 49 ft (15 m)	3 × 49 ft (15 m)	207
Resisted march	2 × 15m	3 × 49 ft (15 m)	4 × 49 ft (15 m)	2 × 49 ft (15 m)	209
Falling acceleration	N/A	4 × 33 ft (10 m)	6 × 33 ft (10 m)	3 × 33 ft (10 m)	211
Acceleration to base	N/A	N/A	N/A	4 × 33 ft (10 m)	225
	Day 2 lateral				
	Week 1	Week 2	Week 3	Week 4	Page
Rudimentary hop series: lateral, double-leg	1 × 6 each way	1 × 7 each way	1 × 8 each way	1 × 10 each way	69
Drop squat	2 × 3	2 × 3	N/A	N/A	159
Drop squat, eyes closed	N/A	2 × 3	1 × 4	N/A	159
Drop squat, single-leg	N/A	N/A	2 × 3 each side	2 × 3 each side	159
Drop squat, single-leg, eyes closed	N/A	N/A	N/A	1 × 3 each side	159
Lateral noncountermovement jump, over 6-in. (15 cm) hurdles	N/A	1 × 6 each way	1 × 6 each way	N/A	149
Lateral countermovement jump, over 6-in. (15 cm) hurdles	N/A	N/A	1 × 6 each way	1 × 6 each way	163

(continued)

Table 13.7 *(continued)*

	Day 2 lateral *(continued)*				
	Week 1	**Week 2**	**Week 3**	**Week 4**	**Page**
Lateral double-contact jump, over 6-in. (15 cm) hurdles	N/A	N/A	N/A	1 × 6 each way	167
Noncountermovement lateral bound	2 × 5 each side (low amplitude)	1 × 5 each side	2 × 5 each side	2 × 5 each side	155
Stationary skater stride	1 × 5 each side	1 × 6 each side	1 × 7 each side	1 × 5 each side	191
Low skater lateral stride	2 × 49 ft (15 m) each way	2 × 49 ft (15 m) each way	2 × 49 ft (15 m) each way	2 × 49 ft (15 m) each way	193
Side skate jumps	N/A	2 × 33 ft (10 m) each way	2 × 33 ft (10 m) each way	2 × 49 ft (15 m) each way	195
Resisted explosive lateral stride (non-continuous)	N/A	1 × 49 ft (15 m) each way	2 × 49 ft (15 m) each way	3 × 66 ft (20 m) each way	196
Continuous resisted explosive lateral stride	N/A	1 × 49 ft (15 m) each way	2 × 49 ft (15 m) each way	2 × 49 ft (15 m) each way	197
Half-kneeling lateral acceleration	N/A	2 × 33 ft (10 m) each way	2 × 33 ft (10 m) each way	3 × 33 ft (10 m) each way	197
	Day 3 linear				
	Week 1	**Week 2**	**Week 3**	**Week 4**	**Page**
Rudimentary hop series: linear, single-leg forward	1 × 5 each side	1 × 5 each side	1 × 5 each side	1 × 5 each side	69
Rudimentary hop series: linear, single-leg backward	1 × 5 each side	1 × 5 each side	1 × 5 each side	1 × 5 each side	69
Countermovement hop to box	N/A	1 × 4 each side	1 × 5 each side	1 × 5 each side	162
Medicine ball slam	1 × 3	1 × 4	1 × 5	1 × 3	186
Single-arm medicine ball chest toss	1 × 3 each side	1 × 4 each side	1 × 5 each side	1 × 5 each side	186
Speed skater strides	2 × 10 each side	2 × 10 each side	3 × 10 each side	3 × 10 each side	193

	Day 3 linear *(continued)*				
	Week 1	**Week 2**	**Week 3**	**Week 4**	**Page**
Walking acceleration lunge	2 × 98 ft (30 m)	2 × 98 ft (30 m)	3 × 98 ft (30 m) (add band resistance)	N/A	208
Resisted march	N/A	2 × 66 ft (20 m)	3 × 66 ft (20 m)	2 × 66 ft (20 m)	209
Resisted high-knee run	N/A	N/A	2 × 49 ft (30 m)	3 × 49 ft (30 m)	210
Acceleration to base	N/A	3 × 33 ft (10 m)	4 × 33 ft (10 m)	4 × 33 ft (10 m)	225
Falling acceleration	N/A	3 × 33 ft (10 m)	4 × 33 ft (10 m)	4 × 33 ft (10 m)	211
	Day 4 crossover				
	Week 1	**Week 2**	**Week 3**	**Week 4**	**Page**
Rudimentary hop series: lateral, single-leg	1 × 5 each way	1 × 5 each way	1 × 5 each way	1 × 5 each way	69
Single-leg drop squat	2 × 3 each side	2 × 3 each side	2 × 3 each side	2 × 3 each side	159
Lateral noncountermovement hop, over 6-in. (15 cm) hurdles, inside foot	N/A	1 × 6 each way	N/A	N/A	149
Lateral countermovement hop, over 6-in. (15 cm) hurdles	N/A	N/A	1 × 6 each way	1 × 6 each way	30
Lateral single-leg double-contact jump, over 6-in. (15 cm) hurdles, inside foot	N/A	N/A	N/A	1 × 6 each way	167
Noncountermovement lateral bound	2 × 5 each side (low amplitude)	1 × 5 each side	2 × 5 each side	2 × 5 each side	155
Stationary skater crossover	1 × 5 each side	1 × 6 each side	1 × 7 each side	1 × 5 each side	198
Low skater crossover	2 × 49 ft (15 m) each way	2 × 49 ft (15 m) each way	2 × 49 ft (15 m) each way	2 × 49 ft (15 m) each way	199
Crossover to base	N/A	2 × 3 each way	1 × 3 each way	N/A	202

(continued)

Table 13.7 *(continued)*

	Day 4 crossover *(continued)*				
	Week 1	Week 2	Week 3	Week 4	Page
Crossover to base and return	N/A	1 × 3 each way	2 × 3 each way	3 × 3 each way	203
Resisted explosive crossover	N/A	N/A	2 × 66 ft (20 m) each way	3 × 66 ft (20 m) each way	201
Corner skate jump	N/A	2 × 33 ft (10 m) each way	2 × 33 ft (10 m) each way	2 × 33 ft (10 m) each way	203
Half-kneeling cross over acceleration	N/A	2 × 33 ft (10 m) each way	2 × 33 ft (10 m) each way	3 × 33 ft (10 m) each way	204

Table 13.8 Sample Phase 2: Four-Day Advanced Off-Season (Preparatory Phase) Movement Strength and Skill Training Program

	Day 1 linear				
	Week 1	Week 2	Week 3	Week 4	Page
Rudimentary hop series: linear, double-leg forward	1 × 10	1 × 10	1 × 10	1× 10	69
Rudimentary hop series: linear, double-leg backward	1 × 10	1 × 10	1 × 10	1 × 10	69
Countermovement jump, over 12-in. (30 cm) hurdles	2 × 6	N/A	N/A	N/A	30
Double-contact jump, over 12-in. (30 cm) hurdles	2 × 6	N/A	N/A	N/A	167
Continuous jump: double-leg, over 12-in. (30 cm) hurdles	N/A	2 × 6	2 × 6	2 × 6	168
Rotational countermovement jump	N/A	2 × 4 each way	1 × 4 each way	1 × 4 each way	163
Rotational double-contact jump	N/A	1 × 4 each way	2 × 4 each way	2 × 4 each way	167
Medicine ball chest toss, split stance	1 × 5	2 × 5	1 × 5	1 × 5	185

	Day 1 linear *(continued)*				
	Week 1	**Week 2**	**Week 3**	**Week 4**	**Page**
Medicine ball slam	1 × 5	2 × 5	1 × 5	1 × 5	186
Medicine ball perpendicular toss	N/A	2 × 5 each way	1 × 5 each way	1 × 5 each way	180
Resisted march	2 × 49 ft (15 m)	2 × 49 ft (15 m)	1 × 49 ft (15 m)	N/A	209
Resisted march to resisted high-knee run (transition)	2 × 30 ft (10 m) + 30 ft (10 m)	2 × 30 ft (10 m) + 30 ft (10 m)	3 × 30 ft (10 m) + 30 ft (10 m)	4 × 30 ft (10 m) + 30 ft (10 m)	209, 210
Resisted high-knee run	N/A	2 × 49 ft (15 m)	4 × 49 ft (15 m)	4 × 15m	210
Acceleration to base	3 × 30 ft (10 m)	4 × 30 ft (10 m)	4 × 30 ft (10 m)	N/A	225
Get-up acceleration	4 × 30 ft (10 m)	4 × 49 ft (15 m)	4 × 49 ft (15 m)	4 × 49 ft (15 m)	212
Falling acceleration	N/A	4 × 30 ft (10 m)	4 × 30 ft (10 m)	4 × 30 ft (10 m)	211
	Day 2 lateral				
	Week 1	**Week 2**	**Week 3**	**Week 4**	**Page**
Rudimentary hop series: lateral, double-leg	1 × 10 each way	1 × 10 each way	1 × 10 each way	1 × 10 each way	69
Drop squat, single-leg, eyes closed	3 × 3 each side	N/A	N/A	N/A	150
Lateral double-contact jump, over 12-in. (30 cm) hurdles	1 × 6 each way	N/A	N/A	N/A	167
Continuous jump: lateral, double-leg, over 12-in. (30 cm) hurdles	N/A	1 × 6 each way	1 × 6 each way	1 × 6 each way	168
Double-contact lateral bound	2 × 4 each side	2 × 4 each side	2 × 4 each side	2 × 4 each side	167
Noncontinuous resisted explosive lateral stride	2 × 66 ft (20 m) each way	N/A	N/A	N/A	197
Continuous resisted explosive lateral stride	2 × 49 ft (15 m) each way	4 × 49 ft (15 m) each way	5 × 49 ft (15 m) each way	3 × 66 ft (20 m) each way	196
Lateral shuffle to linear acceleration	3 × 33 ft (10 m) each way	4 × 33 ft (10 m) each way	5 × 33 ft (10 m) each way	3 × 33 ft (10 m) each way	227

(continued)

Table 13.8 *(continued)*

	Day 3 linear				
	Week 1	**Week 2**	**Week 3**	**Week 4**	**Page**
Rudimentary hop series: linear, single-leg forward	1 × 5 each side	1 × 5 each side	1 × 5 each side	1 × 5 each side	69
Rudimentary hop series: linear, single-leg backward	1 × 5 each side	1 × 5 each side	1 × 5 each side	1 × 5 each side	69
Countermovement hop, over 12-in. (30 cm) hurdles	1 × 6 each side	N/A	N/A	N/A	162
Double-contact hop, over 12-in. (30 cm) hurdles	1 × 6 each side	1 × 6 each side	N/A	N/A	167
Continuous jump: linear, single-leg, over 12-in. (30 cm) hurdles	N/A	1 × 6 each side	2 × 6 each side	1 × 6 each side	168
Medicine ball slam	1 × 4	1 × 4	1 × 4	1 × 4	186
Medicine ball chest toss, single-arm, split stance	1 × 4 each side	1 × 4 each side	1 × 4 each side	1 × 4 each side	185
Resisted march to resisted high-knee run (transition)	4 × 33 ft (10 m) + 33 ft (10 m)	4 × 33 ft (10 m) + 33 ft (10 m)	N/A	N/A	209
Resisted high-knee run	N/A	N/A	4 × 49 ft (15 m)	4 × 49 ft (15 m)	210
Acceleration to base and return	5 × 49 ft (15 m)	6 × 49 ft (15 m)	6 × 49 ft (15 m)	4 × 33 ft (10 m)	225
Falling acceleration	4 × 33 ft (10 m)	4 × 33 ft (10 m)	4 × 49 ft (15 m)	3 × 49 ft (15 m)	211
	Day 4 crossover and drop step				
	Week 1	**Week 2**	**Week 3**	**Week 4**	**Page**
Rudimentary hop series: lateral, single-leg	1 × 5 each way	1 × 5 each way	1 × 5 each way	1 × 5 each way	69
Drop squat, single-leg, eyes closed	3 × 3 each side	N/A	N/A	N/A	150
Lateral countermovement hop, over 12-in. (30 cm) hurdles	1 × 6 each side	N/A	N/A	N/A	30

	Day 4 crossover and drop step *(continued)*				
	Week 1	Week 2	Week 3	Week 4	Page
Lateral double-contact jump, over 12-in. (30 cm) hurdles, inside foot	1 × 6 each side	1 × 6 each side	N/A	N/A	167
Continuous jump: lateral (inside foot), single-leg, over 12-in. (30 cm) hurdles	N/A	1 × 6 each side	2 × 6 each side	1 × 6 each side	168
Noncountermovement rotational bound	2 × 5 each side	N/A	N/A	N/A	157
Countermovement rotational bound	N/A	2 × 5 each side	2 × 5 each side	2 × 5 each side	116
Crossover to base and return	2 × 3 each way	3 × 3 each way	3 × 3 each way	3 × 3 each way	203
Resisted explosive crossover	2 × 66 ft (20 m) each way	3 × 66 ft (20 m) each way	3 × 66 ft (20 m) each way	3 × 66 ft (20 m) each way	201
Acceleration and deceleration 90 runs	2 × each way	3 × each way	3 × each way	2 × each way	226
Lateral shuffle to linear acceleration to drop step	N/A	N/A	4 × 33 ft (10 m) each way	4 × 33 ft (10 m) each way	228

Table 13.9 Sample Phase 3: Four-Day Advanced Off-Season (Preparatory Phase) Movement Strength and Skill Training Program

	Day 1 linear				
	Week 1	Week 2	Week 3	Week 4	Page
Rudimentary hop series: linear, double-leg forward	1 × 10	1 × 10	1 × 10	1 × 10	69
Rudimentary hop series: linear, double-leg backward	1 × 10	1 × 10	1 × 10	1 × 10	69
Continuous jump: double-leg, over 12-in. (30 cm) hurdles	2 × 6	N/A	N/A	N/A	168

(continued)

Table 13.9 *(continued)*

	Day 1 linear *(continued)*				
	Week 1	**Week 2**	**Week 3**	**Week 4**	**Page**
Rotational counter-movement jump	1 × 4 each way	N/A	N/A	N/A	163
Rotational double-contact jump	2 × 4 each way	N/A	N/A	N/A	167
Continuous rotational jump	N/A	2 × 4 each way	1 × 4 each way	N/A	169
Medicine ball chest toss with step	1 × 6	1 × 6	1 × 6	N/A	186
Medicine ball slam	1 × 5	1 × 5	1 × 5	N/A	186
Resisted march to resisted high-knee run (transition)	2 × 33 ft (10 m) + 33 ft (10 m)	2 × 33 ft (10 m) + 33 ft (10 m)	N/A	N/A	209
Resisted high-knee run	2 × 49 ft (15 m)	3 × 49 ft (15 m)	3 × 49 ft (15 m)	1 × 49 ft (15 m)	210
Acceleration to base, continuous	3 × (2 × 33 ft [10 m])	3 × (3 × 33 ft [10 m])	2 × (2 × 33 ft [10 m])	N/A	225
Partner mirroring, linear	2 × 49 ft (15 m)	3 × 49 ft (15 m)	3 × 49 ft (15 m)	N/A	232
Get-up acceleration	4 × 49 ft (15 m)	4 × 49 ft (15 m)	4 × 49 ft (15 m)	N/A	212
Falling acceleration	4 × 33 ft (10 m)	5 × 33 ft (10 m)	4 × 33 ft (10 m)	4 × 33 ft (10 m)	211
	Day 2 lateral stride				
	Week 1	**Week 2**	**Week 3**	**Week 4**	**Page**
Rudimentary hop series: lateral, double-leg	1 × 10 each way	1 × 10 each way	1 × 10 each way	1 × 10 each way	69
Drop squat, single-leg, eyes closed	3 × 3 each side	N/A	N/A	N/A	150
Continuous jump: lateral, double-leg, over 12-in. (30 cm) hurdles	2 × 6 each way	N/A	N/A	N/A	68
Continuous lateral bound	2 × 4 each side	1 × 4 each side	N/A	N/A	169
Continuous resisted explosive lateral stride	3 × 66 ft (20 m) each way	2 × 66 ft (20 m) each way	1 × 66 ft (20 m) each way	N/A	196

	Day 2 lateral stride *(continued)*				
	Week 1	**Week 2**	**Week 3**	**Week 4**	**Page**
Read and react 45-degree cut	3 × 49 ft (15 m) each way	3 × 49 ft (15 m) each way	4 × 33 ft (10 m) each way	1 × 33 ft (10 m) each way	230
Four-cone drill with visual cues, 33 ft (10 m) spacing	3 × 15 sec	4 × 15 sec	4 × 15 sec	2 × 15 sec	231
	Day 3 linear				
	Week 1	**Week 2**	**Week 3**	**Week 4**	**Page**
Rudimentary hop series: linear, single-leg forward	1 × 5 each side	1 × 5 each side	1 × 5 each side	1 × 5 each side	69
Rudimentary hop series: linear, single-leg backward	1 × 5 each side	1 × 5 each side	1 × 5 each side	1 × 5 each side	69
Continuous jump: linear, single-leg, over 12-in. (30 cm) hurdles	2 × 6 each side	N/A	N/A	N/A	168
Medicine ball slam	1 × 4	1 × 4	1 × 4	N/A	186
Medicine ball chest toss with step, single-arm	1 × 4 each side	1 × 4 each side	1 × 4 each side	N/A	186
Resisted high-knee run	2 × 49 ft (15 m)	3 × 49 ft (15 m)	3 × 49 ft (15 m)	1 × 49 ft (15 m)	210
Acceleration to base, continuous	3 × (2 × 33 ft [10m])	3 × (3 × 33 ft [10m])	2 × (2 × 33 ft [10m])	N/A	225
Partner mirroring, lateral	3 × 49 ft (15 m)	5 × 49 ft (15 m)	3 × 49 ft (15 m)	N/A	232
Falling acceleration	4 × 33 ft (10 m)	5 × 33 ft (10 m)	4 × 33 ft (10 m)	4 × 33 ft (10 m)	211
	Day 4 crossover and drop step				
	Week 1	**Week 2**	**Week 3**	**Week 4**	**Page**
Rudimentary hop series: lateral, single-leg	1 × 5 each way	1 × 5 each way	1 × 5 each way	1 × 5 each way	69
Continuous jump: lateral (inside foot), single-leg, over 12-in. (30 cm) hurdles	2 × 6 each side	N/A	N/A	N/A	168
Countermovement rotational bound	2 × 5 each side	2 × 5 each side	2 × 5 each side	1 × 5 each side	116

(continued)

Table 13.9 *(continued)*

	Day 4 crossover and drop step *(continued)*				
	Week 1	**Week 2**	**Week 3**	**Week 4**	**Page**
Resisted explosive crossover	3 × 49 ft (15 m) each way	2 × 66 ft (20 m) each way	2 × 66 ft (20 m) each way	1 × 66 ft (20 m) each way	201
Lateral shuffle to linear acceleration to drop step	4 × 33 ft (10 m) each way	3 × 33 ft (10 m) each way	2 × 33 ft (10 m) each way	N/A	228
Four-cone partner mirror drill	3 × 15 sec	4 × 15 sec	4 × 15 sec	2 × 15 sec	231

Advanced Strength and Power

As is true for the beginner and intermediate athlete, the advanced athlete's power and strength training is designed to balance movement patterns. Being great at the basics remains a critical tenet for advanced athletes; however, movement complexity is often added to keep the training stimulus and psychological motivation high. Tables 13.10 through 13.13 outline sample advanced power and strength training programs for the macrocycle's preparatory phase.

Table 13.10 Sample Phase 1, Block 1: Advanced Off-Season (Preparatory Phase) Power and Strength Training Program With an Eccentric Strength Focus

			Day 1		
	Tempo	**Rest**	**Week 1**	**Week 2**	**Page**
A1. Single-arm dumbbell snatch	Explosive		3 × 5 each side	3 × 5 each side	179
A2. Stability ball rollout	2-0-1-0		3 × 10 each side	3 × 12 each side	96
A3. Hip distraction and glide	Controlled	120 sec	3 × 10 each side	3 × 10 each side	57
B1. Trap bar deadlift	5-0-1-0	30 sec	4 × 2 @ 85% RM	4 × 2 @ 85% RM	125
B2. Pull-up	5-0-1-0		4 × 2 @ 85% RM	4 × 2 @ 85% RM	27
B3. Side plank	N/A		3 × 30 sec each side	3 × 45 sec each side	99
B4. Hip rotations	Controlled	90 sec	3 × 3 each side	3 × 3 each side	58

Day 1 (continued)					
	Tempo	**Rest**	**Week 1**	**Week 2**	**Page**
C1. Staggered stance single-arm dumbbell row	2-0-1-0	20 sec	3 × 8 each side	4 × 8 each side	137
C2. Skater squat, half repetition	2-0-1-0		3 × 6 each side	4 × 6 each side	121
C3. Skater squat to hip lock (bottom up)	2-0-1-0	90 sec	3 × 8 each side	4 × 8 each side	121
D1. Upward cable X to extension	2-0-1-0		3 × 12	3 × 12	105
D2. Half-kneeling stability lift	2-0-1-0	60 sec	3 × 8 each side	3 × 10 each side	102
Day 2					
	Tempo	**Rest**	**Week 1**	**Week 2**	**Page**
A1. Kettlebell complex (staggered stance single-arm kettlebell row, RDL, goblet squat, continuous jump squat)	AFAP		3 × 5 each movement	3 × 5 each movement	141
A2. Half-kneeling hip flexor AIS	1-2-1-0	60 sec	3 × 10 each side	3 × 12 each side	48
B1. Dumbbell bench press	5-0-1-0		4 × 2 @ 85% RM	4 × 2 @ 85% RM	132
B2. Groin squeeze	1-1-1-10		3 × (2 × 10 sec hold)	3 × (2 × 10 sec hold)	107
B3. Banded overhead AIS	Controlled	60 sec	3 × 10 each side	3 × 10 each side	54
C1. Half-kneeling landmine press	2-0-1-0		3 × 8 each side	3 × 8 each side	133
C2. Linear wall drill, hold, miniband around feet	1-0-1-5		3 × 3 each side	3 × 4 each side	207
C3. Butterfly adductor PNF stretch	Controlled	60 sec	3 × 3	3 × 4	50
D1. Slide board finisher, isometric hold			2 × 4	2 × 4	142
D2. Half-kneeling Pallof press	1-1-1-2		2 × 10 each side	2 × 10 each side	101
D3. Downward cable X to extension	2-0-1-0	60 sec	2 × 10	2 × 10	106

(continued)

Table 13.10 *(continued)*

	Tempo	Rest	Week 1	Week 2	Page
Day 3					
A1. Noncounter-movement trap bar jump, bottom up	Explosive		3 × 5 each movement	3 × 5 each movement	171
A2. Cable single-leg RDL to Y	2-0-1-0		3 × 10 each side	3 × 10 each side	113
A3. Bodyweight squat, hold bottom position	2-10-1-0	120 sec	3 × 3	3 × 3	116
B1. Rear foot–elevated split squat	5-0-1-0	30 sec	4 × 2 @ 85% RM	4 × 2 @ 85% RM	121
B2. Rings row	5-0-1-0		4 × 2 @ 85% RM	4 × 2 @ 85% RM	135
B3. Side plank	N/A	90 sec	3 × 30 sec each side	3 × 45 sec each side	99
C1. Single-leg RDL to hip lock	2-0-1-0		3 × 10 each side	3 × 10 each side	127
C2. Quadruped adductor rock back	Controlled	60 sec	3 × 10 each side	3 × 12 each side	50
D1. Kneeling cable pull-down	2-0-1-0		3 × 12	3 × 12	138
D2. Half-kneeling stability chop	2-0-1-0	60 sec	3 × 8 each side	3 × 8 each side	101

	Tempo	Rest	Week 1	Week 2	Page
Day 4					
A1. Dumbbell complex (RDL, reverse lunge to hip lock, continuous jump squat)	AFAP		3 × 5 each movement	3 × 5 each movement	141
A2. Hip distraction and glide	Controlled	90 sec	3 × 10 each side	3 × 10 each side	57
B1. Rings push-up	5-0-1-0		4 × 2 @ 85% RM	4 × 2 @ 85% RM	133
B2. Wheel rollout	2-0-2-0		3 × 10	3 × 10	96
B3. T-spine distraction and glide	Controlled		3 × 12	3 × 12	59
C1. Dumbbell overhead press, single-arm	2-0-1-0		3 × 8 each side	3 × 8 each side	135

Day 4 *(continued)*					
	Tempo	**Rest**	**Week 1**	**Week 2**	**Page**
C2. Front plank	N/A		3 × 45 sec	3 × 45 sec	94
C3. Linear wall drill, hold, miniband around feet	1-0-1-2		3 × 8 each side	3 × 8 each side	207
D1. Front squat, half rep, bottom to half-way up	1-0-1-0		3 × 15	3 × 15	118
D2. Antirotation chop	2-0-1-1		2 × 10 each side	2 × 10 each side	103
D3. Shoulder external rotation	2-0-2-0		2 × 10 each side	2 × 10 each side	104

Table 13.11 Sample Phase 1, Block 2: Advanced Off-Season (Preparatory Phase) Power and Strength Training Program With a Concentric Strength Focus

Day 1					
	Tempo	**Rest**	**Week 1**	**Week 2**	**Page**
A1. Single-arm dumbbell snatch	Explosive		3 × 5 each side	3 × 5 each side	179
A2. Stability ball rollout	2-0-1-0		3 × 10 each side	2 × 12 each side	96
A3. Hip distraction and glide	Controlled	120 sec	3 × 10 each side	2 × 10 each side	57
B1. Trap bar deadlift, bottom up	2-1-X-0	30 sec	4 × 5 @ 85% RM	3 × 5 @ 85% RM	125
B2. Pull-up	2-0-X-0		4 × 5 @ 85% RM	3 × 5 @ 85% RM	27
B3. Side plank	N/A		3 × 45 sec each side	2 × 60 sec each side	99
B4. Hip rotations	Controlled	90 sec	3 × 3 each side	2 × 3 each side	58
C1. Staggered stance single-arm dumbbell row	2-0-1-0	20 sec	4 × 8 each side	2 × 8 each side	137
C2. Skater squat, half repetition	2-0-1-0		4 × 6 each side	2 × 6 each side	121
C3. Skater squat to hip lock (bottom up)	2-0-1-0	90 sec	3 × 6 each side	2 × 6 each side	121

(continued)

Table 13.11   *(continued)*

	Day 1 *(continued)*				
	Tempo	**Rest**	**Week 1**	**Week 2**	**Page**
D1. Upward cable X to extension	2-0-1-0		3 × 12	2 × 12	105
D2. Half-kneeling stability lift	2-0-1-0	60 sec	3 × 8 each side	2 × 10 each side	102
	Day 2				
	Tempo	**Rest**	**Week 1**	**Week 2**	**Page**
A1. Kettlebell complex (staggered stance single-arm kettlebell row, RDL, goblet squat, continuous jump squat)	AFAP		3 × 5 each movement	3 × 5 each movement	141
A2. Half-kneeling hip flexor AIS	1-2-1-0	60 sec	3 × 10 each side	3 × 12 each side	48
B1. Dumbbell bench press	2-0-X-0		4 × 5 @ 85% RM	3 × 5 @ 85% RM	132
B2. Groin squeeze	1-1-1-10		3 × (2 × 10 sec hold)	3 × (2 × 10 sec hold)	107
B3. Banded overhead AIS	Controlled	60 sec	3 × 10 each side	3 × 10 each side	54
C1. Half-kneeling landmine press	2-0-1-0		3 × 8 each side	2 × 8 each side	133
C2. Linear wall drill, hold, miniband around feet	1-0-1-5		3 × 3 each side	2 × 4 each side	207
C3. Butterfly adductor PNF stretch	Controlled	60 sec	3 × 3	2 × 4	50
D1. Slide board finisher, isometric hold			2 × 4	2 × 4	142
D2. Half-kneeling Pallof press	1-1-1-2		2 × 10 each side	2 × 10 each side	101
D3. Downward cable X to extension	2-0-1-0	60 sec	2 × 10	2 × 10	106
	Day 3				
	Tempo	**Rest**	**Week 1**	**Week 2**	**Page**
A1. Noncountermovement trap bar jump, bottom up	Explosive		3 × 5 each movement	3 × 5 each movement	171

	Tempo	Rest	Week 1	Week 2	Page
Day 3 *(continued)*					
A2. Cable single-leg RDL to Y	2-0-1-0		3 × 10 each side	3 × 10 each side	113
A3. Bodyweight squat, hold bottom position	2-10-1-0	120 sec	3 × 3	3 × 3	116
B1. Rear foot–elevated split squat, bottom up	2-1-X-0	30 sec	4 × 5 each side @ 85% RM	3 × 5 each side @ 85% RM	121
B2. Rings row	2-0-X-0	30 sec	4 × 5 @ 85% RM	3 × 5 @ 85% RM	135
B3. Side plank	N/A	90 sec	3 × 45 sec each side	2 × 60 sec each side	99
C1. Single-leg RDL to hip lock	2-0-1-0		3 × 10 each side	2 × 10 each side	127
C2. Quadruped adductor rock back	Controlled	60 sec	3 × 10 each side	2 × 12 each side	50
D1. Kneeling cable pull-down	2-0-1-0		3 × 12	2 × 12	138
D2. Half-kneeling stability chop	2-0-1-0	60 sec	3 × 8 each side	2 × 8 each side	101
Day 4					
	Tempo	Rest	Week 1	Week 2	Page
A1. Dumbbell complex (RDL, reverse lunge to hip lock, continuous jump squat)	AFAP		3 × 5 each movement	3 × each movement	141
A2. Hip distraction and glide	Controlled	90 sec	3 × 10 each side	3 × 10 each side	57
B1. Rings push-up	2-0-X-0		4 × 5 @ 85% RM	3 × 5 @ 85% RM	133
B2. Wheel rollout	2-0-2-0		3 × 10	2 × 10	59
B3. T-spine distraction and glide	Controlled		3 × 12	2 × 12	59
C1. Dumbbell overhead press, single-arm	2-0-1-0		3 × 8 each side	2 × 8 each side	135
C2. Front plank	N/A		3 × 45 sec	2 × 45 sec	94
C3. Linear wall drill, hold, miniband around feet	1-0-1-2		3 × 8 each side	2 × 8 each side	207

(continued)

Table 13.11 *(continued)*

	Day 4 *(continued)*				
	Tempo	Rest	Week 1	Week 2	Page
D1. Front squat, half rep, bottom to half way up	1-0-1-0		3 × 15	2 × 15	118
D2. Antirotation chop	2-0-1-1		2 × 10 each side	2 × 10 each side	103
D3. Shoulder external rotation	2-0-2-0		2 × 10 each side	2 × 10 each side	104

Table 13.12 Sample Phase 2: Advanced Off-Season (Preparatory Phase) Power and Strength Training Program With a Rate of Force Development Focus

	Day 1						
	Tempo	Rest	Week 1	Week 2	Week 3	Week 4	Page
A1. Continuous jump: single-leg, over 12-in. (30 cm) hurdles	Explosive		3 × 4 each side	3 × 4 each side	3 × 4 each side	2 × 4 each side	168
A2. Drop jump, 12-in. (30 cm)	Explosive		3 × 3	3 × 3	3 × 3	2 × 3	169
A3. T-spine glide, rotation	Controlled	120 sec	3 × 10 each side	3 × 10 each side	3 × 10 each side	2 × 10 each side	59
B1. Trap bar deadlift	2-0-1-0		5 @ 60% RM; 3 @ 70% RM; 1 @ 80% RM	5 @ 60% RM; 3 @ 70% RM; 1 @ 80% RM	5 @ 60% RM; 3 @ 70% RM; 1 @ 80% RM	5 @ 60% RM; 3 @ 70% RM	125
B2. Hip flexor and quadriceps combination AIS	Controlled	90 sec	3 × 12 each side	3 × 12 each side	3 × 12 each side	2 × 12 each side	49
C1. Trap bar deadlift, banded (accommodating resistance)	1-0-X-0		4 × 6 @ 65% RM	4 × 6 @ 65% RM	4 × 6 @ 65% RM	2 × 6 @ 65% RM	125
C2. Resisted explosive lateral stride	Explosive	120 sec	4 × 5 each side	4 × 5 each side	4 × 5 each side	2 × 5 each side	196
D1. Skater squat to hip lock	2-1-X-0		3 × 6 each side	3 × 6 each side	3 × 6 each side	2 × 6 each side	121

			Day 1 *(continued)*				
	Tempo	Rest	Week 1	Week 2	Week 3	Week 4	Page
D2. Single-leg RDL to hip lock (with torsion)	2-0-X-0	90 sec	3 × 6 each side	3 × 6 each side	3 × 6 each side	2 × 6 each side	127
E1. Cable resisted slide board lateral lunge	1-0-X-0		3 × 6 each side	3 × 6 each side	3 × 6 each side	2 × 6 each side	109
E2. Split stance antirotation chop	2-0-1-0	60 sec	3 × 10 each side	3 × 10 each side	3 × 10 each side	2 × 10 each side	103
			Day 2				
	Tempo	Rest	Week 1	Week 2	Week 3	Week 4	Page
A1. Staggered stance single-arm dumbbell row	1-0-X-0		3 × 6 each side	4 × 6 each side	4 × 6 each side	2 × 6 each side	137
A2. Split cable reach to T	2-0-1-0		3 × 6 each side	3 × 6 each side	3 × 6 each side	2 × 6 each side	111
A3. Linear wall drill, hold, mini-band around feet	1-0-1-2	90 sec	3 × 8 each side	3 × 8 each side	3 × 8 each side	2 × 8 each side	207
B1. Dumbbell bench press, single-arm	2-0-X-0		3 × 6 each side	3 × 6 each side	3 × 6 each side	2 × 6 each side	132
B2. Countermovement medicine ball chest toss, single-arm	Explosive		3 × 4 each side	3 × 4 each side	3 × 4 each side	2 × 4 each side	186
B3. Wheel rollout	2-0-1-0		3 × 12	3 × 12	3 × 12	2 × 12	59
B4. Shoulder external rotation	2-0-2-0	120 sec	3 × 12 each side	3 × 12 each side	3 × 12 each side	2 × 12 each side	104
C1. Kneeling cable pull-down	2-0-X-0		3 × 10	3 × 10	3 × 10	2 × 10	138
C2. Half-kneeling stability chop	3-0-1-0		3 × 10 each side	3 × 10 each side	3 × 10 each side	2 × 10 each side	101
C3. Copenhagen side plank	N/A	60 sec	3 × 30 sec each side	3 × 40 sec each side	3 × 45 sec each side	2 × 30 sec each side	100
D1. Front squat, half rep, bottom to halfway up	1-0-X-0	120 sec	3 × 30 sec @ 50% RM	3 × 45 sec @ 50% RM	3 × 60 sec @ 50% RM	2 × 30 sec @ 50% RM	118

(continued)

Table 13.12 *(continued)*

	Tempo	Rest	Week 1	Week 2	Week 3	Week 4	Page
Day 3							
A1. Rear foot–elevated split squat	2-0-X-0		5 @ 55% RM; 3 @ 70% RM; 3 @ 80% RM	5 @ 55% RM; 3 @ 70% RM; 3 @ 80% RM	5 @ 55% RM; 3 @ 70% RM; 3 @ 80% RM	5 @ 55% RM; 3 @ 75% RM	121
A2. Hip flexor inhibition, lax ball or foam roller	N/A	120 sec	3 × 30 sec each side	3 × 30 sec each side	3 × 30 sec each side	2 × 30 sec each side	43
B1. Rear foot–elevated split squat	1-0-X-0		4 × 4 each side @ 70% RM	4 × 4 each side @ 70% RM	4 × 4 each side @ 70% RM	2 × 4 each side @ 70% RM	121
B2. Countermovement hop to box	Explosive		4 × 4 each side	4 × 4 each side	4 × 4 each side	2 × 4 each side	162
B3. Single-leg drop squat	Explosive	120 sec	4 × 4 each side	4 × 4 each side	4 × 4 each side	2 × 4 each side	159
C1. Resisted crossover bound	Explosive		3 × 5 each side	3 × 5 each side	3 × 5 each side	2 × 5 each side	177
C2. Continuous lateral bound	Explosive	120 sec	3 × 3 each side	3 × 3 each side	3 × 3 each side	2 × 3 each side	169
D1. Nordic hamstring curl	Controlled		3 × 6	3 × 6	3 × 6	2 × 6	130
D2. Bottom-up skater jump	Explosive	90 sec	3 × 4 each side	3 × 4 each side	3 × 4 each side	2 × 4 each side	152
E1. Single-leg hip thrust	1-0-X-0		3 × 6 each side	3 × 6 each side	3 × 6 each side	2 × 6 each side	126
E2. Lateral mini-band walk	Controlled		3 × 10 each side	3 × 10 each side	3 × 10 each side	2 × 10 each side	64
E3. Drop squat	Explosive	120 sec	3 × 5	3 × 5	3 × 5	2 × 5	159
Day 4							
A1. Pull-up	2-0-X-0		4 × 6	4 × 6	4 × 6	2 × 6	27
A2. Countermovement single-arm explosive cable row	Explosive		4 × 5 each side	4 × 5 each side	4 × 5 each side	2 × 5 each side	188
A3. Split stance antirotation chop	2-0-1-0	90 sec	3 × 10 each side	3 × 10 each side	3 × 10 each side	2 × 10 each side	103

	Day 4 *(continued)*						
	Tempo	Rest	Week 1	Week 2	Week 3	Week 4	Page
B1. Dumbbell bench press, single-arm	1-0-X-0		3 × 6 each side	3 × 6 each side	3 × 6 each side	2 × 6 each side	132
B2. Countermovement medicine ball chest toss	Explosive		3 × 5	3 × 5	3 × 5	2 × 5	186
B3. Forward step medicine ball perpendicular toss	Explosive		3 × 5 each side	3 × 5 each side	3 × 5 each side	2 × 5 each side	181
B4. Shoulder external rotation	2-0-2-0	120 sec	3 × 10 each side	3 × 10 each side	3 × 10 each side	2 × 10 each side	104
C1. Shoulder Ts	2-0-1-0		3 × 10	3 × 10	3 × 10	2 × 10	63
C2. Split cable reach to T	2-0-1-0		3 × 10 each side	3 × 10 each side	3 × 10 each side	2 × 10 each side	111
C3. Body saw	2-0-1-0	60 sec	3 × 10	3 × 12	3 × 12	2 × 12	97
D1. Low skater walk + continuous jump	N/A	120 sec	3 × (2 × 164 ft [50 m] walk + 5 jumps)	3 × (2 × 164 ft [50 m] walk + 5 jumps)	3 × (2 × 164 ft [50 m] walk + 5 jumps)	2 × (2 × 164 ft [50 m] walk + 5 jumps)	207

Table 13.13 Sample Phase 3: Advanced Off-Season (Preparatory Phase) Power and Strength Training Program With a High-Velocity Power Development Focus

	Day 1						
	Tempo	Rest	Week 1	Week 2	Week 3	Week 4	Page
A1. Trap bar deadlift, isometric pull			3 × 5 sec	3 × 5 sec	3 × 5 sec	2 × 5 sec	125
A2. Ankle distraction and glide	Controlled	90 sec	3 × 12 each side	3 × 12 each side	3 × 12 each side	2 × 12 each side	55
B1. Drop jump	Explosive	15 sec	3 × 5	3 × 5	3 × 5	2 × 5	169
B2. Rear foot–elevated jump	Explosive	90 sec	2 × 10 each side @ 35% RM	2 × 10 each side @ 35% RM	2 × 10 each side @ 35% RM	1 × 10 each side @ 35% RM	174
C1. Rear foot–elevated jump	Explosive	20 sec	3 × 10 each side @ 35% RM	3 × 10 each side @ 35% RM	2 × 10 each side @ 35% RM	1 × 10 each side @ 35% RM	174

(continued)

Table 13.13　*(continued)*

	Day 1 *(continued)*					
	Tempo	**Rest**	**Week 1**	**Week 2**	**Week 3**	**Week 4**	**Page**
C2. Linear wall drill, single exchange with miniband	Explosive		3 × 5 each side	3 × 5 each side	3 × 5 each side	2 × 5 each side	207
C3. Forward step horizontal cable chop	Explosive	90 sec	3 × 6 each side	3 × 6 each side	3 × 6 each side	2 × 6 each side	184
D1. Hip thrust	Explosive		3 × 10 @ 35% RM	3 × 10 @ 35% RM	2 × 10 @ 35% RM	1 × 10 @ 35% RM	122
D2. Glute bridge groin squeeze	1-0-1-1	90 sec	3 × (15 × 1 sec hold)	3 × (15 × 1 sec hold)	2 × (15 × 1 sec hold)	1 × (15 × 1 sec hold)	108
	Day 2					
	Tempo	**Rest**	**Week 1**	**Week 2**	**Week 3**	**Week 4**	**Page**
A1. Rings row, isometric hold	1-0-1-5	15 sec	3 × 5 sec	3 × 5 sec	3 × 5 sec	2 × 5 sec	135
A2. Shoulder Y	1-0-1-0	90 sec	3 × 10	3 × 10	3 × 10	2 × 10	63
B1. Rings row	Explosive		3 × 10 @ 55% RM	3 × 10 @ 55% RM	2 × 10 @ 55% RM	1 × 10 @ 55% RM	135
B2. Medicine ball slam	Explosive	90 sec	3 × 6	3 × 6	2 × 6	1 × 6	186
C1. Dumbbell bench press	Explosive	15 sec	3 × 12 @ 35% RM	3 × 12 @ 35% RM	2 × 12 @ 35% RM	1 × 12 @ 35% RM	132
C2. Single-arm medicine ball chest toss	Explosive	15 sec	3 × 4	3 × 4	2 × 4	1 × 4	186
C3. Single-leg squat roll to back and return	Controlled	90 sec	3 × 5 each side	3 × 5 each side	2 × 5 each side	1 × 5 each side	115
D1. Medicine ball slam	Explosive		3 × 6	3 × 6	2 × 6	1 × 6	186
D1. Cable single-leg squat Pallof hold	2-0-X-0	90 sec	3 × 8 each side	3 × 8 each side	1 × 8 each side	1 × 8 each side	112
	Day 3					
	Tempo	**Rest**	**Week 1**	**Week 2**	**Week 3**	**Week 4**	**Page**
A1. Trap bar deadlift, isometric pull		15 sec	3 × 5 sec	3 × 5 sec	3 × 5 sec	2 × 5 sec	125

			Day 3 *(continued)*				
	Tempo	**Rest**	**Week 1**	**Week 2**	**Week 3**	**Week 4**	**Page**
A2. Rudimentary hop series: single-leg, in place	Explosive	90 sec	3 × 10 each side	3 × 10 each side	3 × 10 each side	2 × 10 each side	69
B1. Half-kneeling lateral bound	Explosive	15 sec	3 × 5 each side	3 × 5 each side	3 × 5 each side	2 × 5 each side	153
B2. Rear foot–elevated split squat	Explosive	120 sec	2 × 12 each side @ 35% RM	2 × 12 each side @ 35% RM	2 × 10 each side @ 35% RM	1 × 10 each side @ 35% RM	121
C1. Rear foot–elevated split squat	Explosive	15 sec	3 × 12 each side @ 35% RM	3 × 12 each side @ 35% RM	2 × 10 each side @ 35% RM	1 × 10 each side @ 35% RM	121
C2. Cable resisted slide board lateral lunge	Explosive		3 × 6 each side	3 × 6 each side	2 × 6 each side	1 × 6 each side	109
C3. Split stance antirotation chop	2-1-2-0	90 sec	3 × 10 each side	3 × 10 each side	2 × 10 each side	1 × 10 each side	103
D1. Stability ball leg curl	Explosive		3 × 10	3 × 10	2 × 10	1 × 10	129
D2. Resisted high-knee run	Explosive	90 sec	3 × 49 ft (15 m)	3 × 49 ft (15 m)	2 × 49 ft (15 m)	1 × 49 ft (15 m)	210
			Day 4				
	Tempo	**Rest**	**Week 1**	**Week 2**	**Week 3**	**Week 4**	**Page**
A1. Rings row, iso-metric hold	1-0-1-5	15 sec	3 × 5 sec	3 × 5 sec	3 × 5 sec	2 × 5 sec	135
A2. Shoulder external rotation	1-0-1-0	90 sec	3 × 12 each side	3 × 12 each side	3 × 12 each side	2 × 12 each side	104
B1. Staggered stance single-arm dumbbell row	Explosive	15 sec	3 × 12 each side @ 35% RM	3 × 12 each side @ 35% RM	2 × 12 each side @ 35% RM	1 × 12 each side @ 35% RM	137
B2. Downward cable X to exten-sion	1-0-X-0	90 sec	3 × 10	3 × 10	2 × 10	1 × 10	106
C1. Rings row	Explosive	15 sec	3 × 12 @ 35% RM	3 × 12 @ 35% RM	2 × 12 @ 35% RM	1 × 12 @ 35% RM	135
C2. Countermove-ment medicine ball slam	Explosive		3 × 6	3 × 6	2 × 6	1 × 6	187

(continued)

Table 13.13 *(continued)*

	Tempo	Rest	Week 1	Week 2	Week 3	Week 4	Page
Day 4 *(continued)*							
C3. Single-arm farmer's carry	Controlled	90 sec	3 × 30 sec each side	3 × 30 sec each side	2 × 30 sec each side	1 × 30 sec each side	100
D1. Half-kneeling landmine press	Explosive	15 sec	3 × 12 each side @ 35% RM	3 × 12 each side @ 35% RM	2 × 12 each side @ 35% RM	1 × 12 each side @ 35% RM	133
D2. Cable single-leg RDL to Y	Controlled	90 sec	3 × 8 each side	3 × 8 each side	1 × 8 each side	1 × 8 each side	135

SUMMARY

The off-season or preparatory phase of the yearly training plan is when athletes can make the most physical and physiological improvements. A thorough physical and psychological examination and ongoing monitoring of the individual athlete should help in the development of a thoughtful and balanced training plan. When designing these training plans and programs, several principles, including the following, should serve as a guide.

1. Strive for a balance between the fundamental movement patterns.
2. Focus on movements, not muscles.
3. Master the basics before advancing to more complex movements.
4. If time is a constraint, use an exercise selection that provides the most bang for your buck, such as unilateral compound movements that also challenge aspects of stability and range of motion.

Following these principles and the programming structure outlined in this chapter will ensure your athletes have a successful and productive off-season training plan.

Chapter 14

Preseason Training

The stabilization or competition phase of the macrocycle in hockey includes precompetition (preseason) and main competition (in-season) components. The preseason element in the stabilization phase is typically two to three weeks long, depending on playing level. The physical capacities developed during the preparatory phase are maintained while focusing on the execution of technical and tactical skills on the ice. During the preseason, off-ice training volume is significantly reduced, and an emphasis is placed on the intensity of the exercise performed off the ice. The preseason is also a period of high psychological stress for hockey players because they are continuously evaluated on and off the ice. They often feel uncertain about their place on the team, and this additional psychological stress must be accounted for when designing training plans for the preseason. Training during this period should follow several principles outlined throughout this chapter.

PRESEASON TRAINING PRINCIPLES

Due to the paradigm shift of prioritizing on-ice technical and tactical skills over off-ice power and strength development, the following principles should guide off-ice programming.

- *Volume:* Because the volume of on-ice work is significantly increased, off-ice training volume consequently must be reduced. This reduction in training volume is guided by the volume of training performed on the ice.
- *Intensity:* Although the volume of off-ice training is significantly reduced, the intensity should remain high, albeit in smaller doses.
- *Sagittal plane focus:* Because the volume of skating is significantly increased during the preseason and in-season, the volume of frontal plane training should be minimized while emphasizing the sagittal plane (linear

flexion and extension) to offset or balance the frontal plane workload experienced on the ice.

- *Movement pattern balance:* The exercise selection used in preseason training should balance the movement patterns outlined in chapter 5.
- *Movement capacity:* Movement capacity training is to be performed daily during the preseason. This training structure might vary depending on the on-ice training schedule. See chapter 3 for specific examples of how to design this training.

PRESEASON TRAINING COMPONENTS

Physical training during the preseason should include movement capacity, power and strength, acceleration and change of direction (COD), and energy systems development.

Movement capacity training should be performed six or seven days a week during the preseason for all athlete levels. The on-ice practice and game schedule dictate the volume and structure of this training. See chapter 3 for specific examples of how to structure these sessions in certain scenarios.

Preseason power and strength training for the beginner or intermediate athlete should be performed one or two times per week, depending on the on-ice schedule. These workouts concurrently combine power and strength development. Preseason power and strength training for the advanced athlete should be performed approximately three times per week. Each of these days will have a specific strength quality focus: Day 1 is maximum strength maintenance, day 2 is heavy power, and day 3 is light power.

Acceleration and COD or agility training for the beginner or intermediate athlete takes the form of small-sided games. These small-sided games are performed approximately two times per week, and they also account for the additional energy systems training for the beginner or intermediate level. At the advanced level, acceleration or speed and COD training are performed approximately two times per week. This type of activity includes specific acceleration and speed drills and various small-sided games.

Additional energy systems development training is not required for the beginner or intermediate athlete. This type of training is incorporated into the practice and small-sided games. The advanced athlete should perform two additional days of on-ice energy systems development training in addition to the acceleration or speed and COD (small-sided games) training. These days include lactate production and lactate capacity training.

Preseason Weekly Breakdown

The structure of the preseason training week is typically guided by ice time availability and placement of preseason games. Therefore, the training components outlined earlier are adaptable to fit any given scenario. Figures 14.1 and 14.2 outline a sample weekly breakdown of training components for both

Session	Day 1	Day 2	Day 3	Day 4	Day 5	Day 6	Day 7
Pre-ice	Movement capacity						
On-ice	Skill and tactical	Small-sided games	Off	Skill and tactical	Small-sided games	Off	Preseason game
Off-ice	Power and strength: day 1			Power and strength: day 2			

Figure 14.1   Sample beginner or intermediate preseason weekly training break-down with four practice days and one game. The two skill or tactical on-ice sessions represent low- to moderate-intensity practices, and the sessions, including small-sided games, represent higher-intensity workloads.

Session	Day 1	Day 2	Day 3	Day 4	Day 5	Day 6	Day 7
Pre-ice	Movement capacity						
On-ice	Speed and agility	Lactate capacity	Off	Lactate production	Speed and agility	Skill and tactical	Preseason game
Off-ice	Power and strength: day 1		Power and strength: day 2		Power and strength: day 3		

Figure 14.2   Sample advanced preseason weekly training breakdown with five on-ice practice days and one game. Skill and tactical training are performed every on-ice session.

beginner or intermediate and advanced players, assuming the first preseason game is at the end of the first week.

Beginner or Intermediate Preseason Power and Strength Training

As mentioned earlier, power and strength are concurrently trained during the preseason at the beginner or intermediate level. Performing these training sessions one or two times per week is advised; however, the frequency of training is adaptable depending on the on-ice schedule. For example, if the team has only one practice and one game in a given week, the strength and conditioning coach can increase off-ice power and strength training frequency. At this level of the game, there is less emphasis on wins and losses and more emphasis on the athletes' overall development. Tables 14.1 and 14.2 outline the general off-ice power and strength training template and a sample beginner or intermediate preseason training program.

Table 14.1 Sample Beginner or Intermediate Preseason Power and Strength Training Template

Day 1	Day 2
A1. Power movement	A1. Power movement
A2. Core	A2. Core
B1. Lower body: squat pattern	B1. Lower body: hinge pattern
B2. Upper body: horizontal push	B2. Upper body: vertical push
B3. Upper body: vertical pull	B3. Upper body: horizontal pull

Table 14.2 Sample Beginner or Intermediate Preseason Training Program With a Concurrent Power and Strength Focus

	Day 1				
	Tempo	**Rest**	**Sets**	**Reps**	**Page**
A1. Countermovement jump to box	Explosive		2-3	3-5	162
A2. Stability ball rollout	2-1-1-0	90 sec	2-3	10-12	96
B1. Split squat (weighted at 65%-90% 1-repetition max)	2-1-X-0		2-3	5-10 each side	119
B2. Dumbbell bench press (weighted at 65%-90% 1-repetition max)	2-1-X-0		2-3	5-10	132
B3. Kneeling cable pull-down (weighted at 65%-90% 1-repetition max)	2-1-X-0	90 sec	2-3	5-10	138
	Day 2				
	Tempo	**Rest**	**Sets**	**Reps**	**Page**
A1. Countermovement hop to box	Explosive		2-3	3-5 each side	162
A2. Half-kneeling stability chop	2-0-1-0	90 sec	2-3	10-12 each side	101
B1. Romanian deadlift (weighted at 65%-90% 1-repetition max)	2-1-X-0		2-3	5-10	123
B2. Half-kneeling land-mine press (weighted at 65%-90% 1-repetition max)	2-1-X-0		2-3	5-10 each side	133
B3. Rings row	2-1-X-0	90 sec	2-3	8-12	135

Beginner or Intermediate Preseason Acceleration, Agility, and Energy Systems Training

Acceleration, COD or agility, and energy systems development training are accomplished through small-sided games at the beginner or intermediate level. The main goal of this training is to incorporate the training variables in a fun and exciting way. As outlined previously in this book, these drills can take any form with various rules and rule changes along the way. The coach's responsibility is to be creative in the drill design, emphasizing enjoyment and fun. These small-sided games are to be performed approximately two times per week after the technical and tactical goals are accomplished for the day but can be adapted to fit any schedule. Table 14.3 outlines two variations of work-to-rest ratios that incorporate energy systems development.

Table 14.3 Sample Beginner or Intermediate Preseason Acceleration, Agility, and Energy Systems Development Training

	Training	Rest	Sets	Duration	Page
Day 1	Small-sided games	60 sec	5-10	15-30 sec	235
Day 2	Small-sided games	60-120 sec	5-10	30-45 sec	235

Advanced Preseason Power and Strength Training

The frequency of power and strength training for the advanced athlete during the preseason is approximately three times per week. As in all cases, the training frequency is adaptable depending on the on-ice practice and game schedule. These off-ice training sessions often focus on power and strength concurrently; however, various power and strength qualities are emphasized at different times throughout a week. As mentioned previously, the three training days typically include maximum strength maintenance, heavy power, and light or reactive power focus. At the advanced level, the priority during the preseason is performance on the ice. Therefore, these different training days must be structured to optimize on-ice performance. Tables 14.4 and 14.5 outline the general off-ice power and strength training template and a sample advanced preseason training program.

Table 14.4 Sample Advanced Preseason Power and Strength Training Template

Day 1: strength maintenance focus	Day 2: heavy power focus	Day 3: light or reactive power focus
A1. Lower body: squat or hinge pattern	A1. Lower body: squat or hinge pattern	A1. Lower body: squat or hinge pattern
A2. Core	A2. Core	A2. Core
B1. Upper body: horizontal or vertical push	B1. Upper body: horizontal or vertical push	B1. Upper body: horizontal or vertical pull
B2. Hip and groin	B2. Hip and groin	B2. Upper body: horizontal or vertical pull (high velocity)
C1. Upper body: horizontal or vertical pull	C1. Upper body: horizontal or vertical pull	C1. Upper body: horizontal or vertical push
C2. Rotator cuff	C2. Rotator cuff	C2. Upper body: horizontal or vertical push (high velocity)

Table 14.5 Sample Advanced Preseason Training Program

	Day 1: maximum strength maintenance focus				
	Tempo	Rest	Sets	Reps	Page
A1. Trap bar deadlift (weighted at 85%-90% 1-repetition max)	2-1-X-0		2	3-5	125
A2. Wheel rollout	2-0-1-0	120 sec	2	10-12	59
B1. Dumbbell bench press (weighted at 85%-90% 1-repetition max)	2-1-X-0		2	5	132
B2. Glute bridge groin squeeze	2-2-1-0	90 sec	2	10-12	108
C1. Chin-up (weighted at 85-90% 1-repetition max)	2-1-X-0		2	5	139
C2. Shoulder external rotation	2-1-2-0	90 sec	2	10-12 each side	104
	Day 2: heavy power focus				
	Tempo	Rest	Sets	Reps	Page
A1. Reverse lunge to hip lock (weighted at 60%-70% 1-repetition max)	1-0-X-0		2	3-5 each side	120
A2. Half-kneeling stability chop	2-0-1-0	120 sec	2	10-12 each side	101

	Day 2: heavy power focus *(continued)*				
	Tempo	Rest	Sets	Reps	Page
B1. Half-kneeling landmine press (weighted at 60%-70% 1-repetition max)	1-0-X-0		2	3-5 each side	133
B2. Four-way cable hip series	Controlled	90 sec	2	5 each way	108
C1. Staggered stance single-arm dumbbell row (weighted at 60%-70% 1-repetition max)	1-0-X-0		2	3-5 each side	137
C2. Upward cable X to extension	2-0-1-1	90 sec	2	10	105
	Day 3: light or reactive power focus				
	Tempo	Rest	Sets	Reps	Page
A1. Countermovement jump squat (weighted at 20%-40% 1-repetition max)	Explosive		2	5	174
A2. Half-kneeling Pallof press	2-0-1-2	120 sec	2	10-12 each side	101
B1. Single-arm explosive cable row (weighted at 20%-40% 1-repetition max)	1-0-X-0		2	5 each side	187
B2. Medicine ball slam	Explosive	90 sec	2	5	186
C1. Rings push-up (weighted at 20%-40% 1-repetition max)	1-0-X-0		2	5	133
C2. Medicine ball chest toss	Explosive	90 sec	2	5	185

Advanced On-Ice Preseason Acceleration, Agility, and Energy Systems Training

In contrast to the beginner or intermediate level of athlete, advanced hockey players must perform specific acceleration and energy systems training in addition to performing small-sided games for agility and the technical and tactical aspects of practice. These drills are typically conducted after the technical and tactical goals are accomplished for the day. Table 14.6 outlines two sample days of acceleration and agility training, in which the small-sided games can be structured appropriately for the skills the coaching staff wishes to improve. Table 14.7 outlines the parameters for the additional energy systems development training to be performed on the ice. This energy systems training can be completed in any fashion, but incorporating hockey-specific skills and tactics within the drills is preferred. As with the previous plans, these sessions' frequency must be dictated by the on-ice practice and game schedule.

Table 14.6 Sample Advanced Preseason Acceleration and Agility Training

	Training	Rest	Sets	Distance or duration	Page
Day 1	Flying acceleration (skating positions) or goalie butterfly to lateral shuffle (goalie)	30 sec	5-10	Blue line to blue line (skating positions) or 5-10 sec (goalies)	217
	Small-sided games	60 sec	5-10	15-30 sec	235
Day 2	Crossover acceleration (forwards), backward crossover start (defense), or goalie butterfly to lateral shuffle with shot (goalie)	30 sec	5-10	Blue line to blue line (skating positions) or 5-10 sec (goalies)	218
	Small-sided games	60-120 sec	5-10	30-45 sec	235

Table 14.7 Sample Advanced Preseason Energy Systems Development Training

Day's focus	Intensity	Rest	Sets	Duration
Lactate capacity	Maximal effort	60-90 sec	6	30-45 sec
Lactate production	Maximal effort	45-60 sec	6	15-30 sec

SUMMARY

During the preseason, the training priorities typically shift from off-ice physical capacities to on-ice technical and tactical qualities. Therefore, off-ice training volume is reduced and on-ice training volume is increased concurrently. However, hockey players must regularly train the various physical qualities while following a carefully structured plan to maintain or improve physical performance without hindering on-ice development. With that in mind, the following training principles must be followed:

- Reduced off-ice training volume
- High off-ice training intensity
- Sagittal plane bias in the off-ice training, particularly in the lower body
- Maintenance of movement pattern balance within the training program
- Movement capacity training performed daily

By following these specific principles, we give the athlete the best chance of optimizing their performance on the ice. As with any training plan, it must remain adaptable to suit the team's or individual's specific requirements.

Chapter 15

In-Season Training

The main competition or in-season component of the stabilization phase typically ranges from five to eight months, depending on the level of play and success of the team. During this phase of the annual calendar, the physical training's primary goal is to maintain many of the physical qualities developed during the preparatory phases of training. However, this rule is not always set in stone. For younger and less experienced athletes, the in-season is still a time when improvements can be made even though the off-ice training volume remains low. As mentioned in the previous chapter, overall athlete development (which includes physical development) for beginner and even intermediate athletes should be prioritized over wins and losses. Therefore, the importance of off-ice physical training during the season cannot be understated. The general philosophy during the season is to accomplish some form of training every day. This activity can take many forms, ranging from essential movement capacity work to power and strength development.

IN-SEASON TRAINING PRINCIPLES

In-season training for hockey players is a balancing act due to the nature of the game schedule. There is a fine line between generating training stimulus and fatigue that can compromise on-ice performance. As a result, several training principles should be followed in-season, including microdosing, minimum frequency, frequency of power and strength qualities, sagittal plane bias, movement balance, the "keep it simple" (KIS) principle, and monitoring.

Microdosing refers to performing off-ice training frequently but in low-volume training sessions. Rather than completing one or two long-duration sessions in a given week, players perform multiple short-duration sessions within the same time frame to accumulate the same training volume but minimize excessive fatigue accumulation. Microdosing is particularly important at the advanced levels of hockey, where games occur more frequently.

Players perform in-season off-ice training with a minimum frequency of one training session per week. One session per week is not necessarily ideal from a training stimulus standpoint, but it should be the goal to minimize detraining effects. Again, the goal is to perform some form of training every day. However, in a real-world application, this option might not always be accessible.

Various power and strength qualities are often trained concurrently within the in-season training program. However, qualities such as strength maintenance, power, light, and reactive power can be emphasized at different microcycle points depending on the game schedule. Training these specific power and strength qualities regularly will minimize the detraining effects within each variable and maintain performance improvements realized in the preparation phase.

Due to the volume of the frontal plane skating movement on the ice, off-ice training (notably lower-body exercises) must have a sagittal plane bias to offset or balance the frontal plane skating load. That is not to say that frontal plane training off the ice is entirely off-limits, but most of the heavy and demanding strength training should be performed in the sagittal plane.

As discussed in previous chapters, all training programs must strive for movement balance for healthy individuals. Balancing the movement patterns outlined in chapter 5 is essential to avoid inadvertently creating structural imbalances.

Follow the KIS principle: keep it simple. It is not advisable to add novel exercises, loading patterns, or training techniques during the in-season. A general rule is that if the athletes have not performed a specific type of activity or loading in the preparation phase and preseason, it should not be added during the in-season. Do not attempt to reinvent the wheel during this time. Instead, players should perform familiar, simple, and effective training techniques.

As outlined in chapter 2, it is essential to monitor athletes' health and readiness regularly. Ongoing monitoring of athletes allows strength and conditioning professionals to make microadjustments to the training plan to ensure optimal on-ice performance is attainable.

TRAINING WITH INTENT

Games, practices, and travel significantly add to the workload each athlete experiences. Due to this additional workload and subsequent fatigue, athletes often struggle to perform off-ice training with the same sense of purpose as they do in the off-season. However, athletes must strive to use each training session as an opportunity to improve. They must approach each exercise with the same mindset as during the off-season and perform each repetition with intent and a specific purpose to improve.

BEGINNER OR INTERMEDIATE IN-SEASON PROGRAMMING

In-season programming for beginner and intermediate hockey players generally follows the same formula as preseason training. The training frequency is approximately one or two sessions per week using a concurrent power and strength model. Training volume and intensity can also be changed from week to week, depending on the player's training level. Off-ice training volume can be higher than for advanced players due to several factors, including the priority of overall athlete development and a lower number of games played than at the advanced levels of the game. Aim to perform this off-ice power and strength training at least two days before the next game to allow for adequate recovery. Movement capacity training can be completed daily following the guidelines in chapter 3. Additional energy systems training typically is not required at these levels because practices and games generally provide enough stimulus to maintain or improve these qualities. Table 15.1 outlines the beginner or intermediate in-season off-ice training template, and table 15.2 is a sample two-day training program.

Table 15.1   Beginner or Intermediate In-Season Off-Ice Training Template

Day 1	Day 2
A1. Power movement	A1. Power movement
A2. Core	A2. Core
B1. Lower body: squat pattern	B1. Lower body: hinge pattern
B2. Upper body: horizontal push	B2. Upper body: horizontal pull
B3. Upper body: vertical pull	B3. Upper body: vertical push

Table 15.2   Sample Beginner or Intermediate Off-Ice Training With Concurrent Power and Strength Focus

	Day 1				
	Tempo	Rest	Sets	Reps or duration	Page
A1. Countermovement jump to box	Explosive		2-3	3-5	162
A2. Side plank	N/A	90 sec	2-3	30 sec each side	99
B1. Goblet squat (weighted at 65%-90% 1-repetition max)	2-1-X-0		2-3	5-10	117

(continued)

Table 15.2 *(continued)*

	Day 1 *(continued)*				
	Tempo	Rest	Sets	Reps or duration	Page
B2. Push-up or rings push-up	2-1-X-0		2-3	8-15	131, 133
B3. Chin-up or kneeling cable pull-down	2-1-X-0	90 sec	2-3	5-10	139, 138
	Day 2				
	Tempo	Rest	Sets	Reps	Page
A1. Forward step medicine ball perpendicular toss	Explosive		2-3	3-5 each side	181
A2. Half-kneeling Pallof press	2-0-1-1	90 sec	2-3	8-12 each side	101
B1. Single-leg Romanian deadlift to hip lock (weighted at 65%-90% 1-repetition max)	2-1-X-0		2-3	5-10 each side	127
B2. Rings row	2-1-X-0		2-3	8-15	135
B3. Dumbbell overhead press	2-1-X-0	90 sec	2-3	5-10	135

ADVANCED IN-SEASON PROGRAMMING

The game schedule typically dictates in-season programming at the advanced levels of the game. The frequency of power and strength training for advanced hockey players ranges from two to five sessions per week. The specific nature of these sessions is guided by the number of days until the next game. Generally, advanced in-season training follows a concurrent power and strength model; however, specific qualities such as strength maintenance, power, and light or reactive power are emphasized depending on timing. Table 15.3 highlights possible training focus relative to the number of days until the next game. Table 15.4 outlines the advanced in-season off-ice training template, and tables 15.5 to 15.7 are sample training programs for the three days listed.

Table 15.3 Specific Training Focus Relative to the Number of Days Until the Next Game

Number of days until game	Training focus
Three or more (game – 3+)	Strength maintenance
Two (game – 2)	Power
One (game – 1)	Light or reactive power

Table 15.4 Advanced In-Season Off-Ice Training Template

<tch>Game – 3+	Game – 2	Game – 1
<tb>A1. Lower body: squat or hinge pattern	A1. Power movement: loaded	A1. Power movement: loaded or unloaded
A2. Core	A2. Core	A2. Core
B1. Upper body: horizontal or vertical push	B1. Lower body: squat or hinge pattern	B1. Upper body: power
B2. Upper body: horizontal or vertical pull	B2. Upper body: horizontal or vertical push	B2. Upper body: power
B3. Core or rotator cuff	B3. Upper body: horizontal or vertical pull	B2. Rotational power

Table 15.5 Sample Game – 3+ Advanced Off-Ice Training With a Strength Maintenance Focus

	Tempo	Rest	Sets	Reps	Page
A1. Split squat (weighted at 80%-90% 1-repetition max)	3-1-X-0		2-3	4-8 each side	119
A2. Stability ball rollout	2-0-1-0	120 sec	2-3	10-12	96
B1. Dumbbell bench press (weighted at 80%-90% 1-repetition max)	2-1-X-0		2-3	5	132
B2. Pull-up (weighted at 80%-90% 1-repetition max)	2-1-X-0		2-3	5	27
B3. Shoulder external rotation	2-1-2-0	90 sec	2-3	10-12 each side	104

Table 15.6 Sample Game – 2 Advanced Off-Ice Training With Power Focus

	Tempo	Rest	Sets	Reps	Page
A1. Noncountermovement trap bar jump (weighted at 20%-80% 1-repetition max)	Explosive		2-3	3-6	171
A2. Split stance antirotation chop	2-0-1-0	120 sec	2	10-12 each side	103
B1. Skater squat to hip lock	1-0-X-0		2	5-8 each side	121
B2. Half-kneeling landmine press	1-0-X-0		2	5-8 each side	133
B3. Rings row	1-0-X-0	90 sec	2	6-10	135

Table 15.7 Sample Game – 1 Advanced Off-Ice Training With Light or Reactive Power Focus

	Tempo	Rest	Sets	Reps	Page
A1. Countermovement hop to box	Explosive		2-3	5 each side	162
A2. Side plank	N/A	120 sec	2	30-45 sec each side	99
B1. Staggered stance single-arm dumbbell row (weighted at 20%-60% 1-repetition max)	1-0-X-0		1-2	5-8 each side	137
B2. Medicine ball slam	Explosive		1-2	5	186
B3. Forward step medicine ball perpendicular toss	Explosive	90 sec	1-2	5 each side	181

Advanced hockey players should also perform movement capacity training six or seven days per week. The movement capacity work structure varies depending on the day, and these scenarios are outlined in chapter 3. Typically, additional energy systems training is not required at the advanced level. Practice and game volumes usually provide enough stimulus in these areas. However, in some cases athletes will require supplemental energy systems training. These include times when athletes acquire low playing minutes (i.e., less than 10-12 minutes) during games. Also, using low-level aerobic training, primarily as a recovery modality, provides aerobic energy system benefits. If a player is consistently playing low minutes during games, consider the addition of supplemental lactate production and lactate capacity work, potentially after a game. The volume of this additional work should remain low (i.e., 3-6 sets).

It is currently common practice at the game's advanced levels to perform strength training immediately following games. The rationale behind this is that the density of games is so high, often occurring every other night at the professional level, that training immediately after a game will maximize the amount of recovery time before the next game. However, this topic is hotly debated. Along with the purported benefits, there are also several drawbacks to training at this time. These limitations include physical and mental fatigue, which might not allow the athletes to optimize their gym time. That said, during times of high game density, this is a time when athletes can accumulate training volume during a hectic game schedule in microdosed sessions. Typically, these postgame training sessions do not include any high-intensity power movements, but preferably three or four exercises focusing on the lower body, upper body, and core patterns using different strength methods in an undulating fashion. Table 15.8 outlines a general template for postgame training, and table 15.9 is a sample postgame workout for advanced players with a high-density game schedule. Postgame strength training should not be performed at the beginner and intermediate levels. Additionally, training

Table 15.8 Advanced Postgame Strength Training Template

Postgame strength training
A1. Lower body: squat or hinge pattern
A2. Core
B1. Upper-body pull: vertical or horizontal
B2. Upper-body push: vertical or horizontal

Table 15.9 Sample Advanced Postgame Strength Training Workout

Postgame strength training				
Exercise	Rest	Sets	Reps	Page
A1. Split squat (weighted at 50%-85% 1-repetition max)		1-2	5-8 each side	119
A2. Stability ball rollout	60-90 sec	1-2	10	96
B1. Rings row		1-2	5-10	135
B2. Half-kneeling landmine press	60-90 sec	1-2	5-10 each side	133

after games should be avoided at the advanced levels when the team is playing back-to-back games.

SUMMARY

Many challenges are associated with in-season off-ice training, particularly at the game's advanced levels. At the advanced levels, the priority is on winning games and less on long-term development. In contrast, the focus at the beginner and intermediate levels is primarily long-term development. These challenges mainly revolve around accumulating enough power and strength training volume to maintain the off-season developments while minimizing fatigue accumulation. These factors will ensure the athletes are physically ready to perform during games. Several in-season training principles were outlined in this chapter, including the following:

- Using a microdosed program structure
- Attaining a minimum training frequency of one training session per week
- Frequently training different power and strength qualities to minimize the detraining effects of each specific variable
- Off-ice training with a sagittal plane bias to offset the frontal plane load accumulated during skating
- Balancing movement patterns outlined in chapter 5 within the off-ice training

- Following the KIS principle by not overcomplicating things and adding novel exercises or training stimuli that athletes have not been previously exposed to during the in-season
- Daily and weekly monitoring of physiological and psychological variables to allow for reevaluation and adjustment of the training plan to meet the athlete's needs

By following these principles, athletes will benefit from a well-balanced off-ice training program that can be performed with confidence. As a result, they will be ready to perform on demand.

References

Abbott, K. 2014. "Injuries in Women's Ice Hockey: Special Considerations." *Curr Sports Med Rep* 13 (6): 377-382. https://doi.org/10.1249/jsr.0000000000000102.

Andersen, J.L., and P. Aagaard. 2010. "Effects of Strength Training on Muscle Fiber Types and Size: Consequences for Athletes Training for High-Intensity Sport." *Scand J Med Sci Sports* 20 (S2): 32-38. https://doi.org/10.1111/j.1600-0838.2010.01196.x.

Andersen, L.L., J.L. Andersen, S.P. Magnusson, C. Suetta, J.L. Madsen, L.R. Christensen, and P. Aagaard. 2005. "Changes in the Human Muscle Force–Velocity Relationship in Response to Resistance Training and Subsequent Detraining." *J Appl Physiol* 99 (1): 87-94. https://doi.org/10.1152/japplphysiol.00091.2005.

Bastos, F.N., L.C.M. Vanderlei, F.Y. Nakamura, M. Bertollo, M.F. Godoy, R.A. Hoshi, J.N. Junior, and C.M. Pastre. 2012. "Effects of Cold Water Immersion and Active Recovery on Post-Exercise Heart Rate Variability." *Int J Sports Med* 33 (11): 873-879. https://doi.org/10.1055/s-0032-1301905.

Beelen, A., and A.J. Sargeant. 1991. "Effect of Fatigue on Maximal Power Output at Different Contraction Velocities in Humans." *J Appl Physiol* 71 (6): 2332-2337. https://doi.org/10.1152/jappl.1991.71.6.2332.

Behm, D.G., M.J. Wahl, D.C. Button, K.E. Power, and K.G. Anderson. 2005. "Relationship Between Hockey Skating Speed and Selected Performance Measures." *J Strength Cond Res* 19 (2): 326-331. https://doi.org/10.1519/r-14043.1.

Best, T.M., R. Hunter, A. Wilcox, and F. Haq. 2008. "Effectiveness of Sports Massage for Recovery of Skeletal Muscle From Strenuous Exercise." *Clin J Sport Med* 18 (5): 446-460. https://doi.org/10.1097/jsm.0b013e31818837a1.

Bishop, D., O. Girard, and A. Mendez-Villanueva. 2011. "Repeated Sprint Ability—Part II: Recommendations for Training." *Sports Med* 41 (9): 741-756. https://doi.org/10.2165/11590560-000000000-00000.

Black, S., K. Black, A. Dhawan, C. Onks, P. Seidenberg, and M. Silvis. 2019. "Pediatric Sports Specialization in Elite Ice Hockey Players." *Sports Health* 11 (1): 64-68. https://doi.org/10.1177/1941738118800446.

Bompa, T.O., and G.G. Haff. 2009. *Periodization: Theory and Methodology of Training*. 5th ed. Champaign, IL: Human Kinetics.

Bond, C.W., E.M. Willaert, and B.C. Noonan. 2017. "Comparison of Three Timing Systems: Reliability and Best Practice Recommendations in Timing Short-Duration Sprints." *J Strength Cond Res* 31 (4): 1062-1071. https://doi.org/10.1519/jsc.0000000000001566.

Boyle, M. 2010. *Advances in Functional Training: Training Techniques for Coaches, Personal Trainers, and Athletes*. Santa Cruz, CA: On Target Publications.

Brughelli, M., and J. Cronin. 2007. "Altering the Length–Tension Relationship With Eccentric Exercise: Implications for Performance and Injury." *Sports Med* 37 (9): 807-826. https://doi.org/10.2165/00007256-200737090-00004.

Burkhart, K., and J.R. Phelps. 2009. "Amber Lenses to Block Blue Light and Improve Sleep: A Randomized Trial." *Chronobiology International* 26 (8): 1602-1612. https://doi.org/10.3109/07420520903523719.

Burr, J.F., R.K. Jamnik, J. Baker, A. Macpherson, N. Gledhill, and E.J. McGuire. 2008. "Relationship of Physical Fitness Test Results and Hockey Playing Potential in Elite-Level Ice Hockey Players." *J Strength Cond Res* 22 (5): 1535-1543. https://doi.org/10.1519/JSC.0b013e318181ac20.

Cabré-Riera, A., M. Torrent, D. Donaire-Gonzalez, M. Vrijheid, E. Cardis, and M. Guxens. 2019. "Telecommunication Devices Use, Screen Time and Sleep in Adolescents."

Environmental Research 171: 341-347. https://doi.org/https://doi.org/10.1016/j.envres.2018.10.036.

Calder, A. 2003. "Recovery." In *Strength and Conditioning for Tennis*, edited by M. Reid, A. Quinn, and M. Crespo. London: International Tennis Federation.

Cannon, A., K. Finn, and Z. Yan. 2018. "Comparison of Hip Internal and External Rotation Between Intercollegiate Distance Runners and Non-Running College Students." *Int J Sports Phys Ther* 13 (6): 956-962.

Causer, J., N.J. Smeeton, and A.M. Williams. 2017. "Expertise Differences in Anticipatory Judgements During a Temporally and Spatially Occluded Task." *PloS ONE* 12 (2): e0171330-e0171330. https://doi.org/10.1371/journal.pone.0171330.

Chang, M., L.V. Slater, R.O. Corbett, J.M. Hart, and J. Hertel. 2017. "Muscle Activation Patterns of the Lumbo-Pelvic-Hip Complex During Walking Gait Before and After Exercise." *Gait Posture* 52: 15-21. https://doi.org/10.1016/j.gaitpost.2016.11.016.

Chang, Y.W., F.C. Su, H.W. Wu, and K.N. An. 1999. "Optimum Length of Muscle Contraction." *Clin Biomech* 14 (8): 537-542. https://doi.org/10.1016/s0268-0033(99)00014-5.

Cintineo, H.P., M.A. Arent, J. Antonio, and S.M. Arent. 2018. "Effects of Protein Supplementation on Performance and Recovery in Resistance and Endurance Training." *Frontiers in Nutrition* 5: 83. https://doi.org/10.3389/fnut.2018.00083.

Cook, G. 2003. *Athletic Body in Balance*. Champaign, IL: Human Kinetics.

Davidson, R.J., J. Kabat-Zinn, J. Schumacher, M. Rosenkranz, D. Muller, S.F. Santorelli, F. Urbanowski, A. Harrington, K. Bonus, and J.F. Sheridan. 2003. "Alterations in Brain and Immune Function Produced by Mindfulness Meditation." *Psychosomatic Medicine* 65 (4): 564-570. https://journals.lww.com/psychosomaticmedicine/Fulltext/2003/07000/Alterations_in_Brain_and_Immune_Function_Produced.14.aspx.

Delaney, J.A., G.M. Duthie, H.R. Thornton, and D.B. Pyne. 2018. "Quantifying the Relationship Between Internal and External Work in Team Sports: Development of a Novel Training Efficiency Index." *Science and Medicine in Football* 2 (2): 149-156. https://doi.org/10.1080/24733938.2018.1432885.

Delisle-Houde, P., N.A. Chiarlitti, R.E.R. Reid, and R.E. Andersen. 2019. "Predicting On-Ice Skating Using Laboratory- and Field-Based Assessments in College Ice Hockey Players." *Int J Sports Physiol Perform* 14 (9): 1184-1189. https://doi.org/10.1123/ijspp.2018-0708.

Deschenes, M.R., and W.J. Kraemer. 2002. "Performance and Physiologic Adaptations to Resistance Training." *Am J Phys Med Rehabil* 81 (11 Suppl): S3-S16. https://doi.org/10.1097/00002060-200211001-00003.

Dorado, C., J. Sanchis-Moysi, and J.A.L. Calbet. 2004. "Effects of Recovery Mode on Performance, O_2 Uptake, and O_2 Deficit During High-Intensity Intermittent Exercise." *Can J Appl Physiol* 29 (3): 227-244. https://doi.org/10.1139/h04-016.

Dunn, J., and M.H. Grider. 2020. *Physiology, Adenosine Triphosphate*. Treasure Island, FL: StatPearls Publishing.

Durocher, J.J., D.D. Jensen, A.G. Arredondo, D.T. Leetun, and J.R. Carter. 2008. "Gender Differences in Hockey Players During On-Ice Graded Exercise." *J Strength Cond Res* 22 (4): 1327-1331. https://doi.org/10.1519/JSC.0b013e31816eb4c1.

Epstein, D.M., M. McHugh, M. Yorio, and B. Neri. 2013. "Intra-Articular Hip Injuries in National Hockey League Players: A Descriptive Epidemiological Study." *Am J Sports Med* 41 (2): 343-348. https://doi.org/10.1177/0363546512467612.

Flouris, A.D., G.S. Metsios, and Y. Koutedakis. 2005. "Enhancing the Efficacy of the 20 m Multistage Shuttle Run Test." *Br J Sports Med* 39 (3): 166-170. https://doi.org/10.1136/bjsm.2004.012500.

Fogt, D.L., P.J. Cooper, C.N. Freeman, J.E. Kalns, and W.H. Cooke. 2009. "Heart Rate Variability to Assess Combat Readiness." *Mil Med* 174 (5): 491-495. https://doi.org/10.7205/milmed-d-02-6808.

Ford, P., M. De Ste Croix, R. Lloyd, R. Meyers, M. Moosavi, J. Oliver, K. Till, and C. Williams. 2011. "The Long-Term Athlete Development Model: Physiological Evidence and Application." *J Sports Sci* 29(4): 389-402. https://doi.org/10.1080/02640414.2010.536849.

Fullagar, H.H., R. Duffield, S. Skorski, A.J. Coutts, R. Julian, and T. Meyer. 2015. "Sleep and Recovery in Team Sport: Current Sleep-Related Issues Facing Professional Team-Sport Athletes." *Int J Sports Physiol Perform* 10 (8): 950-957. https://doi.org/10.1123/ijspp.2014-0565.

Gaitanos, G.C., C. Williams, L.H. Boobis, and S. Brooks. 1993. "Human Muscle Metabolism During Intermittent Maximal Exercise." *J Appl Physiol* 75 (2): 712-719. https://doi.org/10.1152/jappl.1993.75.2.712.

García-Ramos, A., B. Feriche, C. Calderón, X. Iglesias, A. Barrero, D. Chaverri, T. Schuller, and F.A. Rodríguez. 2015. "Training Load Quantification in Elite Swimmers Using a Modified Version of the Training Impulse Method." *Eur J Sport Sci* 15 (2): 85-93. https://doi.org/10.1080/17461391.2014.922621.

Gilenstam, K.M., K. Thorsen, and K.B. Henriksson-Larsén. 2011. "Physiological Correlates of Skating Performance in Women's and Men's Ice Hockey." *J Strength Cond Res* 25 (8): 2133-2142. https://doi.org/10.1519/JSC.0b013e3181ecd072.

Haddad, M., G. Stylianides, L. Djaoui, A. Dellal, and K. Chamari. 2017. "Session-RPE Method for Training Load Monitoring: Validity, Ecological Usefulness, and Influencing Factors." *Front Neurosci* 11: 612. https://doi.org/10.3389/fnins.2017.00612.

Hellsten, Y., and M. Nyberg. 2015. "Cardiovascular Adaptations to Exercise Training." *Compr Physiol* 6 (1): 1-32. https://doi.org/10.1002/cphy.c140080.

Hill, J., G. Howatson, K. van Someren, J. Leeder, and C. Pedlar. 2014. "Compression Garments and Recovery From Exercise-Induced Muscle Damage: A Meta-Analysis." *Br J Sports Med* 48 (18): 1340. https://doi.org/10.1136/bjsports-2013-092456.

Irish, L.A., C.E. Kline, H.E. Gunn, D.J. Buysse, and M.H. Hall. 2015. "The Role of Sleep Hygiene in Promoting Public Health: A Review of Empirical Evidence." *Sleep Medicine Reviews* 22: 23-36. https://doi.org/https://doi.org/10.1016/j.smrv.2014.10.001.

Issurin, V. 2008. *Block Periodization: Breakthrough in Sport Training.* Muskegon, MI: Ultimate Athlete Concepts.

Jäger, R., C.M. Kerksick, B.I. Campbell, P.J. Cribb, S.D. Wells, T.M. Skwiat, M. Purpura, T.N. Ziegenfuss, A.A. Ferrando, S.M. Arent, A.E. Smith-Ryan, J.R. Stout, P.J. Arciero, M.J. Ormsbee, L.W. Taylor, C.D. Wilborn, D.S. Kalman, R.B. Kreider, D.S. Willoughby, J.R. Hoffman, J.L. Krzykowski, and J. Antonio. 2017. "International Society of Sports Nutrition Position Stand: Protein and Exercise." *J Int Soc Sports Nutr* 14: 20. https://doi.org/10.1186/s12970-017-0177-8.

Kavanagh, M.F., and I. Jacobs. 1988. "Breath-by-Breath Oxygen Consumption During Performance of the Wingate Test." *Can J Sport Sci* 13 (1): 91-93.

Kibler, W.B., J. Press, and A. Sciascia. 2006. "The Role of Core Stability in Athletic Function." *Sports Med* 36 (3): 189-198. https://doi.org/10.2165/00007256-200636030-00001.

Kraemer, W.J., R.S. Staron, F.C. Hagerman, R.S. Hikida, A.C. Fry, S.E. Gordon, B.C. Nindl, L.A. Gothshalk, J.S. Volek, J.O. Marx, R.U. Newton, and K. Häkkinen. 1998. "The Effects of Short-Term Resistance Training on Endocrine Function in Men and Women." *Eur J Appl Physiol Occup Physiol* 78 (1): 69-76. https://doi.org/10.1007/s004210050389.

Kuhn, A.W., B.C. Noonan, B.T. Kelly, C.M. Larson, and A. Bedi. 2016. "The Hip in Ice Hockey: A Current Concepts Review." *Arthroscopy* 32 (9): 1928-1938. https://doi.org/10.1016/j.arthro.2016.04.029.

Lamberts, R.P., J. Swart, B. Capostagno, T.D. Noakes, and M.I. Lambert. 2010. "Heart Rate Recovery as a Guide to Monitor Fatigue and Predict Changes in Performance Parameters." *Scand J Med Sci Sports* 20 (3): 449-457. https://doi.org/https://doi.org/10.1111/j.1600-0838.2009.00977.x.

Laursen, P.B., and D.G. Jenkins. 2002. "The Scientific Basis for High-Intensity Interval Training: Optimising Training Programmes and Maximising Performance in Highly Trained Endurance Athletes." *Sports Med* 32 (1): 53-73. https://doi.org/10.2165/00007256-200232010-00003.

Lerebours, F., W. Robertson, B. Neri, B. Schulz, T. Youm, and O. Limpisvasti. 2016. "Prevalence of Cam-Type Morphology in Elite Ice Hockey Players." *Am J Sports Med* 44 (4): 1024-1030. https://doi.org/10.1177/0363546515624671.

Lignell, E., D. Fransson, P. Krustrup, and M. Mohr. 2018. "Analysis of High-Intensity Skating in Top-Class Ice Hockey Match-Play in Relation to Training Status and Muscle Damage." *J Strength Cond Res* 32 (5): 1303-1310. https://doi.org/10.1519/jsc.0000000000001999.

Lloyd, R.S., P. Read, J.L. Oliver, R.W. Meyers, S. Nimphius, and I. Jeffreys. 2013. "Considerations for the Development of Agility During Childhood and Adolescence." *Strength Cond J* 35 (3): 2-11. https://doi.org/10.1519/SSC.0b013e31827ab08c.

Mangus, B.C., L.A. Hoffman, M.A. Hoffman, and P. Altenburger. 2002. "Basic Principles of Extremity Joint Mobilization Using a Kaltenborn Approach." *J Sport Rehabil* 11 (4): 235-250. https://doi.org/10.1123/jsr.11.4.235.

Martarelli, D., M. Cocchioni, S. Scuri, and P. Pompei. 2011. "Diaphragmatic Breathing Reduces Exercise-Induced Oxidative Stress." *Evidence-Based Complementary and Alternative Medicine* 2011: 932430. https://doi.org/10.1093/ecam/nep169.

Maud, P.J., and B.B. Shultz. 1986. "Gender Comparisons in Anaerobic Power and Anaerobic Capacity Tests." *Br J Sports Med* 20 (2): 51-54. https://doi.org/10.1136/bjsm.20.2.51.

Maughan, R.J., and S.M. Shirreffs. 1997. "Recovery From Prolonged Exercise: Restoration of Water and Electrolyte Balance." *J Sports Sci* 15 (3): 297-303. https://doi.org/10.1080/026404197367308.

McCall, G.E., W.C. Byrnes, S.J. Fleck, A. Dickinson, and W.J. Kraemer. 1999. "Acute and Chronic Hormonal Responses to Resistance Training Designed to Promote Muscle Hypertrophy." *Can J Appl Physiol* 24 (1): 96-107. https://doi.org/10.1139/h99-009.

McGill, S. 2007. *Low Back Disorders*. 2nd ed. Champaign, IL: Human Kinetics.

McMorris, T. 2014. *Acquisition and Performance of Sports Skills*. New York: John Wiley & Sons.

Melkonian, E.A., and M.P. Schury. 2020. *Biochemistry, Anaerobic Glycolysis*. Treasure Island, FL: StatPearls Publishing.

Mohammed, W.A., A. Pappous, and D. Sharma. 2018. "Effect of Mindfulness Based Stress Reduction (MBSR) in Increasing Pain Tolerance and Improving the Mental Health of Injured Athletes." *Front Psychol* 9 (May): 722-722. https://doi.org/10.3389/fpsyg.2018.00722.

Moore, M.K. 2004. "Upper Crossed Syndrome and Its Relationship to Cervicogenic Headache." *J Manipulative Physiol Ther* 27 (6): 414-420. https://doi.org/10.1016/j.jmpt.2004.05.007.

Moreside, J.M., and S.M. McGill. 2012. "Hip Joint Range of Motion Improvements Using Three Different Interventions." *J Strength Cond Res* 26 (5): 1265-1273. https://doi.org/10.1519/JSC.0b013e31824f2351.

Moritani, T., and H.A. deVries. 1979. "Neural Factors Versus Hypertrophy in the Time Course of Muscle Strength Gain." *Am J Phys Med* 58 (3): 115-130.

Murray, B., and C. Rosenbloom. 2018. "Fundamentals of Glycogen Metabolism for Coaches and Athletes." *Nutrition Reviews* 76 (4): 243-259. https://doi.org/10.1093/nutrit/nuy001.

Nicholls, R.A. 2004. "Intra-Articular Disorders of the Hip in Athletes." *Phys Ther Sport* 5 (1): 17-25. https://doi.org/https://doi.org/10.1016/j.ptsp.2003.09.004.

Nimmerichter, A., N.J.R. Weber, K. Wirth, and A. Haller. 2015. "Effects of Video-Based Visual Training on Decision-Making and Reactive Agility in Adolescent Football Players." *Sports* 4 (1): 1. https://doi.org/10.3390/sports4010001.

Ohya, T., Y. Aramaki, and K. Kitagawa. 2013. "Effect of Duration of Active or Passive Recovery on Performance and Muscle Oxygenation During Intermittent Sprint Cycling Exercise." *Int J Sports Med* 34 (7): 616-622. https://doi.org/10.1055/s-0032-1331717.

Paul, D.J., T.J. Gabbett, and G.P. Nassis. 2016. "Agility in Team Sports: Testing, Training and Factors Affecting Performance." *Int J Sports Med* 46 (3): 421-442. https://doi.org/10.1007/s40279-015-0428-2.

Philippaerts, R.M., R. Vaeyens, M. Janssens, B. Van Renterghem, D. Matthys, R. Craen, J. Bourgois, J. Vrijens, G. Beunen, and R.M. Malina. 2006. "The Relationship Between Peak Height Velocity and Physical Performance in Youth Soccer Players." *J Sports Sci* 24 (3): 221-230. https://doi.org/10.1080/02640410500189371.

Pournot, H., F. Bieuzen, R. Duffield, P.-M. Lepretre, C. Cozzolino, and C. Hausswirth. 2011. "Short-Term Effects of Various Water Immersions on Recovery From Exhaustive Intermittent Exercise." *Eur J Appl Physiol* 111 (7): 1287-1295. https://doi.org/10.1007/s00421-010-1754-6.

Price, P.C., R. Jhangiani, and I.-C.A. Chiang. 2019. *Research Methods in Psychology*. 2nd ed. Pressbooks.com.

Robbins, S.M., P.J. Renaud, and D.J. Pearsall. 2018. "Principal Component Analysis Identifies Differences in Ice Hockey Skating Stride Between High- and Low-Calibre Players." *Sports Biomech* 20 (2): 131-149. https://doi.org/10.1080/14763141.2018.1524510.

Robinson, R., and P. Gribble. 2008. "Kinematic Predictors of Performance on the Star Excursion Balance Test." *J Sport Rehabil* 17 (4): 347-357. https://doi.org/10.1123/jsr.17.4.347.

Roca, A., P.R. Ford, A.P. McRobert, and A.M. Williams. 2011. "Identifying the Processes Underpinning Anticipation and Decision-Making in a Dynamic Time-Constrained Task." *Cognitive Processing* 12 (3): 301-310. https://doi.org/10.1007/s10339-011-0392-1.

Rose, C., K.M. Edwards, J. Siegler, K. Graham, and C. Caillaud. 2017. "Whole-Body Cryotherapy as a Recovery Technique After Exercise: A Review of the Literature." *Int J Sports Med* 38 (14): 1049-1060. https://doi.org/10.1055/s-0043-114861.

Samuels, C. 2009. "Sleep, Recovery, and Performance: The New Frontier in High-Performance Athletics." *Phys Med Rehabil Clin N Am* 20 (1): 149-159. https://doi.org/https://doi.org/10.1016/j.pmr.2008.10.009.

Sandler, D. 2005. *Sports Power*. Champaign, IL: Human Kinetics.

Schroeder, A.N., and T.M. Best. 2015. "Is Self-Myofascial Release an Effective Preexercise and Recovery Strategy? A Literature Review." *Curr Sports Med Rep* 14 (3): 200-208. https://doi.org/10.1249/jsr.0000000000000148.

Shell, J.R., S.M.K. Robbins, P.C. Dixon, P.J. Renaud, R.A. Turcotte, T. Wu, and D.J. Pearsall. 2017. "Skating Start Propulsion: Three-Dimensional Kinematic Analysis of Elite Male and Female Ice Hockey Players." *Sports Biomech* 16 (3): 313-324. https://doi.org/10.1080/14763141.2017.1306095.

Shindle, M.K., B.G. Domb, and B.T. Kelly. 2007. "Hip and Pelvic Problems in Athletes." *Oper Tech Sports Med* 15 (4): 195-203. https://doi.org/https://doi.org/10.1053/j.otsm.2007.10.003.

Smith, D.J. 2003. "A Framework for Understanding the Training Process Leading to Elite Performance." *Sports Med* 33 (15): 1103-1126. https://doi.org/10.2165/00007256-200333150-00003.

Spiteri, T., S. Nimphius, N.H. Hart, C. Specos, J.M. Sheppard, and R.U. Newton. 2014. "Contribution of Strength Characteristics to Change of Direction and Agility Performance in Female Basketball Athletes." *J Strength Cond Res* 28 (9): 2415-2423. https://doi.org/10.1519/jsc.0000000000000547.

Stone, M.H., H.S. O'Bryant, B.K. Schilling, R.L. Johnson, K.C. Pierce, G.G. Haff, A.J. Koch, and M. Stone. 1999. "Periodization: Effects of Manipulating Volume and Intensity. Part 1." *Strength Cond J* 21 (2): 56-62. https://doi.org/10.1519/1533-4295(1999)021<0056:PE OMVA>2.0.CO

Taber, C., C. Bellon, H. Abbott, and G.E. Bingham. 2016. "Roles of Maximal Strength and Rate of Force Development in Maximizing Muscular Power." *Strength Cond J* 38 (1): 71-78. https://doi.org/10.1519/ssc.0000000000000193.

Thorpe, R.T., G. Atkinson, B. Drust, and W. Gregson. 2017. "Monitoring Fatigue Status in Elite Team-Sport Athletes: Implications for Practice." *Int J Sports Physiol Perform* 12 (S2): S2-27. https://doi.org/10.1123/ijspp.2016-0434.

Tibor, L.M., and J.K. Sekiya. 2008. "Differential Diagnosis of Pain Around the Hip Joint." *Arthroscopy* 24 (12): 1407-1421. https://doi.org/10.1016/j.arthro.2008.06.019.

Tricoli, V., L. Lamas, R. Carnevale, and C. Ugrinowitsch. 2005. "Short-Term Effects on Lower-Body Functional Power Development: Weightlifting vs. Vertical Jump Training Programs." *J Strength Cond Res* 19 (2): 433-437. https://journals.lww.com/nsca-jscr/Fulltext/2005/05000/short_term_effects_on_lower_body_functional_power.32.aspx.

Upjohn, T., R. Turcotte, D.J. Pearsall, and J. Loh. 2008. "Three-Dimensional Kinematics of the Lower Limbs During Forward Ice Hockey Skating." *Sports Biomech* 7 (2): 206-221. https://doi.org/10.1080/14763140701841621.

Váczi, M., J. Tollár, B. Meszler, I. Juhász, and I. Karsai. 2013. "Short-Term High-Intensity Plyometric Training Program Improves Strength, Power and Agility in Male Soccer Players." *H Hum Kinet* 36 (1): 17-26. https://doi.org/https://doi.org/10.2478/hukin-2013-0002.

Verschueren, J., B. Tassignon, K. De Pauw, M. Proost, A. Teugels, J. Van Cutsem, B. Roelands, E. Verhagen, and R. Meeusen. 2020. "Does Acute Fatigue Negatively Affect Intrinsic Risk Factors of the Lower-Extremity Injury Risk Profile? A Systematic and Critical Review." *Int J Sports Med* 50 (4): 767-784. https://doi.org/10.1007/s40279-019-01235-1.

Versey, N.G., S.L. Halson, and B.T. Dawson. 2013. "Water Immersion Recovery for Athletes: Effect on Exercise Performance and Practical Recommendations." *Int J Sports Med* 43 (11): 1101-1130. https://doi.org/10.1007/s40279-013-0063-8.

Vigotsky, A.D., G.J. Lehman, C. Beardsley, B. Contreras, B. Chung, and E.H. Feser. 2016. "The Modified Thomas Test Is Not a Valid Measure of Hip Extension Unless Pelvic Tilt Is Controlled." *PeerJ* 4: e2325. https://doi.org/10.7717/peerj.2325.

Wall, M., and J. Côté. 2007. "Developmental Activities That Lead to Dropout and Investment in Sport." *Phys Educ Sport Pedagogy* 12 (1): 77-87. https://doi.org/10.1080/17408980601060358.

Williams, C. 2004. "Carbohydrate Intake and Recovery From Exercise." *Science & Sports* 19 (5): 239-244. https://doi.org/10.1016/j.scispo.2004.05.005.

Winke, M., and S. Williamson. 2018. "Comparison of a Pneumatic Compression Device to a Compression Garment During Recovery from DOMS." *Int J Exerc Sci* 11 (3): 375-383. https://pubmed.ncbi.nlm.nih.gov/29795729

Young, W., M.J. Davies, D. Farrow, and A. Bahnert. 2013. "Comparison of Agility Demands of Small-Sided Games in Elite Australian Football." *Int J Sports Physiol Perform* 8 (2): 139-147. http://ezproxy.lib.ucalgary.ca/login?url=http://search.ebscohost.com/login.aspx?direct=true&db=s3h&AN=86152838&site=ehost-live.

About the Author

Ryan van Asten is the director of sports performance for the Calgary Flames and has been the head strength and conditioning coach for the organization for the past seven years.

Prior to joining the Flames, van Asten spent three seasons as the head strength and conditioning coach of the Los Angeles Kings, winning Stanley Cups in 2012 and 2014. He was also the head strength and conditioning coach and coordinator for Hockey Canada and the Canadian Sport Centre–Calgary, where he was part of the 2010 Olympic gold medal–winning women's hockey team. In addition, van Asten was fortunate to be a part of three world championship teams and 10 World Cup winners in hockey and luge.

At the University of Calgary van Asten earned a master of science degree in exercise physiology. He also holds a bachelor of science degree in life sciences and a bachelor of physical and health education degree from Queen's University in Kingston, Ontario. He holds the Certified Strength and Conditioning Specialist credential from the National Strength and Conditioning Association (NSCA).

You read the book—now complete the companion CE exam to earn continuing education credit!

Find and purchase the companion CE exam here:
US.HumanKinetics.com/collections/CE-Exam
Canada.HumanKinetics.com/collections/CE-Exam

50% off the companion CE exam with this code

CCH2023